Treatment Courts

Treatment Courts

Solving the Recidivism Problem

Christopher Salvatore

Professor of Justice Studies
Montclair State University

CAROLINA ACADEMIC PRESS
Durham, North Carolina

Library of Congress Cataloging-in-Publication Data

Names: Salvatore, Christopher, 1974- author.
Title: Treatment courts : solving the recidivism problem / Christopher
Salvatore.
Description: Durham, North Carolina : Carolina Academic Press, LLC, [2023]
| Includes bibliographical references and index.
Identifiers: LCCN 2023047339 | ISBN 9781531025229 (paperback) | ISBN
9781531025236 (ebook)
Subjects: LCSH: Recidivism — United States. | Courts of special
jurisdiction — United States. | Crime prevention — United States. |
Crime — United States--Sociological aspects.
Classification: LCC HV6049 .S27 2024 | DDC 364.3 — dc23/eng/20231024
LC record available at https://lccn.loc.gov/2023047339

Carolina Academic Press, LLC
700 Kent Street
Durham, North Carolina 27701
(919) 489-7486
www.cap-press.com
Printed in the United States of America

This book is dedicated to the memory of Evelyn Asevero, someone who truly embodied kindness and justice. Evelyn, thank you for your friendship, laughter and knowing smile. You are remembered and missed.

Contents

Preface   xiii

Introduction: Treatment Courts and Making a Difference   xv

Chapter 1 · The Crime Problem and the Incarceration "Fix"   3
   How Much Crime and What Does It Cost?   5
      How Much Crime Occurs?   5
      What Does Crime Cost?   7
      The Cost of the Criminal Justice System   8
   The Main Response: Mass Incarceration   9
      The Incarceration Boom   9
      Has Mass Incarceration Worked to Reduce Crime?   11
      Key Conceptual Issues About Incapacitation   11
   Mass Incarceration: The Costs to Society   13
      Costs to Families and Communities   13
      Race/Ethnicity Inequality   14
      Post-Conviction Punishments   14
   Conclusion   15
   References   16

Chapter 2 · Therapeutic Jurisprudence and the
      Evolution of Treatment Courts   19
   What Is a Problem-Oriented/Specialty/Treatment Court?   20
   Evolution of Treatment Courts   21
      How Treatment Courts Are Funded   22
      Therapeutic Jurisprudence Defined   22
      The Role of the Judge in Treatment Courts   23

Collaboration and Treatment Goals   24
Court Process   25
Brief Summary of Programs   26
    Animal Courts   26
    Drug Courts   27
    Domestic Violence Courts   28
    Fathering Courts   28
    Homeless Courts   29
    Mental Health Courts   29
    Prostitution Courts   30
    Reentry Courts   30
    Teen Courts   31
    Veterans' Courts   32
Pros and Cons of Treatment Courts   32
Conclusions   34
References   34

Chapter 3 · Theoretical Applications: Overview   39
Therapeutic Jurisprudence   40
Social Bonding Theory   41
Theoretical Orientation: Deterrence Theory and
    Risk-Need-Responsivity Model   43
Life Course Theory   45
Restorative Justice   46
Towards an Integrated Theory of Treatment Courts   48
    An Integrated Theory of Treatment Courts to Promote
      Program Compliance and Rehabilitation   49
Theoretical Implications/Conclusion   52
References   53

Chapter 4 · Adult and Juvenile Drug Courts: Overview   57
Drug Court Program Phase Structure   59
10 Key Components   61
Juvenile Drug Courts   63
The Role of Social Bonds and Attachments in Drug Courts   65
Drug Courts and Life Course Theory   70
Do Drug Courts Work?   72
    Support for Drug Courts   73
    Evidence Challenging Drug Court Programs'
      Effectiveness   76

Future Research   77
Conclusions   78
References   80

Chapter 5 · Mental Health Courts: Overview   89
Mental Health Court Program Model Example:
    Manhattan Mental Health Court   91
Defining Mental Health Courts: Key Characteristics
    and Elements   93
Juvenile MHCs   97
Mental Health Court Theoretical Orientation   99
Mental Health Courts: Do They Work?   100
Evidence Supporting Their Effectiveness   100
Evidence Challenging Their Effectiveness   104
Future Research   107
Conclusions   108
References   110

Chapter 6 · Domestic Violence Courts: Overview   115
Domestic Violence Courts Requirements,
    Goals, and Program Structure   118
    Program Requirements   119
    Goals   120
    Program Structure   122
Theoretical Orientation   124
Critical Factors Needed for DVCs to Work   125
Evidence Supporting the Effectiveness of Domestic
    Violence Courts   130
Evidence Challenging the Effectiveness of Domestic
    Violence Courts   131
Future Research   132
Conclusions   133
References   135

Chapter 7 · Veterans' Court: Overview   141
Veterans' Court Requirements and Program Structure   144
Theoretical Orientation   147
    Peer Mentors in VTCs   148
    Peer Mentoring as a Form of
        Social Bonding/Attachment   150

Restorative Justice   151
Identity Theory Approach   152
Evidence of Veterans' Courts' Effectiveness   153
Evidence of Veterans' Courts' Ineffectiveness   154
Future Research   155
Conclusions   157
References   159

Chapter 8 · Reentry Courts: Overview   163
Reentry Court Requirements and Program Structure   164
    Active Ingredients of Reentry Courts   165
    Program Requirements and Program Structure
        Example: ReNew Reentry Court,
        Newark, New Jersey   167
Theoretical Orientation: Deterrence Theory and
    Risk-Need-Responsivity Model   169
    The Role of Social Bonds   170
The Role of Social Capital   172
Evidence Supporting the Effectiveness of Reentry Courts   174
Evidence Refuting the Effectiveness of Reentry Courts   175
Future Research   176
Conclusions   177
References   179

Chapter 9 · Teen Courts: Overview   183
Development of the Juvenile Justice System   185
Teen Court Characteristics   191
Teen Court Theoretical Orientation   193
    Peer Justice   193
    Differential Association   194
    Restorative Justice   194
    Labeling   195
Evidence for the Effectiveness of Teen Courts   195
Problems in Teen Courts, Evidence Not Supporting
    the Effectiveness of Teen Courts, and Criticisms 198
Future Research   200
Conclusions   202
References   204

Chapter 10 · Prostitution Courts: Overview 209
Prostitution Court Structure 211
Sex or Human Trafficking Courts 214
Prostitution Court Theoretical Orientation 216
Prostitution Courts: Do They Work? 218
Support for Prostitution Courts 218
Evidence Challenging Prostitution Court
Programs' Effectiveness 219
Future Research 220
Conclusions 221
References 223

**Chapter 11 · Policy Applications/Implications for
Policy and Change** 227
Introduction 227
General Benefits of Treatment Courts 229
Cost Savings 229
Maintain Social Bonds 230
Avoiding Stigma 232
Shift Towards Greater Social Justice 233
Policy Recommendations 234
Adoption of Standardized Models 234
Target Youth Populations: Special Program Needs
of Today's Youth 235
Target Overlooked Populations: LGBTQIA+
Populations 236
Increasing Aftercare 237
Conclusion 238
References 239

Chapter 12 · Conclusions 241

Index 249

Preface

Everytime I start to write a project, be it a book, an article or a commentary, I always ask myself, "would I want to read this?" "Would reading this be worth my time as a researcher, teacher, or just a regular everyday person?" "Will this book enlighten me? Help me learn something new, or just be an interesting read?" Hopefully this book will do some or all of these things for you the reader. Many of us have at least some understandings of what a courtroom is and what goes on in it, but not everyone may be familiar with the concept of a courtroom as an arena that can help instead of punishing. While treatment or problem-oriented courts have been around for over 30 years, they are still considered by many a relatively recent innovation in the criminal justice system. There has been some mainstream press and attention from high profile political leaders like President Obama's visit to the ReNew Reentry Court in Newark, NJ in 2015, but many in the general public, including students in criminal justice, criminology, justice studies, sociology, public health, political science, psychology, law, and other fields may not be familiar with treatment courts and the exciting opportunity they offer clients. These programs can help in so many areas including drug treatment, housing, education, employment as well as so many others you will read about in these pages.

My own journey to treatment courts started as a graduate student in criminal justice at Temple University in Philadelphia, PA. One summer, I was hired as a project manager for a research project examining the Philadelphia Juvenile Drug Court. Part of my duties involved attending court sessions to document what was going on during the court sessions.

I was instantly transfixed by the commitment of the judge and the treatment court workgroup in assisting the youths in the program. So many of the young people in their caseload faced a multitude of challenges from family dysfunction to drug use, trouble doing well in school to finding jobs. The compassion the judge and treatment court had for these youth, and the visible impact they had was impressive, even to my objective researcher's mind. My work on that project culminated in two articles and several presentations and gave me the experience to conduct another observational study of the ReNew Reentry Court in Newark, NJ, another impressive program. As will be discussed in the coming chapters, both programs helped on so many levels and ways. My experience in these programs also left me wanting to do more for treatment courts. I decided to write this book to help educate and inform readers about these courts.

The purpose of this book is to act as a relatively short introduction to the various types of treatment courts, the philosophy behind them, and to discuss their benefits and limitations. This book would be a perfect supplement for college courses looking at treatment programs, courts, and the criminal justice system in general. Practitioners like judges, prosecutors and defense attorneys, police, social workers, and others who work with clients of the criminal justice system, may also gain valuable insights and knowledge about treatment courts. Finally, the public, who tend to get their information about the criminal justice system from fictional media representations and short news stories in the media, can also benefit from a deeper understanding of what treatment courts are and how they can help solve some of the challenges facing our society when it comes to rehabilitation and recidivism of criminal offenders. It should be noted that as a fairly short, supplementary text, this book is not conceptualized as the final word on any of the treatment court models. As research is ongoing in these areas, there will always be new sources to review and studies to provide insights into these programs.

I hope you enjoy this book and gain an understanding of treatment courts and the potential benefits they offer the criminal justice system, clients of these programs, and our general society.

Thanks for reading!

Christopher Salvatore
Montclair, NJ

Treatment Courts and Making a Difference: The Personal Touch Matters

Turn on a computer, smartphone, or television, or just pick up an old-fashioned newspaper, and you will see crime remains a major challenge in the United States. The criminal justice system faces an endless list of challenges, ranging from limited resources to ever-changing public opinion, and the need to provide effective treatment and prevention services. Three of the biggest challenges in the criminal justice system are: (1) finding alternatives to incarceration that can address public safety, (2) providing cost savings to the community, and (3) finding what can be done to help those leaving jails and prisons succeed once released back into the community. Without successful strategies in these areas, the "revolving door" of offending, incarceration, then release, followed by the same cycle, will repeat itself, generation to generation, in communities worldwide. The criminal justice system needs solutions, not only to lighten the load of practitioners such as police, prosecutors, judges, and probation and parole officers, but also to alleviate criticisms of its ineffectiveness in dealing with repeat offenders and to provide opportunities for long-term success for clients of the criminal justice system, which ultimately saves time and money for both society and the criminal justice system and may also spare potential victims. Practitioners like police and judges, policymakers, and the public need to know that solutions to these challenges exist in the form of treatment courts.

Over the last 30 years, treatment-oriented courts like drug and reentry courts have become a popular way to divert offenders from the criminal justice system. They support those seeking treatment for various issues like substance use disorders (drug courts), provide treatment and support for mental health issues (mental health courts), and help upon reentry for those released from prison (reentry courts) (Salvatore et al., 2020). While these programs may all have a different area of focus and utilize various types of treatment, they all have in common that they are grounded in the therapeutic jurisprudence model. This model engages actors and agencies across multiple areas of the client's life. These areas may include education, drug treatment, and housing and employment support to provide judicial intervention and supervision, which connects the client with courtroom workgroup members, including the judge, defense attorney, prosecutor, and others such as a program director and probation officer. These connections are then used to help promote the client's success (Redlich & Han, 2014).

Crime is still very much an issue in the United States. In the year ending 2019, there were 10,085,207 arrests nationwide (FBI, 2019). A large portion of those arrests, 1,553,862, were for drug abuse violations (FBI, 2019), reflecting the ongoing challenges drugs pose for the United States and the need for diversion programs like drug courts. As stated, drug courts provide a sound alternative to incarceration, with ample evidence supporting their use in lowering recidivism. For example, in a 2003 study by the National Institute of Justice, 17,000 drug court graduates from programs throughout the United States had only a 16.4 percent rate of being arrested and charged with a felony within one year of graduating from the program (Roman et al., 2003). Like most treatment-oriented courts, drug courts are grounded in therapeutic jurisprudence, which provides the conceptual key to participants' success.

Reentry is a core challenge for those leaving jails and prisons. Studies have found a decreasing rate of offenders being released in recent years (Kaeble & Cowhig, 2018). However, we still had 443,740 inmates released from state and federal prisons in 2021 (Carson, 2022), demonstrating a substantial population of individuals experiencing not only incarceration but the challenges of reentry. These inmates will face challenges as they reenter society, including housing, education, finances, employment, family reunification, substance abuse disorders, mental health issues, and lingering legal problems (Phillips & Spencer, 2013). With recidivism rates high across the nation, reentry courts provide a much-needed tool to help those returning to the community prevent reoffending (Taylor, 2014).

Therapeutic jurisprudence utilizes judicial actors as agents of therapeutic change in clients' lives (Redlich & Han, 2014). The therapeutic jurisprudence model incorporates a variety of practices, such as involving members of the courtroom workgroup to not only provide supervision but also to devise a treatment plan and provide support across multiple life domains like education, housing, employment, and mental health services, to promote the success of the program participant (Redlich & Han, 2014). Scholars such as Fay-Ramirez (2015) have argued for the benefits of employing therapeutic jurisprudence as a theoretical foundation for the success of treatment court program participants. In practice, therapeutic jurisprudence builds social bonds and provides mentoring and support from the courtroom workgroup to guide the client to the necessary services and support for lasting success. A variety of national evaluation-based studies of treatment court programs grounded in therapeutic jurisprudence, such as Salvatore and colleagues (2011, 2020), as well as international studies, such as McIvor (2009) and Toki (2017), have found treatment-oriented courts may provide the services a client needs, such as drug treatment, educational support, employment services, and mental health counseling. These studies have also shown that these programs create bonds between the client and the treatment team.

Like all treatment and prevention strategies, there are successes and failures, with some evidence suggesting the benefits of treatment courts like drug courts. For example, a multisite evaluation study conducted by the US National Institute of Justice in 2011 examined 23 drug courts and six comparison sites. The results found several promising findings: those who participated in drug courts were less likely to relapse relative to those in the comparison group, had fewer positive drug tests, and had reductions in criminal behaviors (such as being less likely to commit crime versus to those in comparison groups) (Rossman et al. 2011). In another meta-analytic study, Mitchell and colleagues (2012) found that drug court programs have lower recidivism rates. Turning attention to cost-effectiveness, a 2016 report from the Washington State Institute for Public Policy found that drug courts for adult and juvenile populations were more cost-effective than traditional processing. In sum, while evidence regarding the effectiveness of drug courts continues to be an ongoing area of inquiry, there is some evidence to support their utility. An essential aspect of drug and treatment courts is understanding the key to their effectiveness: the social bonds built through the treatment process.

A theme explored throughout this book is the role of specific factors in bringing about successful changes in clients of problem-oriented courts. One such factor that has been identified throughout the criminological and treatment literature is social bonds, which has been found to be crucial in the success or failure of treatment and prevention programs (Salvatore & Taniguchi, 2012). It should be noted that social bonds will be the focus of this example and this introduction but other theoretical orientations will be discussed throughout this book. For example, Gilmore and colleagues (2005) utilized social control theory to study the bonds that influenced desistance in a juvenile drug court program in Maricopa County, Arizona. The study found that anti-social bonds to peers and siblings influenced adverse outcomes, such as a higher number of delinquent acts. Conversely, Salvatore et al. (2011) found greater participation of parents and other family members led to positive outcomes (e.g., lower rates of drug use) in juvenile drug court participants. More recently, Salvatore et al. (2020) found that the influence of treatment team members in a reentry court, in particular the judge, was a critical factor in successful outcomes with the bond between the judge and clients of the program being identified by staff, participants, and graduates of the program as being an essential component of programmatic success. These studies support the notion that a treatment-oriented court can facilitate bonds between the participant and their family and peers and the treatment court workgroup, particularly the judge. As the various types of problem-oriented courts are examined as we move through the chapters, we will find other members of the treatment court also build important bonds with clients in these programs, including probation officers and graduates from the program who act as peer-mentors.

Grounded in Hirschi's (1969) social bond theory, the notion of social bonds is that they connect individuals to mainstream society through attachment and bonds built through education, employment, family, prosocial peers, and in this case, the attachment made by participation in a treatment court program. Hirschi's (1969) core idea is to adopt a stake in conformity or mainstream society to prevent delinquency and crime; individuals are less likely to engage in crime if they have stronger attachments and bonds. It should be noted that this is a fairly basic conceptualization of social bond theory. In a forthcoming chapter, more complex iterations of social bond theory will be discussed.

Salvatore (2013, 2018) argued that social bonds are essential in preventing crime in youth populations. The strength of social bonds may help connect individuals to mainstream society, as fear of losing these bonds prevents engaging in behaviors that endanger them. In other words, if someone has strong bonds to prosocial others, such as parents, peers, coworkers, or their spouse, they will not engage in behaviors that will disappoint those individuals or risk the bonds they have built with them. Regarding treatment courts, participants who have made bonds with judges and other members of the treatment court workgroup may be less apt to reoffend, use drugs, or violate the program's conditions for fear of disappointing these individuals.

Social Bonds Matter

As mentioned above, social bonds and mentoring can be crucial to client success in treatment courts. Numerous studies provide examples of such bonds being meaningful to treatment court participants and leading to successful outcomes. For instance, in a recent study by Salvatore et al. (2020), a participant described the role of the judges being a critical factor in their success. One participant discussed the judge's level of interest in participants' lives and engagement with participants in the reentry court program beyond the program's confines as a life-changing experience. One subject discussed how the judge took them to Lens-Crafters and utilized their social network to help the program participants. This level of dedication and interest builds a connection between the program participant and the judge, not only accomplishing a practical goal but also fostering a social bond and relationship between the justice system and client in a manner that many may not have experienced from a prosocial role model such as a judge in the past.

In another example from Salvatore et al. (2020), a participant in the reentry court program described how the judge married him and his spouse in the same courtroom where the treatment court sessions occurred. Salvatore et al. (2020) discussed how this type of experience demonstrates the judge's investment in clients and gives participants in the program a sense of being valued on a human level that they had never experienced in their prior experiences in the criminal justice system. This sense of value is best reflected in a quotation from the article where a treatment team member reflected on the building of bonds between the judge and participants:

> [There were] times when the judge gave someone a break or listened when team members were talking or absorbed a compliment they were given. Things the team did [to] build up trust and confidence. Judge [one] takes risks with the guys and reveals [themselves]. [Judge one] tells [the participants] … things, gives compliments, gives personal advice, asks disarming and personal questions. (pp. 210–211)

In another quotation, a participant discussed the relationship between participants and the judge as a critical bond:

> [The judges] give them back their trust in humanity. The system is very dehumanizing and stripping. Interaction with the judges gives them back something they have lost. Judges have a power dynamic, [they] sit on the bench, make decisions, talk during sessions, [and] decide about sanctions. [The] guys create close relationships with [the] judges. [The participants] have ambivalent opinions about [program] office, [they are] cautious and ambivalent with the program, but not with the judges, [those relationships] are very different and [the] bonds that get formed. (p. 210)

Both of these quotations reflect the impact that judicial interest and support had on participants in reentry court. These findings suggest the potential influence the connections build between problem-oriented courts' clients, and in the examples discussed the judges are reflective of the philosophical grounding of therapeutic jurisprudence, as well as the role of social bonds in problem-oriented courts.

Taylor's (2010) work further demonstrates judges' interest in participants, humanizing them beyond their current or ex-offender role. In an example from Taylor's (2010) examination of the STAR reentry court in Philadelphia, Pennsylvania, Taylor discussed the importance of the family bond in the court sessions, noting, in one session, that the judge asked a participant, "Now am I gonna get to meet your girlfriend sometime?" (pp. 15–16). Taylor further stated the judge explained he "just want[s] to thank her for all she has done to help the participant stay on the right track" (p. 16). During the STAR court evaluation, the reentry court judges frequently asked about participants' family lives, including children's births, child custody issues, sick parents, and new romantic partnerships.

In a final example, a participant discussed how the judge and treatment group created a "family vibe" in the program that carried over into recreational activities with the judge, treatment group, and current and former participants, including a fishing trip:

> So, for us, it's more or so, like a definite family vibe that they always give us because it's like, when I graduated with my associates and [several of the team members and one of the judges] were on vacation and came [to the graduation ceremony]—these guys all got together and took me out for lunch, and then Judge One was saying, … was talking to my aunt and of all the things they were talking about, they're talking about fish, Judge One telling us fish stories, she's telling Judge One fish stories, and Judge One is like, "Hey, we should go fishing sometimes." I'm not looking to go. Like, I don't fish [laughs]. (p. 211)

Salvatore et al. (2020) also discussed other activities, such as holiday parties, graduation ceremonies, and participating in races with one of the judges. The examples mentioned above reflect the importance of social bonds to clients in treatment courts and show how by going outside the box of the traditional adversarial court, treatment courts can utilize social bonds to create not only a positive programmatic experience for clients of the program but also, help facilitate prosocial bonds, which, as mentioned in Salvatore (2018), can help prevent reoffending and relapse. As we move through the following chapters we will explore other theories and factors that influence success in specialty or treatment court programs.

Conclusion

Treatment courts create a bond and connection between the participant and the treatment workgroup. Most have a vision of the court process as a mostly adversarial one, with a stern judge admonishing a defendant, an aggressive prosecutor, and a diligent defense attorney, all working towards the goal of justice. Many may be unaware of the treatment court approach, grounded in jurisprudence and teamwork to help the offender meet goals and objectives, with the ultimate goal of being a prosocial member of society, not involved in the criminal justice system.

Disrupting common notions of the court and criminal justice process, treatment courts utilize therapeutic jurisprudence to foster bonds and connections that help participants in the programs reach goals like attaining education, employment, and housing. Building bonds between the judge and other treatment courtroom group members also creates a connection that allows the participant to feel the system treats them as human beings, perhaps for the first time. As identified in studies such as Salvatore et al. (2020), this type of treatment, especially by judges, can connect to positive programmatic outcomes.

Through treatment courts, we see that therapeutic jurisprudence is a theoretical orientation that may help resolve underlying challenges and issues for criminal justice system clients. By working with offenders as clients rather than offenders or prisoners, these programs integrate a personal, human touch, allowing participants to not only be viewed as individuals but also for the participants to see members of the courtroom workgroup as mentors and build bonds that can help foster success rather than resentment or frustration.

Programs like Renew in Newark, New Jersey, and STAR Courts in Philadelphia, Pennsylvania, provide a model through which other treatment courts can utilize social bonds and prosocial mentoring to steer participants in these programs to success in employment, education, housing, and parenting, all critical aspects of long-term prosocial behavior that prevent reoffending. While research in treatment courts is ongoing, social bonds' utility in preventing and treating offending is well established. It will likely continue to be a vital part of each for those involved in the criminal justice system for years to come.

In the chapters that follow, we will examine therapeutic jurisprudence; the evolution and history of treatment courts; the various types of treatment courts used throughout the United States, including discussing their benefits and limitations; theoretical implications of treatment courts; and finally, policy recommendations. Throughout these chapters we will see the common elements in each type of treatment court, examples from studies which help illustrate the potential benefits of these programs, and how they may help provide a solution to challenges around recidivism in the United States.

References

Carson, E. A. (2022). *Prisoners in 2021.* NCJ 305125. US Department of Justice, Bureau of Justice Statistics. https://bjs.ojp.gov/sites/g/files/xyckuh236/files/media/document/p21st.pdf.

Fay-Ramirez, S. (2014). Therapeutic jurisprudence in practice: Change in family treatment court norms over time. *Law & Social Inquiry, 40*(1), 205–236. https://doi.org/10.1111/lsi.12067.

Federal Bureau of Investigation. (2019). *Crime in the United States, 2018.* Uniform Crime Report. Criminal Justice Information Services Division. https://ucr.fbi.gov/crime-in-the-u.s/2018/crime-in-the-u.s.-2018/topic-pages/persons-arrested.pdf.

Gilmore A. S., Rodriguez, N., & Webb, V. J. (2005). Substance abuse and drug courts: The role of social bonds in juvenile drug courts. *Youth Violence and Juvenile Justice, 3*(4), 287–315. https://doi.org/10.1177/1541204005278803.

Hirschi, T. (1969). *Causes of delinquency.* University of California Press.

Kaeble, D., & Cowhig, M. (2018). *Correctional populations in the United States, 2016.* NCJ 251211. US Department of Justice, Bureau of Justice Statistics. https://www.bjs.gov/content/pub/pdf/cpus16.pdf.

McIvor, G. (2009). Therapeutic jurisprudence and procedural justice in Scottish drug courts. *Criminology & Criminal Justice, 9*(1), 29–49. https://doi.org/10.1177/1748895808099179.

Mitchell, O., Wilson, D. B., Eggers, A., & MacKenzie, D. L. (2011). Assessing the effectiveness of drug courts on recidivism: A meta-analytic review of traditional and non-traditional drug courts. *Journal of Criminal Justice, 40*(1), 60–71. https://doi.org/10.1016/j.jcrimjus.2011.11.009.

Phillips, L. A., & Spencer, W. M. (2013). The challenge of reentry from prison to society. *Journal of Current Issues in Crime, Law & Law Enforcement, 6*(2), 123–133.

Redlich, A. D., & Han, W. (2014). Examining the links between therapeutic jurisprudence and mental health court completion. *Law and Human Behavior, 38*(2), 109–118. https://doi.org/10.1037/lhb0000041.

Roman, J., Townsend, W., & Bhati, A. (2003). *Recidivism rates for drug court graduates: Nationally based estimates, final report.* Urban Institute. https://www.ncjrs.gov/pdffiles1/201229.pdf.

Rossman, S. B., Rempel, M., Roman, J. K., Zweig, J. M., Lindquist, C. H., Green, M., Downey, P. M., Yahner, J., Bhati, A. S., & Farole Jr., D. (2011). *The multisite adult drug court evaluation: The impact of drug courts, Volume 4.* Urban Institute, Policy Justice Center. https://www.ojp.gov/pdffiles1/nij/grants/237112.pdf.

Salvatore, C. (2013). Arrested adolescent offenders: A study of delayed transitions to adulthood. LFB Scholarly Publications.

Salvatore, C. (2018). *Sex, crime, drugs, and just plain stupid behaviors: The new face of young adulthood in America.* Palgrave Macmillan.

Salvatore, C., Henderson, J. S., Hiller, M. A., & White, E. (2010). An observational study of team meetings and status hearings in juvenile drug court. *Drug Court Review, 1*(1), 95–124.

Salvatore, C., Hiller, M. L., Samuelson, B., Henderson, J., & White, E. (2011). A systematic observational study of a juvenile drug court judge. *Juvenile and Family Court Journal, 62*(4),19–36.

Salvatore, C., Michalsen, V., & Taylor, C. (2020). Reentry court judge: The key to the court. *Journal of Offender Rehabilitation, 59*(4), 198–222. https://doi.org/10.1080/10509674.2020.1733164.

Salvatore, C., & Taniguchi, T. (2012). Do social bonds matter for emerging adults? *Deviant Behavior, 33*(9), 738–756. https://doi.org/10.1080/01639625.2012.679888.

Taylor, C. (2010). An investigation of the key components of the supervision to aid reentry (STAR) program. A report submitted to the Federal Probation Department for the Eastern District of Pennsylvania. https://digitalcommons.lasalle.edu/cgi/viewcontent.cgi?article=1003&context=soc_crj_faculty.

Taylor, C. (2014). *Program evaluation of the Federal Reentry Court in the Eastern District of Philadelphia: Report on program effectiveness for the first 164 reentry court participants.* LaSalle University Digital Commons. https://digitalcommons.lasalle.edu/soc_crj_faculty/1/.

Toki, V. (2017). Legal responses to mental health: Is therapeutic jurisprudence the answer? The experience in New Zealand. *Journal of Ethics in Mental Health, 10,* 118.

Washington State Institute for Public Policy. (2016). *Drug courts: Juvenile justice.* http://www.wsipp.wa.gov/BenefitCost/Program/44.

Treatment Courts

CHAPTER 1

The Crime Problem and the Incarceration "Fix"

Have you watched the news lately? Checked Google News? How about Netflix? HULU? HBO Max? Amazon Prime? Apple TV? The Roku Channel? Tubi? Or the rest of the ever-changing and expanding lists of streaming services? Let me guess, each and every one of these platforms has some type of programming focusing on crime. Maybe it was a docudrama about Ted Bundy, or perhaps a rerun of *NYPD Blue* or the various *CSIs*. It could have been a revival of a long-dead series like *Dexter*, a high-end documentary about a cold case like the murder of JonBonét Ramsey, or even a miniseries about a high-profile murder like that of Gianna Versace, complete with popstar casting and exotic locations. Regardless of precisely what it was, it is very likely you wouldn't have to look far for a report, movie, TV series, book, comic book, video game, or podcast about crime. If we were to judge from the media representations just listed, you would think a crime was being committed in every home, every street corner, every college campus, every highway, every Target, every Walmart, every public park, well, just about every day, everywhere, always. After all, just a quick run-through of my recommendations from Netflix, HULU, and Tubi showed me dozens of serial killers, cold cases, crime dramas, and detectives.

Even if you haven't seen any of the above types of drama, you probably speak to friends, relatives, and coworkers who share their fear of crime or perhaps even their own experiences. Maybe it was a horrifying tale of a loved one murdered by a serial killer, or perhaps more likely the victim of a drunk driver. While many fear being a victim of violent crimes, various factors like age, gender, race/ethnicity, and where one lives can influence the chance of victimization by a violent crime like assault, rape, or murder. However, it should be stated there can always be exceptions to the statistical trends and patterns, and all victims of crime should be given support and empathy. That being said, just how bad is the crime problem in the United States? What are the actual numbers and trends in the United States regarding crime and the harm caused by it, and how do demographic factors and criminal justice policy share the crime problem? As the media may represent, is a massive storm always brewing and threatening to harm all of us?

So, just how accurate are the media representations of crime? Are they on or off track? The reality is somewhere in the middle. The U.S. does have one of the highest crime rates compared to other high-income democracies. On the other hand, the crime rate in the U.S. has dropped significantly from its high point in the early 1990s. To truly understand the crime problem in the U.S., we also need to have a firm grasp of one of the primary responses to crime: incarceration. The high rate of incarceration in jails and prisons at local, state, and federal levels across the country is grounded in the "Get Tough" approach, which has dominated much of the rhetoric around crime since the late 1970s. This approach is rooted in the two models of the criminal justice system presented by Herbert Packer in his book, *The Limits of Criminal Sanction* (1968). Packer explained the due process and crime control models in this book. The due process model focuses on protecting defendants' rights and is driven by respect for the formal legal process. At each stage of the criminal justice process, due process presents impediments to the criminal justice system to protect the defendants' rights. From the due process perspective, the criminal justice system is an obstacle course in which the system must meet challenges to make sure the system makes as few mistakes as possible (Packer, 1968).

Conversely, the crime control model focuses on protecting the public from victimization. In other words, unlike the due process model, which focuses on protecting defendants' rights, emphasis is placed on public safety and crime reduction from the crime control model. This model looks to process cases effectively and efficiently, recognizing the limits of time and money in limiting the ability to provide a long, drawn-out process (such as a trial) for all criminals. Packer (1968) stated that the criminal justice process is a screening process. Each stage, pre-arrest through disposition, involves a standardized process whose success is measured by the ability to pass cases along to the conclusion. If the due process model is an obstacle course, then from Packer's perspective the crime control model is an assembly line.

As stated above, the "Get Tough" approach to crime has dominated criminal justice policy since the 1970s (Levitt, 2004). Using the "Get Tough" approach, crime in the U.S. has been met with increased use of law enforcement, and more frequent use of incarceration in jails and prisons for more extended periods (Mauer, 2003). As time went on, there was a need for more jails and prisons to be built across the country to respond to this need (Mauer, 2001). This led to the mass incarceration of more than 2 million people in the United States daily in jails and prisons. Many scholars have argued that mass incarceration does more harm than good, damaging social bonds and ties to communities, removing whole generations of individuals from families, and having relatively little impact on the crime rate. In other words, contrary to popular opinion, putting more people in jails and prisons doesn't fix the crime problem; it usually ends up having the opposite effect. Many argue other strategies such as restorative justice approaches, diversion programs like drug courts, and community-based strategies could be more effective without the downsides of mass incarceration (Weissman, 2009; Wolff et al., 2020).

How Much Crime and What Does It Cost?

To frame any discussion about responses to crime (like treatment courts), we need to understand the scope and costs of crime to society. As mentioned above, there is a lot of crime in the United States, but how much crime is happening? Perhaps it is just as important to know the cost of crime to its victims, the criminal justice system, and general society.

How Much Crime Occurs?

While there are a variety of sources of crime, there are two sources typically cited for crime data: the Uniform Crime Report (UCR) and the National Crime Victimization Survey (NCVS) (Payne et al., 2019). The Federal Bureau of Investigation (FBI) administers the Uniform Crime

Report to over 18,000 police departments across the U.S. to report crimes occurring in their jurisdiction. Police gather crime information primarily from individuals reporting crimes they have witnessed or been a victim of. The FBI compiles this data yearly and disseminated it in a report called *Crime in the United States*. The report provides information on two sets of crimes. Part I crimes are generally viewed as more serious, including criminal homicide (e.g., murder and non-negligent manslaughter), forcible rape, aggravated assault, arson, burglary larceny-theft, and motor vehicle theft. Part II crimes are generally viewed as less severe offenses. They include curfew and loitering violations, fraud, liquor law violations, gambling, driving under the influence (DUI), embezzlement, crimes against family and children, suspicion, vagrancy, vandalism, prostitution and commercial vice, drunkenness, drug abuse violations, buying and selling stolen property, carrying and possessing weapons, and other crimes not explicitly identified as Part I offenses (except traffic violations) (Payne et al., 2019). Per the most recent *Crime in the United States* report available as of the writing of the book, there were approximately 1,203,808 violent crimes in the United States in 2019 (FBI, n.d.b), and an estimated 6,925,677 property crime offenses in the United States in 2019 (FBI, n.d.c).

The above estimates may provide a general idea of how many violent and property crimes occur in the United States. Still, a large number of crimes are unreported to the police. It is estimated that up to 60% of these crimes aren't reported to the police for various reasons. Some victims or witnesses may view the crime as a personal issue and don't want to share it with police or believe there isn't anything the police can do to assist. Others may view the victimization as not severe enough to warrant formal attention from police; some may also be afraid they will be victimized by the perpetrator again if they report the incident to police (Langton et al., 2012). As a result of underreporting to police, many crimes are never reported to the FBI and therefore aren't reported in the UCR. The term "dark figure of crime" is used to describe the crimes not reported (Payne et al., 2019). In practice, some crime data in the UCR, such as homicide data, is likely more accurate than others, since evidence of murder, such as a corpse or reports of a missing person, is likely to attract the attention of police. In contrast, crimes such as sexual assault may go unreported and be caught in the dark figure of crime.

As a result of the dark figure of crime, criminologists also use other sources to collect data about crime. One of the primary sources of this information is the National Crime Victim Survey (NCVS) of the Bureau of Justice Statistics (BJS). The NCVS gathers data from a random sample of households across the U.S. every six months. Survey respondents are aged 12 or older and are asked various demographic questions, including age, sex, race and Hispanic origin, marital status, education level, and income and if they had been victimized. The NCVS collects information for each victimization incident about the offender, including demographic characteristics such as age, race and Hispanic origin, sex, and victim-offender relationship, characteristics of the crime, including the time and where it occurred, if weapons were used, any injuries, as well as economic costs of the crime. The survey also asks respondents if the crime was reported to police, reasons the crime was or was not reported, and victim experiences with the criminal justice system (Bureau of Justice Statistics, n.d.). The NCVS does not collect data on homicide victims (since they are deceased and cannot be surveyed) and is limited to household and personal victimizations (Payne et al., 2019).

The most recent NCVS reported around 46% of violent and 33% of property victimizations were reported to police in 2021. The number of violent crimes (not including simple assault) was approximately 4.5 million in 2021. The number of property crimes including burglary and trespassing victimizations in 2021 was approximately 11.6 million (Thompson & Tapp, 2022). It should be noted that the rates of violent and property victimization were lower than those reported in 2020 in the NCVS, respectively, though as data from both UCR and NCVS demonstrate, crime rates remain relatively high in the United States and reflect a significant crime problem.

What Does Crime Cost?

Crime has costs across a variety of areas for victims. Some victims will struggle with the financial costs of repairing damaged property or the time lost from work to cooperate with police and courts to prosecute perpetrators. Homeowners' or renters' insurance may not always cover the cost of property loss. It can't replace the sentimental value associated with items damaged or stolen during a crime like a burglary or a robbery. There may also be financial costs of medical or mental health care that the victim's health insurance may not cover. Others will face emotional costs, suffering from disorders like posttraumatic stress disorder, which may cause some to be fearful of going out in public or going to areas where they feel vulnerable. Finally, some will face physical health challenges due to injuries incurred during their victimization that may require short- and long-term treatment. Some victims of crimes like rape may have to deal with a lifetime of health challenges and care. These three areas, financial, emotional, and physical, are genuine for victims and can alter how they live their day-to-day lives.

The cost of crime in these areas may be impossible to tabulate as there are both material (e.g., cars, computers, jewelry) and non-material costs (e.g., stress, depression, loss of sentimental objects such as family heirlooms) that don't have a dollar value. In 1996, Miller and colleagues reported that for a crime like rape, the initial costs to victims maybe 7.5 billion dollars per year. Still, when intangible factors like loss of quality of life are considered, this figure may rise to as high as 127 billion dollars (Miller et al., 1996, p. 1). These numbers help us gauge the impact of the victimization experience and show us just how costly intangible losses may be for victims of crime. Others like Wright and Vicneire (2010) estimate the tangible costs of crime to be about $100 billion annually. More recent estimates based on the 120 million crimes committed in the U.S. in 2017 was 2.6 trillion dollars in personal costs to victims, about $1,900 per person in the U.S. (Miller et al., 2021). Regardless of the dollar amount, it is clear that crime costs victims and society a significant amount of money in the United States annually.

The Cost of the Criminal Justice System

Not only does crime cost victims and society, but there is also an additional, massive cost related to crime: the criminal justice system, police, and other law enforcement agencies, the criminal courts, and the correctional system, including jails and prisons. Estimates of the annual costs of the criminal justice system's local, state, and federal branches are in the billions. Using data from 2017, Buehler (2021) reported local, state, and federal governments collectively spent $305 billion on police, courts, and corrections (p. 4), a staggering amount of money for even a large, high-income nation like the United States.

In addition to the shocking costs of the expenditures of the criminal justice system in 2017, is how high these costs have risen since the late 1970s when the United States began its shift to a "Get Tough" approach to crime. For example, from 1997 to 2017, real (inflation-adjusted) expenditures in all three branches of the criminal justice system increased. Policing increased 78%, skyrocketing from $84 billion in 1997 to $149 billion in 2017. Similarly, judicial and legal functions expenditures increased from $41 billion in 1997 to $67 billion in 2012, slightly dropping to $66 billion in 2017. Corrections expenditures increased by 42%, from $63 billion in 1997 to $89 billion in 2017 (Buehler, 2021, p. 1). In a 2015 article in *The New Yorker*, Keller reported politicians across the political aisle were becoming increasingly aware of the need for alternatives to incarceration. In recent years, we have seen an increased use of these alternatives. Along with the focus on states, various scholars have also turned their focus to strategies that may be more cost effective than the use of incarceration. The focus of this book will look at a variety of these strategies in the form of treatment courts.

The Main Response: Mass Incarceration

Before the 1970s, the United States had an incarceration rate on par with many similar nations; however, with the 1970s, we saw marked shifts in correctional philosophies. These changes included the change away from the medical model of incarceration, which focused on managing inmates as if they were ill, and corrections focused on providing treatment to reintegrate offenders into communities once they were "better" (Seiter, 2017).

The Incarceration Boom

A critical moment in the movement away from the medical model and towards the incarceration boom was the *Martinson Report*. Conducted in the early 1970s, Robert Martinson and his colleagues reviewed over 200 correctional treatment programs to gauge their effectiveness in reducing recidivism. Their work did find a few correlations with treatment programs and decreases in recidivism, but there wasn't any finding of any one program significantly decreasing recidivism. As a result,

Martinson's review found that "nothing works." Martinson's work was largely interpreted as "nothing works to successfully treat offenders who are incarcerated," instead of its intended, "nothing works universally to successfully treat offenders who are incarcerated." It may seem like a minor difference in phrasing, but it had a huge impact on corrections. This finding resulted in a significant shift away from using the medical model in corrections and left public officials looking for more cost-effective ways to make corrections more punitive with ample ammunition to shift correctional policy (Seiter, 2017, pp. 9–10).

The incarceration boom has been used to describe the marked increase in incarceration from the 1970s to the present. Why did the "boom" in incarceration happen? There are several key areas that may explain. First, there was the impact of Martinson's report. Next, there was a significant increase in crime rates in the 1970s. Finally, fear of crime in the public increased, and corrections became a hot-button issue with political leaders and the media. Due to these factors, politicians called for the need to "Get Tough" on criminals to keep citizens safe and for offenders to serve "hard" time as punishment. Corrections responded to demands from politicians and the public through the "Get Tough" approach by focusing on public safety over inmate amenities (Seiter, 2017). This approach also led to shifts in sentencing approaches, often incorporating mandatory minimum sentences, mandatory incarceration, and longer prison sentences than in the past (Pfaff, 2017). As a result of these factors, we saw incarceration increase during the 1970s and beyond.

Despite the COVID-19 pandemic, the U.S. still maintains a high population of incarcerated individuals. By the end of March 2021, about 1.8 million people were incarcerated in the United States (Kang-Brown et al., 2021). Pre-pandemic, the United States had an estimated 6,344,000 persons under the supervision of adult correctional systems in the United States. This includes those incarcerated in jails and prisons and those on probation and parole. It should be noted this was a decrease of about 65,000 fewer persons than in 2018.

These numbers are of note because, for the first time since 1999, the correctional population was less than 6.4 million (Minton et al., 2021). While this decrease is notable, it is still far from the 360,0000 correctional system inmates in 1972 (Kaeble & Cowhig, 2018).

Has Mass Incarceration Worked to Reduce Crime?

Two key concepts need to be defined to fully understand the influence of mass incarceration on the crime decline of recent decades. First is incapacitation, which means that mass incarceration has reduced the crime rate because offenders are behind bars and cannot commit additional crimes (Seiter, 2017). If incapacitation has reduced the crime rate, approximately 1.8 to 2 million offenders are prevented from victimizing the public. Second is the notion of deterrence, which is any deterrent effect that the possibility of being arrested, convicted, and sent to jail or prison has on potential offenders (Seiter, 2017). If the deterrence is effective, then harsher punishments such as longer prison terms deter potential offenders from offending.

Since the U.S. has had a relatively high incarceration rate, it seems logical to conclude that mass incarceration works. After all, if the crime rate has dropped over time, then there must be an effective incapacitation effect. Fewer offenders on the street translates to less crime, which seems, at least on the surface, to be the case. On the other hand, if deterrence works, and we see around 2 million people incarcerated in the U.S. yearly, then there may be a significant deterrent effect of mass incarceration as well. However, if we look beneath the surface at incapacitation, we find little support for the incapacitation effect, which is what is the focus of this section. Deterrence is also a key area to examine but less relevant to the focus of this chapter, though we will circle back to it later in this book.

Key Conceptual Issues About Incapacitation

There are three key conceptual issues countering the argument that incapacitation has significantly impacted the crime rate in recent years. The first issue is rooted in the idea, argued by many criminological theories such as Moffitt's (1993) developmental taxonomy, that a relatively small group of offenders commits the bulk of crimes. In her original taxonomy, Moffitt referred to these as life-course-persistent offenders (1993). Given their propensity to commit a crime, it seems statistically likely they will get arrested, processed through the criminal justice system, and end up in jail or prison. Moffitt also identified a second group of offenders who commit fewer, less violent crimes: adolescent-limited offenders. The adolescent-limited offenders usually stop offending earlier and are more likely to engage in illegal drug use. However, with the shift to "Get Tough" policies, the prison boom, and the war on drugs, it is likely more and more low-level offenders also got incarcerated. Locking up lower-level offenders may dilute the incapacitation effect because newer offenders (many of whom were lower level offenders like Moffitt's adolescent-limited type), would have been likely to age out of offending or simply commit fewer crimes than more serious offenders.

A second issue is related to what is referred to by criminologists as the "funnel effect." Mass incarceration simply may not influence the crime rate because many crimes never find their way into the criminal justice system. Typically visualized as a funnel, criminologists have stated that many criminals aren't arrested, and those are typically funneled out at various system stages. Of those arrested, fewer are actually processed through the system. Of those who are charged and processed, some are placed on probation, given fines, or diverted into programs like drug courts. Few end up in prison. Further, few who are sentenced to prison end up serving their entire sentence, leaving relatively few criminals who have been arrested, processed through the system, and served a full prison term; the bulk of criminals are "funneled" out of the system at the various stages described here (Schmalleger, 2016).

The final area involves the aging out of prisoners. As the "Get Tough" era has incarcerated more and more criminals for longer periods, the typical inmate is now older than in the past (Carson & Sabol, 2016). Scholars have continually found that most offenders tend to age out of offending at a relatively young age (Salvatore, 2013). The classic age crime curve has demonstrated that most offenders peak in their late teens and early 20s and then decrease their offending (Gottfredson & Hirschi, 1990). Mass incarceration has led to more and more being incarcerated for longer and longer periods; therefore, many offenders have been incarcerated past their peak offending years, most of whom won't be committing new crimes because they have aged out of offending. In other words, we are keeping offenders in prison longer than they would be offending, thereby incapacitating low-risk individuals who are likely costing far more money to warehouse in prisons than any potential savings to society in crime prevention.

The three above areas show that any influence of an incapacitation effect of mass incarceration is limited. As we will see in the next section, research supports the idea that mass incarceration has not been a successful reduction strategy.

Mass Incarceration: The Costs to Society

It is easy to reduce the costs of mass incarceration to simply the dollars and cents associated with arrest, processing through the criminal justice system, and incarceration. These are, of course, a genuine part of the costs of mass incarceration. However, there are other costs, both tangible and intangible, to communities, progress in racial/ethnic injustice areas, and to former offenders looking to transition into a prosocial life once released back into communities.

Costs to Families and Communities

It is a popular idea with politicians and the public: "lock them up and throw away the key" to keep criminals off our streets and out of our communities. Part of the problem with this thinking is that many forget that the criminals being locked up are parents, children, aunts, uncles, grandchildren, siblings, coworkers, and friends. Locking up criminals cuts them off from the ties of their family and friends, who may rely on them for social support, companionship, and care. The cost to children of incarcerated parents may be especially concerning as there are a variety of consequences for these children. While estimates vary, it is estimated that between 1.7 million and 2.7 million children experience their parents being incarcerated at least once (Shlafer et al., 2013). These children miss out on day-to-day interactions and bonding with their parents. They are also more likely to do poorly in school, experience psychological problems like anxiety, and engage in delinquency.

Lower-income, urban communities may be hit especially hard, as those leaving prison, estimated at over 625,000 from state and federal prisons in 2016 (Carson, 2018), face limited employment opportunities, lingering legal issues such as fines, substance abuse problems, mental health problems, and physical health problems. Many may never have had a job, finished high school, have an employment record, have any form of viable credit, or even have a working draft of a resume (Salvatore et al., 2020). Many of these individuals are still dealing with childhood trauma. Releasing these prisoners back into lower-income communities who are already struggling with high unemployment and other social challenges makes these communities struggle even more, ultimately worsening the conditions (Clear, 2007).

Race/Ethnicity Inequality

People from across the socioeconomic spectrum and every racial/ethnic group have experienced the impact of mass incarceration. However, statistics show that minority groups are disproportionately impacted by mass incarceration, perpetuating the cycle of racial/ethnic inequality in the United States. While the incarceration rate has dropped in recent years, evidence supports that racial disparities continue through the present and impact Black and Hispanic Americans most severely. Carson (2020) reported that in the ten years from 2009 through 2019, the imprisonment rate, which is the portion of U.S. residents in prison, dropped 17% overall. However, at the end of 2019, there were 1,096 black prisoners per 100,000 black residents, 525 Hispanic prisoners per 100,000 Hispanic residents, and 214 white prisoners per 100,000 white residents in the United States (Carson, 2020, p. 1). These numbers further support that while we see a drop in incarceration, the disparities in incarceration rates by race prevail and suggest the use of "Get Tough" approaches like mass incarceration have disproportionately impacted racial minorities (Alexander, 2012).

Post-Conviction Punishments

Many may believe that once someone has completed their sentence in jail or prison their punishment is over. Frequently this isn't the case. Felony disenfranchisement, grounded in the idea of civil death, involves some type of limited or reduced civil rights many felons face once released from conviction. The most common is being prohibited from voting. Chung (2021) reported that over five million Americans had been prohibited from voting due to restrictions on felony voting. Other areas of challenge for those convicted of felony offenses include restrictions in access to public housing, limited employment opportunities, and even limitations on the ability to marry (though that restriction is more of a thing of the past). As will be explored in the coming chapters, there have been innovations in recent years in the form of reentry programs, in particular reentry courts, which work with felony offenders to assist them in overcoming these obstacles and reclaiming their lives, not only to support themselves but also to help stabilize and support their families and communities.

Conclusion

Crime continues to be a significant problem for the United States despite the continuing decreases in the crime rate. The U.S. spends approximately $300 billion yearly dealing with the crime problem. The "Get Tough" approach, which remains popular with the public and politicians, led to the mass incarceration of millions in the U.S., which is unique among other high-income, Western nations. As research has shown, mass incarceration isn't a cost-effective solution and has a variety of collateral consequences. What many have argued is needed are more cost-effective alternatives that provide treatment and support while maintaining the positive life aspects of an offender, such as prosocial bonds and attachments to family, friends, religious congregations, co-workers and jobs, and their community. Treatment courts may be one such alternative.

The following chapters will examine alternatives to incarceration that provide cost-effective solutions. Programs like drug courts, reentry courts, and mental health courts can work with those involved in the criminal justice system to address the causes of their offending, providing support and solutions rather than punishment. These can cost less money (and provide savings to the criminal justice system and taxpayers). Still, they can also prevent collateral costs such as loss of prosocial bonds and felony disenfranchisement, which inhibit so many ex-offenders from succeeding once released from incarceration.

References

Alexander, M. (2012). *The new Jim Crow: Mass incarceration in the age of colorblindness.* The New Press.

Buehler, E. D. (2021). *Justice expenditures and employment in the United States, 2017.* NCJ 256093. US Department of Justice, Bureau of Justice Statistics. https://bjs.ojp.gov/sites/g/files/xyckuh236/files/media/document/jeeus17.pdf.

Bureau of Justice Statistics. (n.d.). National Crime Victims Survey (NCVS). https://bjs.ojp.gov/data-collection/ncvs#18s6hz.

Carson, E. A. (2018). *Prisoners in 2016.* NCJ 251149. US Department of Justice, Bureau of Justice Statistics. https://bjs.ojp.gov/library/publications/prisoners-2016.

Carson, E. A. (2020). *Prisoners in 2019.* NCJ 255115. US Department of Justice, Bureau of Justice Statistics. https://bjs.ojp.gov/content/pub/pdf/p19.pdf.

Carson, E. A., & Sabol, W. J. (2016). *Aging of the state prison population, 1993–2013.* NCJ 248766. US Department of Justice, Bureau of Justice Statistics. https://bjs.ojp.gov/content/pub/pdf/aspp9313.pdf.

Chung, J. (2021). *Voting rights in the era of mass incarceration: A primer.* The Sentencing Project. https://www.sentencingproject.org/publications/felonydisenfranchisement-a-primer/.

Clear, T. (2007). *Imprisoning communities: How mass incarceration makes disadvantaged neighborhoods worse.* Oxford University Press.

Federal Bureau of Investigation. (n.d.b). 2019 Crime in the U.S. Violent Crime. Criminal Justice Information Services Division. https://ucr.fbi.gov/crime-in-the-u.s/2019/crime-in-the-u.s.-2019/topic-pages/violent-crime.

Federal Bureau of Investigation. (n.d.c). 2019 Crime in the U.S. Property Crime. Criminal Justice Information Services Division. https://ucr.fbi.gov/crime-in-the-u.s/2019/crime-in-the-u.s.-2019/topic-pages/property-crime.

Gottfredson, M. R., & Hirschi, T. (1990). *A general theory of crime.* Stanford University Press.

Kaeble, D., & Cowhig, M. (2018). *Correctional populations in the United States, 2016.* NCJ 251211. US Department of Justice, Bureau of Justice Statistics. https://bjs.ojp.gov/library/publications/correctional-populations-united-states-2016.

Kang-Brown, J., Montagnet, C., & Heiss, J. (2021). *People in jail and prison in spring 2021.* VERA Institute of Justice. https://www.vera.org/downloads/publications/people-in-jail-and-prison-in-spring-2021.pdf.

Keller, B. (2015, June 22). Prison revolt. *The New Yorker.* https://www.newyorker.com/magazine/2015/06/29/prison-revolt.

Langton, L., Berofsky, M., Krebs, C., & Smiley McDonald, H. (2012). *Victimizations not reported to the police, 2006–2010.* NCJ 238536. US Department of Justice, Bureau of Justice Statistics. https://bjs.ojp.gov/library/publications/victimizations-not-reported-police-2006-2010.

Levitt, S. D. (2004). Understanding why crime fell in the 1990s: Four factors that explain the decline and six that do not. *The Journal of Economic Perspectives, 18*(1), 163–190. https://doi.org/10.1257/089533004773563485.

Mauer, M. (2001). The causes and consequences of prison growth in the United States. *Punishment and Society, 3,* 920. https://doi.org/10.1177/14624740122228212.

Mauer, M. (2003). *Comparative international rates of incarceration: An examination of causes and trends. Presented to the U.S. Commission on Civil Rights by the Sentencing Project.*

Miller, T., Cohen, M., Swedler, D., Ali, B., & Hendrie, D. (2021). Incidence and costs of personal and property crimes in the USA, 2017. *Journal of Benefit-Cost Analysis, 12*(1), 24–54. https://doi.org/10.1017/bca.2020.36.

Miller, T. R., Cohen, M. A., & Wiersema, B. (1996). *Victims and consequences: A new look.* US Department of Justice, National Institute of Justice. https://www.ojp.gov/pdffiles/victcost.pdf.

Minton, T. D., Beatty, L. G., & Zeng, Z. (2021). *Correctional populations in the United States, 2019: Statistics tables.* NCJ 300655. US Department of Justice, Bureau of Justice Statistics. https://bjs.ojp.gov/sites/g/files/xyckuh236/files/media/document/cpus19st.pdf.

Moffitt, T. E. (1993). Adolescence-limited and life course-persistent antisocial behavior: A developmental taxonomy. *Psychological Review, 100*(4), 674–701. https://doi.org/10.1037/0033-295X.100.4.674.

Packer, H. L. (1968). *The limits of criminal sanction.* Stanford University Press.

Payne, B., Oliver, W. M., & Marion, N. E. (2019). *Introduction to criminal justice: A balanced approach* (2nd ed.). SAGE.

Pfaff, J. (2017). *Locked in: The true causes of mass incarceration and how to achieve real reform*. Basic Books.

Salvatore, C. (2013). *Arrested adolescent offenders: A study of delayed transitions to adulthood*. LFB Scholarly Publications.

Salvatore, C., Michalsen, V., & Taylor, C. (2020). Reentry court judges: The key to the court. *Journal of Offender Rehabilitation, 59*(4), 198–222. https://doi.org/10.1080/10509674.2020.1733164.

Schmalleger, F. (2016). *Criminology* (3rd ed.). Pearson.

Seiter, R. P. (2017). *Correctional administration: Integrating theory and practice* (3rd ed.). Pearson.

Shlafer, R., Gerrity, E., Ruhland, E., & Wheeler, M. (2013). *Children with incarcerated parents: Considering children's outcomes in the context of family experiences*. University of Minnesota.

Thompson, A., & Tapp, S. N. (2022). *Criminal victimization, 2021*. NCJ 305101. US Department of Justice, Bureau of Justice Statistics. https://bjs.ojp.gov/content/pub/pdf/cv21.pdf.

Weissman, M. (2009). Aspiring to the impracticable: Alternatives to incarceration in the era of mass incarceration. *New York University Review of Law & Social Change, 33*(2), 235–270.

Wolff, K. T., Baber, L. M., Dozier, C. A., & Cordeiro, R. (2020). Assessing the efficacy of alternatives to incarceration within seven federal districts. *Justice Evaluation Journal, 3*(1), 27–53. https://doi.org/10.108 0/24751979.2019.1654354.

Wright, E. M., & Vicneire, M. L. (2010). Economic costs of victimization. In B. S. Fisher and S. P. Lab (Eds.), *The encyclopedia of victimology and crime prevention* (pp. 344–348). SAGE.

CHAPTER 2

Therapeutic Jurisprudence and the Evolution of Treatment Courts

There are many images that come to mind when we think about crime and justice; perhaps the one that is most prevalent is that of a stoic judge. When you think about a judge, what do you see? Is it a black-and-white image from an old episode of a TV show like *Perry Mason* of an older man in a black robe sitting behind a bench with a stern look on his face? Or maybe a slightly more current vision of an older man in a black robe with a stern look from a movie like *My Cousin Vinny*? Or perhaps a more recent depiction of a judge such as the female African American judge in the movie *Anger Management*? Regardless of the specifics, your image of a judge and courtroom, in general, is probably a very formal, perhaps stogy environment of rigid legal procedures and processes with lawyers arguing for and against the defendant, court reporters typing away, and bailiffs stoically observing the proceedings. In contrast, the judge sits above it all.

Can you imagine a different kind of court, where there are pleasant conversations about dating, haircuts, and apartment hunting instead of stoic demeanors and rigid procedures? Or what about a court where impromptu birthday parties for the defendant's children occur? How about a court session where instead of arguing for a defendant's guilt or innocence, the prosecutor and defense attorney, along with the judge and other members of the courtroom workgroup, are planning out the education and career goals of a defendant rather than a sentencing strategy? If you can imagine these, you can envision the environment of a problem-oriented or treatment court, a very different kind of court that provides treatment and support rather than punishment. This chapter

19

will look at what a treatment court is and how it differs from traditional courts. We will discuss how these courts evolved, how treatment courts are funded, and define therapeutic jurisprudence, the theoretical orientation in which these courts are grounded; we will then explore the role of judges in the courts and other members of the courtroom workgroup. Finally, a summary of the various treatment courts will be provided.

What Is a Problem-Oriented/Specialty/ Treatment Court?

Over the last three decades, treatment courts, also known as specialty or problem-oriented courts, have become an increasingly common way to process offenders. The focus of these courts varies from animals to drugs (below, a summary will be provided of the various types of treatment courts, and several chapters will be specifically dedicated to the most prevalent types). There is no standard definition of a treatment court that can fully capture all of what the various court models focus on; however, all treatment, problem-oriented, or specialty courts have some common elements. The first is the focus on reducing the recidivism of program participants. Next is using the collaborative approach of a courtroom workgroup to provide support and treatment to address the causes of offending and any underlying challenge areas that cause program participants to end up in the criminal justice system. The third is the use of a judge to provide monitoring and support, using a therapeutic rather than adversarial approach, seen in more traditional courts. Finally, most programs typically work with outside agencies, including employers, educational institutions, mental health and substance abuse counselors, housing programs that deal with issues around domestic abuse, anger management, managing finances, parenting, and general life skills such as computer skills and housekeeping.

Evolution of Treatment Courts

As discussed in the previous chapter, the shift to the crime control model and issues like the war on drugs led to significantly higher rates of arrest and incarceration in the United States, leading to a substantial number of incarcerated persons. For example, in 1980, approximately 580,000 people were arrested for drug offenses. By the decade's end, the number had increased to over 1.3 million (Bureau of Justice Statistics, n.d.a). In response to concerns around the effectiveness of the traditional criminal justice process, especially as it related to drug crime, treatment, specialty, or problem-solving courts (hereafter referred to as treatment courts) emerged with the first drug court in Miami Dade-County in 1989 (Kaplan et al., 2018).

Drug courts were the first treatment court to integrate substance abuse treatment and legal sanctions to divert from traditional criminal justice sentencing into jails and prisons and provide quicker processing. The core idea behind drug courts was that drugs are a key motivating factor in criminal offending, and addressing drug use would benefit the offender and the community (Snedker, 2018). The drug court program utilized judicial supervision for nonviolent felony drug offenders who agreed to participate in the program after being given the voluntary option of either standard processing through the criminal justice system (e.g., trial, plea bargaining) or pleading guilty and joining the drug court program (Lurgio, 2008).

The Miami-Dade County drug court was considered an innovative approach to processing drug offenders and viewed by many as a viable alternative to more traditional criminal justice processing (Lurgio, 2008). The drug court program was celebrated for providing services across multiple life domains by utilizing collaborative relationships with various social services and drug treatment agencies. The programs focused on addressing underlying reasons for offending. However, some still felt this early program needed to be more cohesive and coordinated. Despite this criticism, the Miami-Dade County drug court served as a template for many treatment courts to follow in the coming decades (Lurgio, 2008).

How Treatment Courts Are Funded

Treatment courts require funding to operate, like any criminal justice initiative or program. Drug courts were first provided federal funding for the planning and implementation of the Violent Crime Control Act of 1994; this act also established the Drug Courts Program Office (DCPO) in the Office of Justice Programs (OJP) to administer grant funding to drug courts as they spread throughout the United States (Hiller et al., 2010, p. 933). The Office of Juvenile Justice and Delinquency Prevention (OJJDP) has primarily funded juvenile drug courts and has since 2007 provided $176.5 million to create or expand juvenile drug treatment and related court programs. In 2020, the OJJDP awarded more than $5 million to provide resources to state, local, and tribal governments to create and expand juvenile treatment court programs (OJJDP, n.d.). Federal funding has also been used for reentry courts, which work with offenders as they are transitioning from prison into the community.

Programs like prostitution courts are funded through a variety of sources. For example, PRIDE Court in Dallas, Texas, was initially funded through a three-year, $350,000 implementation grant provided through the Bureau of Justice, which paid for various services, including supplies, training, case management, and counselors (Mueller, 2012). Other problem-oriented courts like mental health courts have also been funded through the Bureau of Justice Assistance (BJA) FY20 Justice and Mental Health Collaboration Program (JMHCP) such as the Seminole County Mental Health Court in Sanford, Florida, which was awarded $748,065 in 2020 (Bureau of Justice Statistics, n.d.b).

Therapeutic Jurisprudence Defined

Treatment courts utilize therapeutic jurisprudence as the theoretical grounding of programs. Therapeutic jurisprudence typically involves using judicial actors as agents of therapeutic change (Redlich & Han, 2014). The primary concern of therapeutic jurisprudence is how the legal systems and actors can provide therapeutic outcomes for clients of the criminal justice system, in this case, those involved in treatment courts (Wexler, 2000). The goal of therapeutic jurisprudence is to empower practitioners to build on aspects of the law to utilize a series of practices such as engaging agencies and actors from a wide range of agencies and services, including drug treatment, mental health services, legal services, employment services, and education services to provide judicial intervention and monitoring of behaviors that engage those in the program with the courtroom workgroup to develop and enact a treatment plan that addresses the participants' needs and promotes their success (Redlich & Han, 2014).

The Role of the Judge in Treatment Courts

Judges are key actors in the treatment court process. Since drug courts are the most established treatment court program in the United States, this section will primarily focus on the role of judges in drug courts to help focus the narrative. Studies such as Salvatore et al. (2020) have found that the role of judges in other treatment courts, such as reentry courts, is similar in function and influence as in drug courts. Many studies have argued that the judge is key to the success of drug court clients. In a 1998 study, Belenko stated that the judge is critical in reinforcing positive behavior in clients (p. 80). More recently, Taylor (2012) identified three areas where the judge plays a significant role in drug courts:

1. The nature of the interactions with participants and judges.
2. Judicial status hearings.
3. The way participants perceive the judge.

Studies have found critical component of participant success in a drug court is the interaction between the judge and the program participant. For example, in their 2000 study Miethe and colleagues examined a Las Vegas drug court. The study found that the poor quality of the relationship between the judge and participants was why the program was less successful than it could have been. The Las Vegas drug court had a treatment-oriented, reintegrative focus, generally found to be beneficial to participants in drug court programs. However, field observations found that the drug court negatively impacted participants because the interactions with the judge were confrontational instead of treatment-oriented and supportive. The Las Vegas drug court had a 10% higher recidivism rate than those not in drug court; it is possible the negative interactions between the drug court and the judge can explain this finding.

Next, studies have found that for some high-risk participants, the simple act of being in front of a judge may be correlated with positive outcomes compared to those at a similar level who are getting some form of treatment services but not interacting with judges (Marlowe et al., 2004). For example, Marlowe and colleagues did a series of studies looking at different drug court programs using random assignment to put high-risk participants in a drug court program in a treatment group who had judicial status hearings consistently or were provided with treatment case manager supervision. Those who appeared before a judge regularly had an increased likelihood of finishing the program and avoiding relapse compared to those who had supervision from a treatment case manager. While scholars like Taylor (2012) pointed out that these studies did not have a qualitative component, it is impossible to know if other factors may have influenced the positive outcome of those who had judicial involvement in their drug court experience. Still, there is a strong suggestion that judicial involvement benefits participants.

Finally, Salvatore et al. (2020) examined the role of the judge in reentry court. The study explored the judge's influence on the program and found that judges were very involved with program participants. The judges utilized their social networks, time, and resources to assist with everything from doctor appointments to finding a job. Participants noted throughout the study the personal commitment and involvement of the judge and how it made a big difference for them and was essential to their success. As we will see with the forthcoming chapters looking at specific types of treatment courts, the role of the judge is critical in treatment courts.

Collaboration and Treatment Goals

The critical difference between traditional and treatment courts is the collaborative relationship between members of the courtroom workgroup to help participants in treatment court programs reach therapeutic goals. In traditional courts, prosecutors act for the state, arguing for the defendant's guilt. Conversely, the defense attorney seeks to protect the defendant's due process rights and argue for their innocence. Judges in traditional courts oversee these arguments and pronounce sentencing. In cases that do not involve a jury, they decide guilt or innocence based on the evidence presented by the defense and prosecution. Treatment courts contain the same actors, but instead of working negatively, members of the courtroom workgroup collaborate to help program participants reach their treatment goals. Instead of arguing for guilt or innocence, prosecutors and defense attorneys may discuss the best way for a participant to find a job, address lingering legal issues, or get a college education. Judges oversee court sessions but in a much more engaged, collaborative manner, often speaking with participants much more informally than we would see in a traditional courtroom.

Court Process

While there may be variation in the day-to-day operations of the various types of treatment courts, many follow the structure of drug courts to provide treatment, intensive supervision, and case management services, including support in areas such as family therapy, education, employment, career planning, and mentoring. The typical drug court has a four-phase structure, with the expectation that the first three phases would take at least six months to complete. During the first two phases, additional types of treatment for issues such as substance abuse may be integrated. In most drug courts, participants are randomly drug tested during the week and must attend two monthly drug court review sessions. Participants in most drug courts advance through the stages by meeting goals outlined in their individualized treatment plans. Supervision was typically reduced as the participant moved through each phase. Once the third phase is complete and the participant moves to phase 4, they attend a graduation program, and supervision shifts to a weekly meeting with the treatment coordinator every week for the first month of this phase, followed by attending a meeting with the drug court every six months for one year to update the treatment team on their progress (Salvatore et al., 2010).

Both sanctions and rewards are employed as part of the treatment court process. Sanctions are typically employed when a participant in a treatment court program fails to meet a treatment goal or violates the conditions of their treatment plans. For example, a participant in a reentry court's treatment plan may state that they must stay within the country under the court's supervision. If it comes to the court's attention that they left the area, they could be given a sanction commensurate with this infraction, such as being pushed back to an earlier program phase.

Lighter infractions, such as failure to complete an updated resume, might result in the participant doing several hours of community service. On the other hand, if participants in the program do well by meeting a treatment plan goal or accomplishing a life goal such as establishing healthy relationships with family members, the participant may be rewarded with verbal praise, being promoted to the next phase of the program, or being taken out to lunch by the treatment court team.

Brief Summary of Programs

Many treatment court programs have been used across the United States since the inception of the modern treatment court in the late 1980s. Below we have a summary of these court programs. It should be noted that this book will focus on the problem-oriented court programs that are commonly found across the United States and have at least some level of empirical evaluations. However, even those discussed below that do not have a chapter dedicated to them are essential and may provide a critical solution to their respective focus areas; they are discussed here to give a sense of how widespread the treatment court model has become and the various areas it is being used to address.

Animal Courts

Animal courts represent an effort of the criminal justice system to address animal abuse and neglect; animal cruelty cases typically receive low priority from the criminal justice system. While the literature on these programs is limited and suggests only a few exist, they provide a unique opportunity for the courts to address the needs of animals in a more humane and focused manner than how traditional criminal justice system approaches have often tried to address animal-related cases (Kaplan et al., 2018).

In Tucson, Arizona, the first animal welfare court started in 2012 and dealt with animal misdemeanor cases. Clients in the court may be mandated to treatment or intervention strategies, given fines, or receive probation or jail. In May 2016, the Pre-Adjudication Welfare Court (PAW) started in New Mexico. The PAW program meets weekly, processing misdemeanor cases involving animals. Participants may complete a 16-

week intervention program in the court programs and have their charges dismissed. The Tucson, Arizona, court, and the PAW program in New Mexico provide judicial oversight. A more recent program established in Botetourt County, Virginia, to address animal cruelty and neglect cases meets quarterly but lacks judicial oversight (Kaplan et al., 2018).

While an exciting addition to the treatment court programs offered, there is little literature available regarding formal evaluation as of this writing. There are only a few programs, as noted above. However, given our society's increased focus on animal welfare and rights, animal welfare courts may be a type of program that will expand in the coming years.

Drug Courts

Drug courts represent the coordinated efforts of the judiciary, prosecution, defense bar, probation, law enforcement, mental health, social service, and treatment communities to actively and forcefully intervene and break the cycle of substance abuse, addiction, and crime. As an alternative to less effective interventions, drug courts quickly identify substance-abusing offenders and place them under strict court monitoring and community supervision, coupled with effective, long-term treatment services.

In this blending of systems, the drug court participant undergoes an intense regimen of substance abuse and mental health treatment, case management, drug testing, and probation supervision while reporting to regularly scheduled status hearings before a judge with specialized expertise in the drug court model (Fox & Huddleston, 2003). In addition, drug courts may provide job skill training, family/group counseling, and many other life skill enhancement services.

Researchers have determined from the earliest evaluations that drug courts provide more direct supervision and more frequent drug testing and monitoring during the program than other forms of community supervision. More importantly, drug use and criminal behavior are significantly reduced while offenders participate in drug court (Belenko, 1998, 2001). Experts have argued that no other justice intervention brings to bear such an intensive response with such dramatic results. These results have been well-documented through the rigors of scientific analysis.

While greater discussion and examination of drug courts will be provided in a forthcoming chapter, drug courts are a popular strategy.

According to a 2021 Bureau of Justice Statistics report, over 350 drug courts operate in the United States, with about half focusing on adults (BJS, 2021). Although not universally supported, studies have found drug courts to be cost-effective alternatives to traditional jail and prison sentences for drug offenders.

Domestic Violence Courts

Established by the Violence Against Women Act, Domestic Violence Courts (DVC) address the high rate of domestic violence in the United States. One of the first DVCs was established in 1996 in Brooklyn, New York. This program set the foundation which many others would follow by providing services for victims such as job training, housing, counseling, and victims advocacy and providing supervision of defendants to ensure compliance with court mandates (Kalpan et al., 2018). Given the focus on victims' needs and safety, DVCs focus more on victim safety than other treatment courts (McLeod, 2012). According to estimates, more than 300 DVCs exist in the U.S. (Keilitz, 2004), with evidence mixed about their effectiveness on recidivism (Kalpan et al., 2018). In a forthcoming chapter, we will examine these programs in more detail, including potential concerns and evidence supporting their effectiveness and limitations.

Fathering Courts

Established in 1997 in Jackson County, Missouri, fathering courts are an innovative approach to encouraging parental responsibility for fathers (Macoubrie & Hall, 2010). The Jackson County Fathering Court population focused on those ordered to appear in court due to child support non-payment. The program focused on a diversion from incarceration for fathers who were delinquent in their child support payments. Since the Jackson County program started, other states, including Texas and Alabama, have opened fathering courts. Other innovations have included hybrid fathering and fathering reentry court programs focusing on education, employment, vocational training, supporting fathers re-entering the community, and non-custodial parents (Lee, 2012). As a relatively new and small innovation in the treatment court arena, there are few formal evaluations of these programs. Still, they provide an intriguing model which scholars and evaluators will likely focus on in the coming years.

Homeless Courts

Homeless Courts started in 1989 in San Diego, California (Binder & Horton-Newell, 2014). Homeless courts focus is on alternative sentencing strategies and plea bargaining to address outstanding misdemeanors. Many clients in homeless courts tend to be veterans, whom the court assists in getting life skills training, education, substance abuse treatment, mental health services, and vocational training (American Bar Association, n.d.). There have only been a handful of evaluations, but results have shown some promising outcomes, including increased permanent housing for program participants and decreased recidivism (Buenaventura, 2018). As stated previously, many homeless courts clients may be veterans who may be diverted into other treatment court programs such as veterans' courts, drug courts, and mental health courts.

Mental Health Courts

Mental illness is one of the most challenging issues in our society that finds its way into the criminal justice system. Researchers have continually found that many jail, state, and federal prisoners have mental health problems (Snedker, 2018); this has led to the need for strategies to address mental health services in the community, such as America's Law Enforcement and Mental Health Project founded in 2000 to expand the use of mental health courts (MHCs) in the United States. Like drug courts, mental health courts focus on addressing underlying issues and providing treatment to help facilitate recovery and decrease recidivism (Lerner-Wren, 2009).

Like drug courts, MHCs are widespread across the country, and by 2012 there were over 200 nationwide (Strong et al., 2016). Evaluations of MHCs are promising, with studies finding participation in MHC related to reduced recidivism. However, conclusions such as this should be interpreted with caution as some studies may have methodological limitations that limit the utility of their findings (Kaplan et al., 2018). As we will see in a forthcoming chapter, MHCs are a much needed and exciting approach to one of the criminal justice system's most significant challenge areas.

Prostitution Courts

Like mental health courts, prostitution courts work to address a population facing a variety of challenges from domestic abuse, human trafficking, substance abuse, childhood abuse and trauma, and sexual exploitation. Some in society consider sex work a victimless crime, but may not consider the experiences of exploitation and victimization of those working within the industry. Through the end the twentieth century and into the twenty-first, a punitive approach was applied to prostitution that did not incorporate the prostitute's experiences with trafficking and sexual exploitation (Muftic & Updegrove, 2019). Starting in New York City in 1993 (Quinn, 2005), prostitution courts are a popular approach to provide prostituted defendants the chance to receive court-supervised, community-based services instead of incarceration (Blakey et al., 2017). Like many types of treatment courts, evidence to date regarding the effectiveness of these programs is mixed. Some studies (e.g., Miner-Romanoff, 2017) suggest these programs are more cost effective than more traditional methods of criminal justice processing, whereas others have pointed out that there is a lack of outcome data for victims (Kulig & Butler, 2019, p. 313).

Reentry Courts

Reentry courts were established to address the high recidivism rate in those released from prison once they return to the community (Taylor, 2013). These programs seek to support many challenging areas of those transitioning back into the community from correctional facilities or parole. These challenges include housing, education, employment, healthcare, lingering fines, and other legal issues (Salvatore et al., 2020). Programs typically operate in a phased structure similar to drug courts, and studies have found mixed evidence of their effectiveness. For example, some studies like Farole (2003) found reentry courts do not influence recidivism. Others, like Hamilton (2010), found that reentry courts may be related to a greater likelihood of revocation (violating conditions of parole). More recently, Salvatore et al. (2020) found reentry courts may provide social bonding and supervision, which have valid impacts upon clients' success.

While a relatively recent innovation in treatment courts, reentry courts can address the still high number of individuals released yearly from state and federal prisons. A forthcoming chapter will explore these programs in greater detail and provide more insights into what empirical evidence has been found regarding the reentry court's effectiveness.

Teen Courts

One if the largest populations the criminal justice system works with are youth, the bulk of whom are committing age-specific types of delinquency, which are typically lower level offenses such as vandalism, being loud and rowdy, and underage drinking (Salvatore, 2013). An innovative approach adopted to work with these populations has been teen courts (sometimes referred to as peer or youth courts), specialized treatment courts developed as an alternative to traditional criminal justice processing for youth offenders. Most youth referred to teen court are typically between the ages of 12 and 15 and are first-time offenders, for delinquent acts like vandalism, stealing, or nonviolent offenses (Butts & Ortiz, 2011). We started to see teen courts the 1970s at a local level, they eventually expanded throughout the U.S. by the 1990s, and, by 2015, were operating in 49 states and the District of Columbia (Gase et al., 2016). Teen courts usually work with low-level and first-time offenders, have volunteer youth who take an active role in providing consequences to offenders (such as acting as attorney, jury, or judge), and have future teen court jury service as a potential sanction (Gase et al., 2016, p. 52). Teen courts offer a variety of strategies focused on repairing the harms caused by the offense, including letters of apology to victims, essays, and community service (Fisher, 1995). While there is no standard format or structure for teen courts, they do share a primary goal of fair and restorative justice in the processing and disposition of youth offenders (Fisher, 1995). Evidence to date regarding their effectiveness is mixed, but promising, with some studies finding they are more cost effective than traditional juvenile justice processing (e.g., Dines, 2017; Stone 2011), and offer anticipatory socialization for those interested in careers in law, or the criminal and juvenile justice systems (e.g., Dines, 2017). Others studies have found teen courts have no effect on recidivism (e.g.,

Schwalbe et al., 2012; Gase et al., 2016) or that those who participate in teen courts self-reported higher levels of delinquent behaviors than those formally processed through the juvenile justice system (Stickle et al., 2008).

Veterans' Courts

Veterans' courts were established to address the increasing number of veterans coming before courts due to mental health and substance abuse-related issues (Kaplan et al., 2018). In 2008, the Veterans Treatment Court in Buffalo, New York, opened. Like drug courts, this program accepted nonviolent offenders with severe mental health issues or substance abuse problems, thereby being a joint drug and veterans' treatment court (Russell, 2009). In addition to incorporating typical treatment court strategies, the program also utilizes peer-to-peer mentoring, which other programs, such as ReNew reentry court in Newark, New Jersey, have also adopted. In general, veterans' courts work with various organizations that serve veterans with services other than treatment, such as job training, housing, and financial assistance (Russell, 2009). Since veterans' courts are a relatively new arena for treatment courts, few studies examine them. Still, some, such as Douds and Ahlin (2019), provide a detailed examination of these programs and suggest they are a promising way to support veterans in crisis.

Pros and Cons of Treatment Courts

Like any innovation, treatment courts have their supporters and critics. While the coming chapters will look at the specific benefits and challenge areas of particular types of treatment courts, there are general benefits and weaknesses of treatment courts. First, treatment court judges (and courtroom workgroups) have specialization and experience in their respective areas, and this may benefit program participants as these judges may be more in tune with the therapeutic needs of program participants and the challenges they face. For example, a drug court judge may be much more aware of the difficulties around addiction and be more sympathetic to issues such as relapse. Next, while generalizing different types of treatment courts, or even one type of treatment court, may be presumptive, there is evidence to suggest that treatment courts like drug courts may be a much more cost-effective way to process offenders relative to criminal justice processing via incarceration (Belenko, 2001). Third, treatment courts may support participants' overall well-being by addressing social and psychological problems (Kaplan et al., 2018). Fourth, judges who oversee treatment courts may be less subject to burnout and have higher levels of job satisfaction (Nolan, 2009). Finally, reducing recidivism by addressing underlying problems like addiction, mental health disorders, and educational deficits may help reduce judicial caseloads and address prison overcrowding (Nolan, 2009).

While treatment courts have the abovementioned pros, there are potential cons. First is net-widening, which is the idea that there is an increased chance of people being arrested after a program like a drug court starts because prosecutors and police may think of arresting people and bringing them into the system for treatment instead of incarceration (Gross, 2010). Net widening may be of particular concern for lower-income offenders, as treatment courts may bring a more significant number of lower-income offenders into treatment than those from higher-income groups (Gross, 2010). Second is the potential for treatment courts to be coercive since many are given a choice between getting processing in a traditional court and having charges dropped if they complete a treatment court program (Nolan, 2009). Next, the start-up costs around treatment court programs, including training for staff and judges, may be quite high (Kaplan et al., 2018). Finally, while many judges find their work in treatment courts fulling and rewarding, often stepping up to provide guidance and support for participants in these programs, there is always the potential for judges in treatment court to experience burnout when dealing with the same types of cases and clients over time (Chase & Hora, 2000).

Conclusions

As this chapter explored, therapeutic jurisprudence provides a non-adversarial approach to treating various courts for specific challenge areas for criminal justice populations. The various models of treatment courts, ranging from the well-established drug court model which has spread across the country, to the newer, more niche type of treatment court like animal courts, have proven to be a popular way to divert offenders from the criminal justice system and provide treatment and support services. As we turn to the next chapter, we will examine some of the most prevalent types of treatment courts, evidence of their effectiveness, and areas of limitation.

References

American Bar Association. (n.d.). About homeless courts. https://www.americanbar.org/groups/public_interest/homelessness_poverty/initiatives/homeless-courts/abouthomeless-courts/.

Belenko, S. (1998). Research on drug courts: A critical review. *National Drug Court Institute Review, I* (1), 1–42.

Belenko, S. (2001). Drug courts. In C. Leukefeld, F. Tims, & D. Farabee (Eds.), *Clinical and policy responses to drug offenders*. Springer.

Binder, S. A., & Horton-Newell, A. (2014). Returning home to homelessness: San Diego's homeless court program models a way to help. *Experience, 23*(3). https://www.americanbar.org/content/dam/aba/publications/division_for_public_services/homelesscourtarticle.authcheckdam.pdf.

Blakey, J. M., Mueller, D. J., & Ritchie, M. (2017). Strengths and challenges of a prostitution court model. *Justice Systems Journal, 38*(4), 364–379. https://doi.org/10.1080/0098261X.2017.1327335.

Buenaventura, M. (2018). Treatment not custody: Process and impact evaluation of Santa Monica homeless court. RAND Corporation. https://www.rand.org/content/dam/rand/pubs/rgs_dissertations/RGSD400/RGSD418/RAND_RGSD418.pdf.

Bureau of Justice Statistics. (n.d.a). Drug use and crime: Drugs and crime facts. US Department of Justice. https://bjs.ojp.gov/drugs-and-crimefacts/enforcement.

Bureau of Justice Statistics. (n.d.b). Mental Health Court grant. US Department of Justice. https://bja.ojp.gov/funding/awards/2020 -mo-bx-0036.

Bureau of Justice Statistics. (2021). *Drug courts*. NCJ 238527. US Department of Justice. https://ojjdp.ojp.gov/sites/g/files/xyckuh176/files/ media/document/drug-courts.pdf.

Butts, J. A., & Ortiz, J. (2011). Teen courts: Do they work and why? *NYSBA Journal*, 18–21.

Chase, D. J., & Fulton Hora, P. (2000). The implications of therapeutic jurisprudence for judicial satisfaction. *Court Review*, *37*(1), 12–20.

Dines, C. (2017). Minors in the major leagues: Youth courts hit a home run for juvenile justice. *Notre Dame Journal of Law, Ethics & Public Policy*, *31*(1), 175–199. https://scholarship.law.nd.edu/ndjlepp/vol 31/iss1/5/.

Douds, A. S., & Ahlin, E. M. (2019). *The veteran's treatment court movement: Striving to serve those who served*. Routledge.

Farole, D. J. (2003). The Harlem parole reentry court evaluation: Implementation and preliminary impacts. Center for Court Innovation. https://www.courtinnovation.org/publications/harlemparole -reentry-court-evaluation-implementation-andpreliminary -impact.

Fischer, M. (1995). Youth courts: Young people delivering justice. Office of Juvenile Justice and Delinquency Prevention. https://www.ojp. gov/pdffiles1/ojjdp/196944.pdf.

Fox, C., & Huddleston, W. (2003). Drug courts in the U.S. http://igml-net.uohyd.ac.in:8000/InfoUSA/politics/ijd e0503/fox.htm.

Gase, L. N., Schooley, T., DeFosset, A., Stoll, M. A. & Kuo, T. (2016). The impact of teen courts on youth outcomes: A systematic review. *Qualitative Review*, *1*, 51–67. https://doi.org/10.1007/s40894 -015-0012-x.

Gross, J. (2010). The effects of net-widening on minority and indigent offenders: A critique of drug courts. *University of Maryland Law Journal of Race, Religion, Gender and Class*, *10*(1), 161–178.

Hamilton, Z. (2010). Do reentry courts work? Center for Court Innovation. https://www.courtinnovation.org/sites/default/files/docu-ments/Reentry_Courts.pdf.

Hiller, M., Belenko, S., Taxman, F., Young, D., Perdoni, M., & Saum, C. (2010). Measuring drug court structure and operations: Key components and beyond. *Criminal Justice and Behavior, 37*(9), 933–950. https://doi.org/10.1177/0093854810373727.

Kaplan, T., Miller, M. K., & Wood, E. F. (2018). Looking backward, looking forward: How the evolution of specialty courts can inform the courts of tomorrow. *Court Review: The Journal of the American Judges Association, 54,* 14–24.

Keilitz, S. (2004). Specialization of domestic violence case management in the courts: A national survey. National Institute of Justice. https://www.ojp.gov/pdffiles1/nij/199724.pdf.

Kulig, T. C., & Butler, L. C. (2019). From "whores" to "victims": The rise and status of sex trafficking courts. *Victims & Offenders, 14*(3), 299–321. https://doi.org/10.1080/15564886.2019.1595242.

Lee, M. C. (2012). Fatherhood in the child support system. *Family Court Review, 50*(1), 59–70. https://doi.org/10.1111/j.1744-1617.2011.01428.x.

Lerner-Wren, G. (2009). Mental health courts: Serving justice and promoting recovery. *Annals Health Law,* 577–593.

Lurgio, A. J. (2008). The first 20 years of drug treatment courts: A brief description of the history and impact. *Federal Probation, 72*(1), 14–20.

Macoubrie, J., & Hall, D. J. (2010). *Achieving the full potential of reentry and fathers' courts.* National Center for State Courts. https://cdm16501.contentdm.oclc.org/digital/collection/spcts/id/214.

Marlowe, D. B., Festinger, D. S., & Lee, P. A. (2004). The judge is a key component of drug court. *Drug Court Review, 4*(2), 91–107.

McLeod, A. M. (2012). Decarceration courts: Possibilities and perils of a shifting criminal law. *Georgetown Law Faculty Publications and Other Works.* 1276. https://scholarship.law.georgetown.edu/facpub/1276.

Miethe, T. D., Lu, H., & Reese, E. (2000). Reintegrative shaming and recidivism risk in drug court. Explanations for some unexpected findings. *Crime & Delinquency, 46*(4), 522–541. https://doi.org/10.1177/0011128700046004006.

Miner-Romanoff, K. (2017). CATCH court: Changing actions to change habits—A preliminary evaluation study. *Journal of Human Trafficking, 3*(2), 136–162. https://doi.org/10.1080/23322705.2016.1194039.

Mueller, D. (2012). *Treatment courts and court-affiliated diversion projects for prostitution courts in the United States.* Chicago Coalition for the Homeless. https://chicagohomeless.issuelab.org/resource/treat-mentcourts-and-court-affiliated-diversion-projects-for-prostitu-tion-in-the-united-states.html.

Muftic, L. R., & Updegrove, A. H. (2019). The effectiveness of a prob-lem-solving court for individuals charged with misdemeanor pros-titution in Harris County, Texas. *Journal of Offender Rehabilitation*, *58*(2), 117–132. https://doi.org/10.1080/10509674.2018.1562506.

Nolan, J. L. (2009). *Legal accents, legal borrowing: The international prob-lem-solving court movement.* Princeton University Press.

Office of Juvenile Justice Delinquency and Prevention (OJJDP). (n.d.). Drug courts. https://ojjdp.ojp.gov/programs/drug-courts.

Quinn, M. C. (2005). Revisiting Anna Moscowitz's Kross's critique of New York City's women's court: The continued problem of solving the "problem" of prostitution with specialized criminal courts. *Ford-ham Urban Law Journal*, *33*(2), 101–160.

Redlich, A. D., & Han, W. (2014). Examining the links between thera-peutic jurisprudence and mental health court completion. *Law and Human Behavior*, *38*(2), 109–118. https://doi.org/10.1037/lhb00000 41.

Russell, R. T. (2009). Veterans treatment courts are developing through-out the nation. All Rise. https://justiceforvets.org/wp-content/uploads/Veterans_Treatment_Courts_Developing _Throughout_the_Nation%20%281%29.pdf.

Salvatore, C. (2013). *Arrested adolescent offenders: A study of delayed transitions to adulthood.* LFB Scholarly Publications.

Schwalbe, C., Gearing, R., MacKenzie, M., Brewer, K., & Ibrahim, R. (2012). A meta-analysis of experimental studies of diversion pro-grams for juvenile offenders. *Clinical Psychology Review*, *32*, 26–33. https://doi.org/10.1177/2F0044118X87018003005.

Salvatore, C., Michalsen, V., & Taylor, C. (2020). Reentry court judges: The key to the court. *Journal of Offender Rehabilitation*, *59*(4), 198–222. https://doi.org/10.1080/10509674.2020.1733164.

Salvatore, C., Henderson, J. S., Hiller, M. A., & White, E. (2010). An observational study of team meetings and status hearings in juvenile drug court. *Drug Court Review*, *1*(1), 95–124.

Snedker, K. A. (2018). *Therapeutic justice: Crime, treatment courts and mental illness.* Palgrave Macmillan.

Stickle, W. P., Connell, N. M., Wilson, D. M., & Gottfredson, D. (2008). An experimental evaluation of teen courts. *Journal of Experimental Criminology, 4*, 137–163.

Stone, E. (2011, June 26). With the right kind of peer pressure, teen courts provide 2nd chance for youth offenders. Noozhawk. https://www.noozhawk.com/article/062011_teen_court.

Strong, S., Rantala, R. R., & Kyckelhahn, T. (2016). *Census of problem-solving courts, 2012*. NCJ 249803. US Department of Justice, Bureau of Justice Statistics. https://bjs.ojp.gov/library/publications/census-problem-solving-courts-2012.

Taylor, C. (2012). Balancing act: The adaption of traditional judicial roles in reentry courts. *Journal of Offender Rehabilitation, 51*(6), 351–369. https://doi.org/10.1080/10509674.2012.677945.

Taylor, C. (2013). Tolerance of minor setbacks in challenging reentry experience: An evaluation of federal reentry court. *Criminal Justice Policy Review, 21*(1), 49–70. https://doi.org/10.1177/0887403411427354.

Wexler, D. B. (2000). Therapeutic jurisprudence: An overview. *Thomas M. Cooley Law Review, 17*, 125–134. https://ssrn.com/abstract=256658.

CHAPTER 3

Theoretical Applications: Overview

One of the goals of any criminological research is to have theoretical implications and ideas that may increase the knowledge and understanding of a particular criminological phenomenon, including increasing the theoretical knowledge of how programs operate (or, in some cases, do not) from a specific theoretical perspective. Throughout our examination of each type of problem-oriented court program, we will be looking at different types of theories; there are a variety of theoretical orientations applied to the various court models, some more applicable than others. Just about all of these programs have a solid theoretical grounding in therapeutic jurisprudence. However, we will also see the influence of various theoretical perspectives, including social bond theory, life course theory, deterrence theory, and restorative justice, some of which will be incorporated into an integrated theory of treatment courts. This chapter will examine the most discussed theories, exploring how they can be applied to various problem-oriented courts and, in some cases, several different programs. Finally, an integrated theory of treatment courts and implications for criminological theory will be presented.

Therapeutic Jurisprudence

In the coming chapters as we work through the various types of treatment courts and applicable theories, we will find time and again that there is one common thread throughout them all: the grounding in therapeutic jurisprudence. Recall that therapeutic jurisprudence utilizes judicial actors as agents of therapeutic change in clients' lives (Redlich & Han, 2014). The therapeutic jurisprudence model ties together a variety of practices of the courtroom workgroup to provide supervision and treatment to provide support across multiple life domains like education, housing, employment, and mental health services, to promote the success of the program participant (Redlich & Han, 2014). In practice, therapeutic jurisprudence incorporates ongoing judicial supervision, monitoring of participant's behaviors, responding to behaviors via sanctions or rewards, working collaboratively with community agencies and other government agencies to address a variety of needs and services, and the integration of treatment services with case processing from the judge (Winick & Wexler, 2015, p. 2). To put it another way, therapeutic jurisprudence works differently from the traditional adversarial process most are likely familiar with—instead, the judge, and frequently in practice prosecutors, defense attorneys, parole officers, and others who are part of the courtroom workgroup, work with the participants in the treatment court program to help address the underlying issues which brought them into the criminal justice system. As we have seen throughout this book, therapeutic jurisprudence is the foundation for every problem-oriented court.

The essential nature of therapeutic jurisprudence is reflected in the foundation of various treatment court models. For example, in the 10 Key Components of Drug Courts (National Drug Court Professionals, 1997)(as well as veterans' courts and mental health courts), the use of the judge (and related members of the courtroom workgroup) is identified as a critical component of problem-solving courts on a philosophical and foundational level. For treatment courts to deliver the needed services and support for clients, there must be a grounding in therapeutic jurisprudence, delivering assistance rather than punishment. The benefits of therapeutic jurisprudence in treatment courts ranging from adult and juvenile drug courts to reentry courts, domestically and internationally, have been found throughout the treatment court literature (e.g., McIvor, 2009; Salvatore et al., 2011; Salvatore et al., 2020; Taylor, 2020; Toki, 2017).

The evidence suggests that therapeutic jurisprudence is an appropriate grounding for treatment court programs. The use of therapeutic jurisprudence to provide the criminal justice system with therapeutic tools to improve the functioning of participants in these programs has been discussed as a significant component of using the law more humanly to address legal issues (Winick & Wexler, 2015, pp. 1–2). Of the various problem-oriented courts examined in this book, almost all have a firm grounding in therapeutic jurisprudence, with only teen courts, with their unique peer structure, having somewhat less of a role for adult participants (though these programs usually have an adult participant providing oversight). *Therapeutic jurisprudence* is the foundation on which all problem-oriented courts are built. Veterans' courts, drug courts, reentry courts, prostitution courts, mental health courts, domestic violence courts, and so forth all utilize therapeutic jurisprudence at the core, providing judicial oversight to address the underlying reasons that brought participants to the court and to provide the treatment and support necessary to prevent reoffending and relapse. However, therapeutic jurisprudence, while the foundation of problem-oriented courts, does not operate in a vacuum; a variety of other theoretical approaches have been integrated into problem-solving court programs. What therapeutic jurisprudence may offer is the first component of an integrated theory of treatment courts which will be presented later. First, several theoretical approaches will be examined, each briefly summarized and discussed, and their use in treatment courts will be examined.

Social Bonding Theory

After the foundation of therapeutic jurisprudence, one of the most frequently occurring ideas in the various treatment court models we have explored is the role of social bonds. Throughout the following book chapters, we will see that social bonds built through the treatment court process may be a critical aspect of what makes these programs work. Recall that Hirschi's (1969) social bond theory argues for the notion of social bonds linking individuals to mainstream society through attachment and bonds built through a variety of agents such as the family, prosocial peers, religious engagement, employment, and, for the purposes of this discussion, bonds made by participation in a treatment courts program like drug courts and reentry courts. Hirschi's (1969) central idea is that adopting a stake in conformity or mainstream society prevents delinquency and crime; individuals are less likely to engage in crime if they have stronger attachments and bonds. If social bonds are strong, they may help connect individuals to mainstream society, as fear of losing these bonds prevents engaging in behaviors that endanger them.

To put it another way, if a person has strong bonds with their parents, peers, coworkers, or their spouse, they are not going to engage in behaviors that will disappoint those individuals or risk the bonds they have built with them. Regarding treatment courts, participants who have made bonds with judges and other members of the treatment court workgroup may be less apt to reoffend, use drugs, or violate the program's conditions for fear of disappointing these individuals. This summation, while simplified, captures the essence of the social bond theory. Over the years, different theories have been integrated into the social bonding discourse. For example, Mears and Stafford (2022) discussed the limitations of Hirschi's (1969) conceptualization of social bonds, including how it does not consider the role of bidirectional change effects, such as how offending behaviors might lower the strength of a social bond (p. 2). Scholars like Thornberry (1987) utilized other theories to look at social bonds, such as interaction theory, which highlighted how bonds could influence delinquency and, conversely, delinquency can influence bonds. Sampson and Laub's (1993) age-graded theory of informal social control looked at how the role of life events and changes (e.g., getting married, having a child) may bring about changes to bonds and, in turn, offending behaviors. These modifications and reconceptualizations of social bond theory help us better understand the role of the relationships built between the participant in a treatment court and members of the courtroom workgroup, as well as engaged peers and family members.

While the role of social bonds in problem-oriented courts can only be hypothesized, we have seen evidence that suggests social bonds may be at least partially responsible for successes found in problem-oriented courts. For example, as discussed in the introduction of this book as well as the chapter dealing with reentry courts, studies such as Salvatore and colleagues (2020) have identified interactions between judges, parole officers, and other participants in the treatment court as being factors cited by participants in these programs as influencing their perception of the treatment court experience and potentially their success in these programs.

As with any hypothesis in the social sciences, there will need to be a definitive test and examination of social bonds' role in treatment court. However, it seems logical and likely that judges, parole officers, defense attorneys, prosecutors, program administrators and peers in the programs, and relatives engaged in the treatment process play some role in the treatment process beyond facilitation. The supportive nature of these programs builds relationships and connections, which foster the desire to meet expectations for participants in these programs.

Social bonding theory and some of its more contemporary variants, like Laub and Sampson's informal theory of social control (2003), provide viable explanations for the "how" of problem-oriented courts on their own. However, what social bonding theory may ultimately be is a component of an integrated theory of treatment courts provided below. However, we will first examine several additional relevant theoretical perspectives.

Theoretical Orientation: Deterrence Theory and Risk-Need-Responsivity Model

While social bonding theory is a core theoretical approach that may apply to treatment courts, others may provide insights into how these programs work to assist participants in making changes. Two theories are the deterrence theory and the risk-need-responsivity (RNR) model. We will see in an upcoming chapter the potential role of deterrence theory, which is grounded in the notion that we are free to choose actions and rationally choose our course of action. In other words, people are rational and have free will. Two types of deterrence have been identified: (1) specific targeting of the individual offender to deter them from committing the same behavior in the future and (2) general deterrence, which looks at society as a whole; when the general society sees someone being punished for behaviors it sends a message to everyone in that society that the behavior will be punished, therefore deterring others from committing the crime (Vito & Holmes, 1994). Reentry courts have incorporated deterrence theory, as it may indeed (along with the swiftness of the punishment) be an effective tool for these programs (Nagin, 2016).

Deterrence may be a valuable tool for treatment courts. Almost all models incorporate some use of sanctions to address infractions. The use of sanctions may provide a deterrent effect for the individual participant and others in the treatment court (who witness the application of these sanctions). For example, suppose a participant in a reentry court program is found to have violated the program's conditions by socializing with gang-involved individuals. In that case, the reentry court judge could publicly admonish the participant in a reentry court session and apply a sanction of downgrading the individual in their phase of the program, say from being at phase 3 of the program back to phase 2. From an individual deterrent perspective, the participant in question would likely not face any additional punishments from the judge and lose any more progress in the program. From a general deterrence perspective, other participants in the reentry court present at this session would not want to engage in similar violation of the rules of the program as they witnessed the judge quickly and decisively providing a verbal sanction as well as the additional punishment of removing time in the program. As such, deterrence will play a role in the below presentation of an integrated theory of tournament courts.

Another theoretical orientation viewed as a theoretical grounding of reentry courts is the risk-need-responsivity (RNR) model. The RNR model assesses inmates for various **risk** factors like education, employment history, and prior substance use. Risk factors help identify what the individual **needs** are once released into the community, and once identified, **responsivity** states treatment provided should be on an individual level and target the offender's specific criminogenic needs (Andrews et al., 2011). The main component of RNR is that higher-risk individuals should be targeted for their specific criminal needs. In other words, the RNR model calls for the use of targeted treatment and support services to address a high-risk offender's needs to prevent future offending (Ndrecka et al., 2017). As many treatment courts tend to apply graduated sanctions throughout the treatment process, the use of an RNR orientation may allow programs to examine those in a problem-oriented court and preemptively direct participants at the highest risk of an infraction, relapse, or re-offense. For example, an individual with an extensive history of gang involvement may be targeting for additional prevention strategies and support, as well as drug treatment in a drug court, relative to another participant who does not have a history of gang involvement. As a component of an integrated theory of treatment courts, both deterrence theory and RNR offer viable components. The use of sanctions can be hypothesized to provide specific and general deterrence through their swift and certain application (though it should be mentioned that the swift and certain application of sanctions may be a challenging area for many judges in practice). RNR may be hypothesized to provide a mechanism through which courts can apply or direct treatment and prevention strategies for participants. Both theoretical orientations may be factored into an integrated model. Our next theoretical perspective, life course theory, also offers valuable contributions to an integrated theoretical approach to treatment courts.

Life Course Theory

Therapeutic jurisprudence, social bonding theory, deterrence theory, and RNR provide viable theoretical explanations for understanding how problem-oriented courts work to help participants make the changes needed to address the underlying behaviors that brought them into the criminal justice system and ultimately reach the goal of living crime-free lives. Life course theory may be one of the most intuitive theories used to understand the underlying mechanisms of treatment courts. This theoretical paradigm views life events like getting married, becoming a parent, military service, reaching educational goals, and getting employed as being able to change the trajectory of an individual's life and change their propensity to participate in criminal behaviors (Elder, 1986; Sampson & Laub, 1993). To briefly recap the core components of life course theory as presented by Sampson and Laub (1993): (1) Social control within the context of family and education can explain criminal behavior in children and adolescents. (2) There is a level of permanency in deviant and criminal behavior seen in adolescence through adulthood across life domains. (3) Informal social ties during adulthood to career, family, and education can explain the shift from delinquent or criminal behavior over the life course regardless of deviance and delinquency earlier in life. From the perspective of life course theory, the informal social controls built in adulthood through parenthood, marriage, employment, and military service can turn people away from a life of offending and towards a non-offending lifestyle (Messer et al., 2016).

Life course theory has been applied to drug courts (see Messer et al., 2016). However, does it provide a logical explanation (or at least part of one) to explain how problem-oriented courts may work to help participants make lasting life changes? Thinking in terms of what a problem court typically offers (keeping in mind that even within the context of one type of treatment court, the exact type of services, format, phase structure, and so forth may vary), we typically see participants offered the opportunity to work with service providers to address deficits in their education, find a job, get mental health services, address lingering legal issues, and get help with finding housing, all usually offered under the judicial oversight provided by therapeutic jurisprudence. Each of these areas, such as enrolling in college or finding a job, could be a turning point for a participant in a treatment court. Through their new job or by going to college classes, as well as the connections they build with the judge and other members of the courtroom workgroup (e.g., parole officer), they could also build prosocial bonds and attachments, a central idea of social bond theory, and one that can serve as another component of an integrated theory of treatment courts.

Restorative Justice

One of the theoretical models we will examine later in this book is restorative justice, which is the belief that punishment can provide benefits for both the offender and the community impacted by crime (Davis & Cates, 2017, p. 252). The Center for Justice & Reconciliation defined restorative justice as a way to heal harm and cultivate transformative change for all those involved in the crime incident (Center for Justice & Reconciliation, 2017). The central idea of restorative justice is that crime is not just a criminal code violation, it includes harm to people, relationships, and the community. As such, a truly just response needs to factor in these areas of harm on top of the harm caused by the crime itself (Center for Justice & Reconciliation, 2017).

Restorative justice has been applied to treatment courts where it provides treatment options for an individual's issues (e.g., mental health counseling), providing restoration for the offender. Working with treatment courts gives counselors and treatment providers a chance to provide individual therapy with vocational counseling, community service options, aftercare supervision, and arbitration and mediation with victims to focus on individual accountability as well, thereby offering the potential for these programs to provide restoration between parties (Haley, 2016). Restorative justice has been examined as a theoretical orientation for problem-oriented courts, such as drug and veterans' courts, but is generally discussed less than other treatment orientations, such as therapeutic jurisprudence. While restorative justice is an essential and valid theoretical framework that has merit and applicability to problem-oriented courts, it may have limitations. A critical challenge when considering restorative justice in the context of problem-oriented courts is that there may be a lack of a victim in these programs. For example, in a drug court, the program may be working with a participant to address the underlying issues of familial dysfunctions as a cause of addiction and crime; there may not be a victim in the traditional sense. Also, in the case of drug courts, the term victim may be muddled, as the participant may be both a victim and offender (Fulkerson, 2009). While it is beyond the scope of this chapter or book to untangle the relationship between restorative justice and treatment courts, we could perhaps more accurately argue that treatment courts are generally more rehabilitative, and as therapeutic jurisprudence is the core foundation of almost all of these programs, the restorative justice aspect of treatment programs (e.g., community service as a sanction) is not as fully integrated as other theoretical orientations. As such, restorative justice, while valued and a potentially vital perspective to be applied to treatment courts, has less direct utility compared to other theoretical orientations (see discussion above) and will not be included in the integrated theory of treatment courts being presented here (though it could certainly be an important component of a future model).

Towards an Integrated Theory of Treatment Courts

Here we present a brief framework for an integrative theoretical model of treatment courts. As we reflect upon the theoretical models applicable to problem-oriented courts, we have examined some of the most applied models. It is important to note that this chapter is not meant to act as an exhaustive review of every potential theory that may be applied to treatment courts; rather it is looking at some of the most commonly applied models and how they may be integrated to provide a more comprehensive theoretical framework for understanding how problem-oriented courts work to provide treatment and support services for participants, as problem-oriented courts are an evolving area, and new types of courts such as fathering courts and homeless courts are developing, which may call for additional theoretical examination.

To present an integrated theoretical model of treatment courts, we need first to understand the nature of an integrated theoretical model. A basic definition of an integrated theoretical model is provided by Bernard, who stated, "integration is achieved based on convergence among the causal arguments in various criminological theories" (1989, p. 137). More recently, Akers and Sellers (2009) provided a similar conceptual framework, stating "theoretical integration is to identify commonalities in two or more theories to produce a synthesis that is superior to one theory individually" (p. 301). Both Bernard's (1989) and Akers and Sellers' (2009) definitions provide a basic but effective understanding of. integrated theoretical models. Others, such as Thornberry (1989), provide a more advanced definition by looking at theoretical integration as "the act of combining two or more sets of logically interrelated propositions into one larger set of propositions in order to provide a more comprehensive explanation of a particular phenomenon" (p. 52). As the goal of this chapter is to present some of the most common theoretical models applied to problem-solving courts and to advance the theoretical discussion of these programs, we will be grounding the integrated theoretical model in the more simplistic conceptualizations provided by Bernard (1989) and Akers and Sellars (2009); that is not to say there is not room for more advanced groundings such as Thornberry's (1989) definition, but providing a more baseline integrated theoretical model for treatment-oriented courts will allow future discussion and examination of these ideas to build upon the foundation provided here.

An Integrated Theory of Treatment Courts to Promote Program Compliance and Rehabilitation

The idea of an integrated theoretical framework for problem-solving courts is a familiar one. Kaiser and Holtfreter (2016) presented a model incorporating therapeutic jurisprudence and procedural justice concepts. In another study, Chuang et al. (2012) examined the use of an integrated model in family dependency treatment courts; as both demonstrate, integrated theoretical models have been utilized in the content of problem-oriented courts in the past. What is different about the model being presented here is that it is an original conceptualization; the goal of presenting it is to provide yet another theoretical lens to examine problem-oriented courts.

The first portion of this model incorporates the five principles of therapeutic jurisprudence, as stated by Winick and Wexler in 2001. These principles include (1) ongoing judicial intervention, (2) close monitoring of participants and quick responses to behaviors, (3) the integration of judicial case processing with treatment services, (4) multidisciplinary involvement, and (5) collaborative involvement of other government agencies/organizations and community-based services. These five principles highlight the critical role of the judge in the treatment process. To put it another way, the role of the judge is paramount in the treatment court process and lays the foundation for all other aspects of the treatment court models.

The second portion of the integrated theory of treatment courts is the social bonding theory. Hirschi's (1969) original social bond theory argues for the notion of social bonds linking individuals to mainstream society through attachment and bonds built through a variety of agents such as the family, prosocial peers, religious engagement, employment, and for this discussion, bonds made by participation in a treatment courts program like drug courts and reentry courts. For this portion of the model, we want to incorporate the idea of the role of bidirectional change effects, as discussed by Mears and Stafford (2022, p. 2). For the integrated model presented here, we conceptualize that the therapeutic interactions with judges, other members of the treatment court, peers or former participants in the treatment court program, and any engaged family members have a positive influence on social bonds between the program participants and these individuals, resulting in an increased desire to engage in conforming behaviors (e.g., meeting treatment court goals and objectives).

The third portion of the model incorporates deterrence theory and risk-need-responsivity (RNR). The idea of deterrence (both specific and generalized) fits into this integrated model well; as judges utilize sanctions in problem-oriented court programs, the individual being directly targeted will modify their behavior. Relatedly, other members of the problem-oriented court program will view the swift application of sanctions for the program and would ideally be influenced not to engage in similar infractions for fear of receiving the same or similar punishment. RNR is also a critical component of the third portion of the integrated theoretical model being presented here—as individuals in the problem-oriented court program who are at the most significant risk of relapse, reoffending, violating program conditions, and will be targeted for the highest level of services such as supervision, judicial engagement/oversight, drug treatment, employment services and so forth (these would vary in practice based on the individual needs of the individual being targeted).

The final component of the integrated theoretical framework being presented here is life course theory. From a life course perspective, participation in a problem-oriented court can not only build social bonds, which can act as a form of social control on participants, but additionally, the experience of being in the problem-oriented court can ultimately act as a turning point away from offending behaviors, substance abuse, and other antisocial behaviors participation in the court is seeking to address.

To illustrate how this integrated model could work in practice, we can take the hypothetical case of "Walter Addison," a 33-year-old participant in a drug court program. As Walter attends drug court sessions, he will go before Judge Smith, who will inquire about Walter's various activities, including his participation in group therapy, his individualized drug counseling, how his job is going, and the state of his marriage. During these interactions, they will provide guidance and insights, helping to keep Walter on track. If needed, the judge will refer Walter to other community-based service providers, work with his probation officer to increase or decrease supervision as needed, and, if necessary, the judge will intervene with sanctions or rewards (depending on if Walter violated a program requirement or met a program goal). These represent the therapeutic jurisprudence component of the integrated theory being presented. The next component is the social bonding theory. Throughout the drug court process, Walter has worked closely with his probation officer, Agnes Viola, a veteran probation officer who has been part of the drug court workgroup since its inception several years ago. In addition, Walter's wife, Alicia, frequently attends drug court sessions with him to provide support. Throughout the drug court process, the support and connection Walter has built with Officer Viola, his wife Alicia, as well as the judge, and the rest of the treatment court has been an invaluable resource to him. During a variety of drug court sessions, Walter frequently mentions how the support and connections he has made through the treatment court process have helped him resist the temptation to relapse and inspire him to meet program goals as he feels everyone believes in him and he does not want to let them down. The third portion, which integrates deterrence and RNR, could be demonstrated during drug court sessions where Walter witnesses those violating drug court program conditions being sentenced to short-term periods in a halfway house, jail, or losing time in the program for violating conditions. In a related manner, Walter could receive more intensive drug treatment services based on the severity of his substance abuse disorder by RNR—as someone with a more severe addiction disorder, Walter would receive more treatment in this area. Life course theory is the final component of the integrated theoretical model being presented here. As discussed above, life course theory focuses on turning points and social bonds as causative factors in bringing about change (typically towards or away from offending behaviors). In the hypothetical scenario discussed here, the drug court program can act as a turning point away from substance abuse for Walter. The treatment services provided, the support and guidance he has been given, and the overall desire to succeed in the program to avoid incarceration as well as letting those down who believe in him, may lead Walter to successfully complete the program, graduate, and (in keeping with most drug courts) have his record expunged if he does not re-offend or relapse within one year of completing the program.

Theoretical Implications/Conclusion

There are a variety of theoretical orientations applicable to treatment courts. As examined in this chapter, social bond theory, restorative justice, life course theory, deterrence theory, and the risk-need-responsivity model all provide an understanding of how treatment courts "work" with participants to provide treatment and rehabilitation services. What seems to be the most consistent theoretical grounding for problem-oriented courts is therapeutic jurisprudence. This theoretical philosophy reflects the mission and operations of just about every type of treatment court examined here and is reflected throughout the treatment court literature There are, of course, many other theories that may be applicable to treatment courts as well. Further studies can continue to examine the role of various theories and their application to treatment courts. Perhaps theories like strain or a general theory of crime, not typically applied to treatment or prevention programs, could be incorporated. It may be that social scientists examining these programs need to incorporate theoretical approaches from outside of criminal justice, criminology, and sociology, perhaps reaching into related disciplines like psychology or even further into areas like economics for the most applicable theoretical approaches to help understand treatment courts. In this chapter, an integrated theoretical model was presented to help start the theoretical inquiries into treatment courts.

The integrated theory provided here gives a model which may explain the underlying mechanisms that make treatment courts work. As mentioned above, there have been other integrated theoretical approaches applied to treatment courts. However, the one discussed here is a new conceptualization reflective of the information and programs discussed in this book. The model presented above serves as a foundation for other conceptualizations of integrated theoretical approaches to treatment courts. Criminological and related theories in sociological, social psychology, psychology, and other fields can be integrated into future integrated theoretical models and approaches. The theoretical models discussed in this chapter and throughout this book provide a valuable look at the various theoretical approaches in which treatment courts may operate. Theoretically grounded research, including tests of specific theories, is a continued area of research needed when examining treatment courts.

In sum, there are several theoretical orientations that have been applied to treatment courts. Empirical studies have found support for some of these theories, and they are reflected throughout the literature. Future research will need to continue to examine the role of theory in treatment courts to better understand how they work in practice and how these models may need to be modified to improve the functioning of treatment courts. It may be that new theoretical models, such as the integrated theoretical model presented here, need to be developed and tested empirically to provide the best possible theoretical match for treatment courts.

References

Akers, R. L., & Sellers, C. S. (2009). *Criminological theories: Introduction, evaluation, and application* (5th ed.). Oxford University Press.

Andrews, D. A., Bonta, J. J., & Wormith, S. (2011). The risk-need -responsivity (RNR) model: Does adding the good lives model contribute to effective crime prevention? *Criminal Justice and Behavior, 38*(7), 735–755. https://doi.org/10.1177/0093854811406356.

Bernard, T. J. (1989). A theoretical approach to integration. In S. F. Messner, M. D. Krohn, & A. E. Liska (Eds.), *Theoretical integration in the study of deviance and crime: Problems and prospects* (pp. 137–160). SUNY Press.

Centre for Justice & Reconciliation. (2017). Lesson 1: What is restorative justice? http://restorative justice.org/restorative-justice/about-restorative-justice/tutorial-intro-to-restorative-justice/lesson-1 -what-isrestorative-justice/#sthash.yTdYUX7Y.dpbs.

Chuang, E., Moore, K., Barrett, B., & Young, M. S. (2012). Effect of an integrated family dependency treatment court on child welfare reunification, time to permanency and reentry rates. *Children and Youth Services Review, 34*, 1896–1902.

Davis, T. O., & Cates, K. A. (2017) Mental health counseling and specialty courts. *The Professional Counselor., 7*(3), 251–258.

Elder, G. H. (1986). Military times and turning points in men's lives. *Developmental Psychology, 22*, 233–245. https://doi.org/10.1037/00 12-1649.22.2.233.

Fulkerson, A. (2009). The drug treatment court as a form of restorative justice. *Contemporary Justice Review, 12*(3) 253–267. https://doi.org/10.1080/10282580903105772.

Haley, M. J. (2016). Drug courts: The criminal justice system rolls the rock. *Loyola Journal of Public Interest Law, 17,* 183–214.

Hirschi, T. (1969). *Causes of delinquency.* University of California Press.

Kaiser, K. A., & Holtfreter, K. (2016). An integrated theory of specialized court programs: Using procedural justice and therapeutic jurisprudence to promote offender compliance and rehabilitation. *Criminal Justice and Behavior, 43*(1), 45–62. https://doi.org/10.1177/0093854815609642.

Laub, J. H., & Sampson, R. J. (2003). *Shared beginnings, divergent lives: Delinquent boys to age 70.* Harvard University Press.

McIvor, G. (2009). Therapeutic jurisprudence and procedural justice in Scottish drug courts. *Criminology & Criminal Justice, 9*(1), 29–49. https://doi.org/10.1177/1748895808099179.

Mears, D. P., & Stafford, M. C. (2022). A reconceptualization of social bond theory to predict change sequences in offending. *Crime & Delinquency,* 1–23. https://doi.org/10.1177/00111287221088000.

Messer, S., Patten, R., & Candela, K. (2016). Drug courts and the facilitation of turning points: An expansion of life course theory. *Contemporary Drug Problems, 43*(1), 6–24. https://doi.org/10.1177/0091450916632545.

National Association of Drug Court Professionals. (1997). Defining drug courts: The 10 key components. Bureau of Justice Statistics, Office of Justice Programs, U.S. Department of Justice, Washington, DC. https://www.ojp.gov/pdffiles1/bja/205621.pdf.

Ndrecka, M., Listwan, S. J., & Latessa, E. (2017). What works in reentry and how to improve outcomes. In S. Stojkovic (Ed.), *Prisoner reentry.* Palgrave Macmillan.

Redlich, A. D., & Han, W. (2014). Examining the links between therapeutic jurisprudence and mental health court completion. *Law and Human Behavior, 38*(2), 109–118. https://doi.org/10.1037/lhb0000041.

Salvatore, C., Hiller, M. L., Samuelson, B., Henderson, J., & White, E. (2011). A systematic observational study of a juvenile drug court judge. *Juvenile and Family Court Journal, 62*(4), 19–36. https://doi.org/10.1111/j.1755-6988.2011.01066.x.

Salvatore, C., Michalsen, V., & Taylor, C. (2020). Reentry court judge: The key to the court. *Journal of Offender Rehabilitation*, *59*(4), 198–222. https://doi.org/10.1080/10509674.2020.1733164.

Sampson, R. J., & Laub, J. H. (1993). *Crime in the making: Pathways and turning points through life*. Harvard University Press.

Taylor C. J. (2020). Beyond recidivism: An outcome evaluation of a federal reentry court and a critical discussion of outcomes that matter. *Justice Evaluation Journal*, *3*(2), 134–154. https://doi.org/10.1080/2 4751979.2020.1721311.

Thornberry, T. P. (1987). Toward an interactional theory of delinquency. *Criminology*, *25*(4), 863–892. https://doi.org/10.1111/j.1745-9125.19 87.tb00823.x.

Thornberry, T. P. (1989). Reflections on the advantages and disadvantages of theoretical integration. In S. F. Messner, M. D. Krohn, & A. E. Liska (Eds.), *Theoretical integration in the study of deviance and crime: Problems and prospects* (pp. 51–60). SUNY Press.

Toki, V. (2017). Legal responses to mental health: Is therapeutic jurisprudence the answer? The experience in New Zealand. *Journal of Ethics in Mental Health*, *10*, 118.

Vito, G., & Homes, R. M. (1994). *Criminology: Theory, research, and policy*. Wadsworth Publishing Company.

Winick, B. J., & Wexler, D. B. (2015). Drug treatment court: Therapeutic jurisprudence applied. *Touro Law Review*, *18*(3), 479–485. https:// digitalcommons.tourolaw.edu/lawreview/vol18/iss3/6.

CHAPTER 4

Adult and Juvenile
Drug Courts: Overview

Since Robert Martinson's controversial report, "What Works?" (1974), there has been a marked curtailment of rehabilitative and treatment programs in American corrections. Interestingly, in the same year Martinson's landmark report was published, New York City was the first jurisdiction to implement a drug court focusing on processing (not treating) drug cases in response to the influx of cases due to the Rockefeller Drug Laws, which quickly overburdened the state's criminal justice system with drug cases (Belenko & Dumanovsky, 1993). However, the more widely known and first drug *treatment* court is the Miami-Dade County Drug Court, which started in 1989; this program is widely considered the start of the modern treatment court movement and serves as the template for most of the treatment or specialized court programs examined in this book. The Miami-Dade County Drug Court represented a shining example of something that "does work." Since the expansion of drug courts to over 3,500 programs across the United States (National Institute of Justice, 2021), studies have found promising results regarding the effect these programs in reducing criminal behavior and drug use while offenders are participating in the program (Belenko, 1998, 2001) and graduates have been shown to have lower rates of recidivism (Goldkamp et al., 2001).

The expansion of drug courts suggests programs can indeed "work" to help drug offenders and may lead to a lower rate of re-offending for participants and lower recidivism rates for graduates of these programs. Further, other studies have shown that drug courts have provided substantial savings to taxpayers in comparison to the cost of incarceration

(Crumpton et al., 2004; Rempel et al., 2003). As the drug court model has shown promise, it has served as the template for many other types of treatment courts, and the development of juvenile drug courts is examined below.

Perhaps more than any other treatment court, drug courts have been thoroughly examined by academics, practitioners, and policymakers and have received a fair amount of attention from the mainstream media. Serving as the model for just about every other treatment court that followed, the Miami-Dade Drug Court has been viewed by many as a successful template for integrating treatment into courtrooms and offering program participants a path to success. Since Miami-Dade County's Drug Court opened in 1989, it has focused on non-serious, nonviolent drug offenders and emphasized judge involvement. By extension, the rest of the treatment workgroup provides treatment and support to program participants (Kaplan et al., 2018). This innovative program relies on voluntary participation from program participants and calls on judges to work with court clients in a new way. Holding frequent hearings, judges provide program participants with a level of attention and monitoring of their progress they likely have never experienced before. Charges can be reduced or dismissed when program participants reach their goals and graduate. On the other hand, if participants fail to comply, they face various consequences ranging from writing essays and community service to incarceration (Berman & Feinblatt, 2001).

As stated above, Miami-Dade County's Drug Court was viewed as an innovative shift away from the punitive approaches to drug offenses to a more treatment and rehabilitative focus to break the cycle of substance use and related criminal behaviors (Belenko, 2019). Drug courts were soon generally celebrated for their successful collaborations addressing drug treatment, as well as a variety of other areas and agencies, including social services, life skills, and job training, to help address the underlying reasons why a participant was engaging in substance use and related criminal activities. It should be noted that some pointed out that Miami-Dade County's Drug Court was not without its faults, including a lack of coordination (Lurgio, 2008). Despite limitations, drug courts have flourished in an environment focused more on mass incarceration than treatment, and they have become an example of "what works" when it comes to providing treatment for criminal justice populations.

In the following sections, we examine drug court programs' phase structures, the 10 key components of drug courts, the addition of juvenile drug courts to drug court programming, and the role of social bonds and attachments in drug courts. We then examine how drug courts connect to life course theory and review evidence supporting the effectiveness of the drug court model, including the cost-effectiveness of drug court programs and the effectiveness of drug courts in reducing recidivism. We conclude with a discussion on areas of needed study and suggestions for future research.

Drug Court Program Phase Structure

Since drug courts began in 1989, drug court programs have spread across the United States. As discussed previously, these courts rely on therapeutic jurisprudence to provide treatment and support instead of punishment in order to address the underlying causes of substance abuse and criminal offending, as well as provide support in a variety of areas across life domains such as housing, education, and employment, in order to ensure long-term success for drug court program participants. We need to understand how programs are structured and operate to discuss drug courts effectively. Drug courts are complicated programs that incorporate a variety of actors and treatment agencies. Further, how programs are structured varies from courtroom to courtroom; this is critical to note as it impacts the ability of researchers to come to generalized conclusions about the effectiveness of these programs. In other words, since there is so much variation in drug court programs, it is challenging to conclude whether these programs "work." Program models vary widely in their design and structure, which may influence the ability of programs to reduce criminal offending and substance use for participants in some programs, but not others (Goldkamp et al., 2002, p. 28).

Since there is such variation in drug court programs, it is challenging to present a standard structure. However, most drug court programs generally follow a three-phase structure: stabilization, intensive treatment, and transition (National Association of Drug Court Professionals, 1997). The stabilization phase involves the immediate detoxification process from alcohol or drugs and the initial assessment screenings for criminal behavior and substance abuse disorders. An arrest is a critical moment for someone with a substance abuse disorder, and quick entrance into a drug court program is essential (Logan & Link, 2019; National Association of Drug Court Professionals, 1997). After stabilization is reached and the individual has formally joined the drug court program, the intensive treatment starts, which typically involves alcohol and drug treatment services combined with programs to address other challenge areas, including health (e.g., medical, dental, vision care) and social issues, housing, employment, and other areas of needed support (Logan & Link, 2019; National Association of Drug Court Professionals, 1997). The program's final phase is the transition phase, which marks the completion of the program. During this phase, efforts are made to provide the participant with the best chances of social integration as the participant disengages from the supervision provided by the drug court judge, treatment workgroup, and related professionals (National Association of Drug Court Professions, 2015).

To help demonstrate how drug court programs may look in practice, we will examine the Philadelphia Juvenile Drug Court phase structure as discussed by Salvatore and colleagues (2010). Their work described an observational study of a juvenile drug court in Philadelphia, Pennsylvania, in the United States. Like most drug courts, the Philadelphia Juvenile Drug Court (JDC) focused on nonviolent substance-abusing clients and on providing drug treatment, intensive supervision, and case management services, including support in areas such as family therapy, education, employment, career planning, and mentoring. The JDC was operated in a four-phase structure, with the expectation that the first three phases would take at least six months to complete. During the first two phases, the JDC participated in intensive outpatient treatment for approximately nine hours per week, was randomly drug tested twice a week, and was required to attend two monthly drug court review sessions. Participants in the JDC advanced through the stages by meeting the goals outlined in their individualized treatment plans. Supervision was typically reduced as the participant moved through each phase. For example, if participants reached phase 3 of the program, their outpatient therapy could be reduced to five hours weekly. Instead of attending two monthly hearings with the drug court to review their progress, they may only have to participate in a hearing every three weeks. Once the 3rd phase is complete and the participant moves to phase 4, they attend a graduation program, and supervision shifts to a weekly meeting with the treatment coordinator for the first month of this phase, followed by attending a meeting with the drug court every six months for one year to update the treatment team on their progress (Salvatore et al., 2010).

As with other treatment courts, sanctions were employed in the Philadelphia JDC. These sanctions were commensurate with the infraction. For example, if a participant missed a drug court review session, they might have needed to write an essay explaining to the judge why they missed the session, then read the essay to the treatment team in the next session. A more severe infraction, such as missing multiple days in school, might have resulted in increased supervision, community service, or verbal reprimand from the judge. Conversely, positive behaviors were rewarded. If a client did well in school, they might have received verbal praise from the judge, been taken out to lunch by a treatment team member, or been promoted to the program's next phase. While drug courts have significant variation in their program models, there are a series of characteristics of drug courts that are distinct and have been summarized in the monograph *Defining Drug Courts: The Key Components* (Office of Justice Programs, 1997, 2004). The monograph was created through the National Association of Drug Court Professionals by the Drug Court Standards Committee, which consisted of researchers, practitioners working in drug courts, and federal administrators, to identify the core elements that define drug courts (Office of Justice Programs, 1997, 2004, p. 4).

10 Key Components

The below list of 10 key components was provided to help guide the implementation of drug courts as they expanded throughout the nation (Hiller et al., 2010). Each component represents how drug court programs conceptually and operationally differ from traditional criminal courts (Hiller et al., 2010, p. 935). The 10 key components help provide tools which help policymakers, researchers, and funders judge to what degree a drug court operates as a drug court reflective of what experts envision (Hiller et al., 2010, p. 935). In other words, the 10 key components help us define which drug court programs meet the standards set by the National Association of Drug Court Professionals in the *Defining Drug Courts: The Key Components Monograph.*

TABLE 4.1: 10 KEY COMPONENTS OF DRUG COURTS

Key Component #1: Drug courts integrate alcohol and other drug treatment services with justice system case processing.
Key Component #2: Using a non-adversarial approach, prosecution and defense counsel promote public safety while protecting participants' due process rights.
Key Component #3: Eligible participants are identified early and promptly placed in the drug court program.
Key Component #4: Drug courts provide access to a continuum of alcohol, drug, and other related treatment and rehabilitation services.
Key Component #5: Abstinence is monitored by frequent alcohol and drug testing.
Key Component #6: A coordinated strategy governs drug court responses to participants' compliance.
Key Component #7: Ongoing judicial interaction with each drug court participant is essential.
Key Component #8: Monitoring and evaluation measure the achievement of program goals and gauge effectiveness.
Key Component #9: Continuing interdisciplinary education promotes effective drug court planning, implementation, and operations.
Key Component #10: Forging partnerships among drug courts, public agencies, and community-based organizations generates local support and enhances drug court program effectiveness.

Source: Office of Justice Programs 1997/2004.

Each of the above-listed components represents an ideal component to be included in drug court programs. The *Defining Drug Courts: The Key Components Monograph* has been used by several studies to juxtapose the ideal representation of a drug court program with the implementation of drug court programs (Carey et al., 2008). It has also influenced which programs receive federal funding, as it has been cited in grant solicitation proposals (Hiller et al., 2010), an impressive feat demonstrating this monograph's significance to the development, practice, study, and funding of drug courts. Of equal note is the influence drug courts have had and their expansion into various other treatment courts, which will be examined in the coming chapters. Next, we will look at their most direct offspring: juvenile drug courts.

Juvenile Drug Courts

As with the adult population, adolescent substance use is a crucial factor in youth offending, costing the juvenile and, in some cases, the adult justice systems financially, as well as using other resources, and is related to a variety of other mental health, behavioral, and social problems. Substance use in adolescent populations has been a longstanding challenge area. For example, recent figures from the Monitoring the Future (2022a, 2022b) study found that while there has been a decrease in substance use in adolescents in the last year, there is still a significant amount of substance use in juvenile populations, as listed below:

- 8th graders: 7.1% reported using marijuana in the past year in 2021, compared to 11.4% in 2020.
- 10th graders: 17.3% reported using marijuana in the past year in 2021, compared to 28.0% in 2020.
- 12th graders: 30.5% reported using marijuana in the past year in 2021, compared to 35.2% in 2020.
- 8th graders: 4.6% reported using any illicit drug (other than marijuana) in the past year in 2021, compared to 7.7% in 2020.
- 10th graders: 5.1% reported using any illicit drug (other than marijuana) in the past year in 2021, compared to 8.6% in 2020.
- 12th graders: 7.2% reported using any illicit drug (other than marijuana) in the past year in 2021, compared to 11.4% in 2020.

The relationship between youth offending and substance use has been well documented (Stein et al., 2015). According to the National Institute of Drug Abuse (NIDA) (2006), about 40% of girls and 56% of boys who are arrested for criminal offense test positive for drugs, with over 50% of youth entering a community supervision program having a substance abuse problem (Scott et al., 2019). In addition, youth substance abuse is related to a variety of other adverse outcomes, including poor school performance (e.g., truancy and dropouts), health issues (e.g., sexually transmitted infections), and family dysfunction (Hicks et al., 2010). Youth involved in the justice system tend to start substance use early and typically have more problems with substance use, as well as involvement with the criminal justice system, relative to other youths (Kandel & Yamaguchi, 2002; Hoeve et al., 2013).

Juveniles are an essential population to address with treatment and prevention strategies as they are at a critical juncture in life. Successful diversion or treatment may steer them onto a prosocial path with success in education, employment, and their personal lives in the future. Conversely, continued involvement with substance use and the criminal justice system may push them further along an antisocial path leading to incarceration and other negative life outcomes. With national rearrest rates for juvenile offenders being reasonably high, especially for those in urban areas (Calvin, 2004; Stein et al., 2015), it is essential to provide strategies that can successfully address the underlying reasons why youth are engaging in substance use and offending behaviors; one such strategy is juvenile drug courts (Stein et al., 2015).

Like adult drug courts, juvenile drug courts focus on providing intensive monitoring and treatment of juveniles along with various services that support educational and employment goals, as well as individual and family counseling (Gilmore et al., 2005). Like adult drug courts, juvenile drug courts have proved to be a popular strategy. As of 2020, there were approximately 308 juvenile drug court programs across the United States (National Drug Court Resource Center, 2021). Early studies of juvenile drug court programs found promising findings, such as significantly reducing recidivism (e.g., Shaw & Robinson, 1998). In contrast, others found reduced criminal offending but increased drug use (Rodriguez & Webb, 2004). Below, we explore the research about the effectiveness of these programs in greater detail.

Juvenile drug courts are different from traditional juvenile courts as they provide highly comprehensive assessments of offenders that incorporate cumulative data on participants, provide a strong focus on family functioning, and integrate coordinated services for program participants and their families (Gilmore et al., 2005, p. 289). Juvenile drug courts, like adult drug courts, have varying models, but voluntary participation is standard (Stein et al., 2015). As the description of the Philadelphia JDC from Salvatore et al. (2010) demonstrated, most programs are usually structured in three or four graduated phases that are typically three months in length (Stein et al., 2015). Juvenile drug courts are grounded in therapeutic jurisprudence, involve rewards and sanctions, and typically require goal-oriented activities (e.g., success in school) (Cooper, 2001). Delivery of sanctions and rewards from judges is a critical component of JDCs, and judges are provided training to offer them (Stein et al., 2015). As with adult drug courts, juvenile drug courts often rely on the social bond and attachments between the program participant and judges whose relationship with participants is a critical component of programmatic success (Salvatore et al., 2010), as well as engaged family members and other members of the treatment court workgroup.

The Role of Social Bonds and Attachments in Drug Courts

Studies of both adult and juvenile drug use have found a variety of factors, such as educational, peer, employment, and familial factors, correlated with substance abuse (Bursik & Grasmick, 1993; Sampson & Laub, 1994). The theoretical reasoning behind how these various relationships influence substance abuse is social control theory, which argues that attachments to peers, education, and family help prevent delinquency and offending behaviors because of the increased informal and external control these attachments provide (Hirschi, 1969). In other words, the informal bonds and attachments built between friends and family, education, and other social institutions can help prevent delinquency and crime by providing more social controls. Laub and colleagues (1998) also found that the strength of social bonds was central in regard to how much they can influence behavior. For example, a robust conventional bond between a teacher and their student can communicate acceptable behaviors to children. Another critical characteristic of social bonds is that they continue to change over time and may provide different levels of control over children and adults. For example, the bonding experience mentioned above of a teacher conveying acceptable behaviors to students may work well for children in grade school but be far less effective for high school students.

Evidence supports that social bonds to family members, peers, education, and others can reduce or increase substance use and other offending behaviors in juvenile and adult samples. Prior studies have found that family-related bonds effectively reduce delinquency (Laub & Sampson, 1993; Sabatine et al., 2017). The role of parents is of particular importance as higher levels of parental supervision have been found to delay the onset of substance use, as well as help reduce substance use (Steinberg et al., 1994). Conversely, social bonds with family members and peers may influence substance use in youth. Studies have found that perceived substance use of family members has been found to influence juvenile drug use in official documents (Gilmore et al., 2005). For example, in their 2000 study, Friedman and colleagues found that the strongest predictor of a child's substance use was the perceived alcohol problem of their mother. As such, we would expect that social bonds with treatment court providers, including the judge, case managers, and other members of the treatment court workgroup, may also help reduce substance use in drug court participants, either alone or in concert with the social bonds participants have across other life domains, including family, employment, peers, and education.

Gilmore et al. (2005) tackled the question of the role of social bonds in juvenile drug courts in their study that examined the influence of social bonds on participants in the JDC program in Maricopa County, Arizona. Gilmore et al. sought to study how peer, school, family, and employment bonds impacted drug use, delinquent behaviors, and the completion of the JDC program (p. 306). In keeping with the social control/bonding literature, the core hypotheses of the study were (1) JDC program participants would be more likely to complete JDC program requirements compared with those on standard probation. (2) JDC participants with strong bonds to peers, family, and school would be more successful in finishing the JDC and desistance from delinquency (Gilmore et al., 2005, p. 306). Results of Gilmore et al.'s 2005 study suggest that social bonds play a vital role in the desistance of delinquent behavior and completing the program. Turning our attention to more specific findings, Gilmore et al. (2005) found that participants in the JDC were more likely to test positive for drugs and less likely to complete JDC programs requirements relative to those on probation, suggesting JDC programs may not be as effective as regular juvenile probation (p. 306). Regarding family bonds, Gilmore et al's (2005) findings were generally in line with the literature, finding that JDC participants with one or more siblings who use drugs committed more delinquent acts. Similarly, JDC participants involved in peer groups that engage in substance abuse will be more likely to do so. The results of the influence of parental drug use were ultimately not significant. Other findings related to parents suggested that parents integrated into treatment may provide additional support for program participants. Interestingly, employment for the Maricopa County, Arizona, JDC program had a negative impact on program completion. This is counter to how we would think social bonding would work, which would be that as a prosocial activity employment should help the JDC participant build bonds and attachments which would prevent delinquency and substance use, but as Gilmore et al. stated, the issue with employment may be that it took time away from the youth's ability to meet program requirements because youth may view employment as more essential or due to work schedule conflicts with program requirements (p. 308). One of the most exciting findings of Gilmore et al's (2005) study was the relationship between gang membership and drug use, with gang membership reducing drug use. This finding was likely a measurement issue or related to the level of drug use of participants in the drug court, as they were screened for the program by probation personnel (Gilmore et al., 2005, pp. 307–208). The findings of Gilmore et al. (2005) provide some valuable insights into how social bonds may influence participants in juvenile drug courts; some reflect what we would expect to find if social bonds in drug court programs works in tune with Hirschi's (1969) theory, though as discussed above, not all of Gilmore et al's (2005) findings support Hirschi's (1969) theory.

Other studies, such as Salvatore et al's (2010) study evaluating the Philadelphia JDC found greater participation of parents and other family members leading to positive outcomes (e.g., lower rates of drug use) in juvenile drug court participants, may provide more direct support for the role of social bonds as being a component of successful treatment in a JDC. Further, being one of the authors of that study, I remember pretty well the guiding influence of the judge and other members of the Philadelphia JDC, and seeing firsthand the impact of the judge taking an interest in a JDC participant, as well as many moments when members of the treatment court workgroup took time out of their day to mentor

JDC participants, take them out to lunch as a reward for program success, or purchase small items like sunglasses or gift certificates for them as rewards, demonstrating their commitment to the JDC program participants and the genuine connections forged between program participants and members of the JDC treatment team.

In a more recent study, Kuehn and Ridener (2016) evaluated the participant experience in a drug court in Pennsylvania. The advantage of qualitative research is that it provides a more in-depth look at a research question; instead of information regarding the significance and direction of a relationship, we get to know why something matters in a study. Kuehn and Ridener (2016) looks at various issues for the drug court, one of which was how social bonds or connections with the treatment workgroup and judge made a difference. For example, the following quotation illustrates how the desire not to let down the judge or get in trouble helped keep a participant accountable:

> I think every week is a bit much, you know what I mean? But I'm about to phase up so it will only be every other week. But, like, what do I have to tell you every single week? But, I mean it *keeps you accountable* [emphasis in original], Like I don't want to get into trouble because I don't want to go in front of that judge and get in trouble in front of everybody." (Kuehn & Ridener, 2016, p. 2252)

The role of other members of the treatment court workgroup may also be a critical component of participants succeeding in drug courts. In the below examples, participants discussed the relationship with the treatment court's parole officer as a critical factor in the success of the program:

> *She goes above and beyond her job* [emphasis in original]…. They do their jobs really well. I can't say enough about them, they're phenomenal." (Kuehn & Ridener, 2016, p. 2253)
> It's more of a *bond* [emphasis in original] with the PO. We are closer than with other POs because of regular visits. I have her personal number, which I have called, she is right there." (Kuehn & Ridener, 2016, p. 2253)
>
> Yeah, it just takes time. When you're an addict and you do that manipulating and lying and all that especially to your fam-

ily ... that's what I did to my probation officer but it takes time and they learn to trust you and that's what happened with my PO. *It's just, she's like family to me and I love her* [emphasis in original]. And I tell her everything that goes on with me and I call her. (Kuehn & Ridener, 2016, p. 2253)

As the above quotations demonstrate, the potential bond between members of the treatment court workgroup, such as a parole officer, may act to help provide support and guidance for a program participant. As participants bond with their parole officer, an attachment is built, one they can rely on for support and understanding through their treatment process and one they may not want to risk by failing to meet programmatic goals.

As discussed above, the role of the judge is often a critical component of a treatment court's success, and this is supported in Kuehn and Ridener's (2016) study. A large portion of the participants stated that the judge was fair, supportive, and understood addiction. Participants' comments suggested that the judge's therapeutic focus was of note. For example, the following quotations point to the engaged, understanding, and supportive role of the judge:

He speaks to me like a human being, Not looking down on me. *He is a judge, but he speaks to me* [emphasis in original], hard to describe, like a counselor, genuinely concerned. I got a couple of self-esteem boosters from the judge. He sees improvements. Even if I don't see them. Meant a lot to me. Pushed me to keep doing what I am doing. *More confident when I leave the courtroom* [emphasis in original]. Usually, when out in front of the judge, I went to jail. Now I leave and I am a free man. (Kuehn & Ridener, 2016, pp. 2253–2254)

He never intimidated me. *He's extremely fair and he will go the extra mile to help you out of a situation* [emphasis in original]. Not where you have a violation, but he will try to get you back on the right path." (Kuehn & Ridener, 2016, p. 2253)

The above comments regarding the role of the judge in drug courts reflect how meaningful the bond between drug court participants and the judge can be (something we will return to when we examine reentry courts). The findings of Gilmore et al. (2005), Salvatore et al. (2010), and

Kuehn and Ridener (2016) provide some support for the idea that social bonds are a critical component of drug court programs. The social controls and attachments provided by judges, other members of the treatment court team, and family, peers, education, and employment all play a role in the effectiveness of drug court programs. Before we turn our attention to the effectiveness of drug court programs, we will briefly examine them from the theoretical perspective of life course theory, which suggests they can act as a turning point away from substance use and criminal offending.

Drug Courts and Life Course Theory

So far, we have explored the roles of therapeutic jurisprudence and social bonds in the context of juvenile and adult drug court programs. We have examined the role these play in drug court programs (and will continue to do so with other treatment court programs in the coming chapters). To briefly recap, therapeutic jurisprudence is the philosophy employed by treatment courts to use the judge and court as an agent of treatment instead of operating in the more traditional adversarial manner of criminal courts. Social bond theory argues that the more attached or bonding an individual is to conventional society through peers, family, education, employment, religion, and other social institutions, the less likely they will be to engage in substance use or other criminal behaviors. However, there may be other criminological theories that may apply to drug courts. One such theory is the life course theory.

Life course theory argues that life events like getting married, becoming a parent, military service, reaching educational goals, and getting employed can alter an individual's life trajectory and change their propensity to participate in criminal behaviors (Elder, 1986; Sampson & Laub, 1993). There are three essential components of life course theory identified by Sampson and Laub (1993): (1) Social control within the context of family and education can explain criminal behavior in children and adolescents. (2) There is a level of permanency in deviant and criminal behavior seen in adolescence through adulthood across life domains. (3) Informal social ties during adulthood to career, family, and education can explain the shift from delinquent or criminal behavior over the life course regardless of deviance and delinquency earlier in life.

In other words, the informal social controls built in adulthood through parenthood, marriage, employment, and military service can act as turning points away from crime towards a more prosocial life (Messer et al., 2016). In prior studies, turning points have been examined within the context of substance use. Studies such as Andersen (2015), Blomqvist (2002), and Kaskutas (1996) have found that turning points can influence decreasing or desistance for substance use through self-motivations as well as the influence of others (Curran et al., 1998; Dawson et al., 2012).

Treatment court programs like drug courts may help facilitate self-motivation and provide support through the social bonds built with the judge and treatment court workgroup, as well as engaged family members, bringing about a shift from a substance-using trajectory to a nonuser. Another potential key factor that may influence turning points is self-perception. Meer et al. (2016) stated that self-perception may be one of the most critical internal turning points. In other words, being able to shift from seeing oneself as a substance abuser to a nonsubstance user may be a critical turning point away from substance use and one of the reasons behind the success of drug court programs.

Moving forward, we now turn our attention to evidence that supports and challenges the effectiveness of drug court programs. In their 2016 study, Messer et al. conducted semi-structured interviews with former participants in drug court programs to see if drug courts may be effective as turning points. During the interviews, a variety of topics were addressed, including how drug courts help increase the self-esteem of participants, improve the former participants' relationships with their children and family, reach educational milestones like getting a general education development certificate (GED), find a job, and get a driver's license. All of these represent factors identified in the life course literature as being able to act as a turning point for those engaged in criminal offending. The findings of Messer et al.'s (2016) study suggest that drug courts may help facilitate turning points; as such, they may be theoretically tied not only into social control theory but potentially life course theory; this may be useful as it may provide a greater understanding of how drug court programs can stimulate participants to make prosocial changes by facilitating turning points like meeting educational goals and finding employment. These help participants, in turn, stop their substance abuse and criminal trajectories, which led them to drug court and could potentially lead them to jail or prison, onto prosocial paths, and successful integration into mainstream society.

Do Drug Courts Work?

The problem of answering a question dealing with the effectiveness of a drug court must begin with an understanding of what a drug court is. Let us briefly recap: compared with methods traditionally employed within the justice system, the aims of the drug court model are much less punitive and more healing and restorative. Unlike traditional court-rooms, drug courts are far more informal, where direct exchanges between the participant and the judge are common and between counsel and the state are non-adversarial. The courtroom functions as a thera-peutic vehicle (similar to a theater in a square), with the judge at the center leading the treatment process (Goldkamp et al., 2001). The judge presides over the drug court and is very much an active participant in the drug court team. Working as a unit, the team provides and links clients with the substance abuse treatment services they need through case management and referral to community agencies. The clients are often intensively supervised through various criminal justice approaches, including random urine tests for illicit drugs, visits to the participant's home, and regular case reviews before the judge. Wrap-around services are focused on a participant's strengths and weaknesses and may include educational and vocational training, mental health treatment, and life skills development (Goldkamp et al., 2001; Butts & Roman, 2004).

Two main justice aims should be examined when considering the effectiveness of drug courts (or any other intervention) "working" in ways that meets the aims defined by Hart (1958). To begin, in a cultural climate where the opinion of criminal justice practitioners and experts is largely ignored (Garland, 2001), it is essential that the benefits for the public in the areas of crime reduction, taxpayer savings, and cost to vic-tims are highlighted. Over the last 30 years, a "culture of fear" has devel-oped in which political leaders who allocate funding are largely influ-enced by public opinion (Garland, 2001). By addressing the justice aims of providing increased safety and savings for the public, the future of drug courts can be made more secure. The next justice aim is to help drug offenders stop offending. By providing treatment and support to drug offenders, not only is the first justice aim of increasing public safety accomplished, but a second equally important aim of providing treatment to help offenders stop offending is met; this redefines both punishment and crime by changing the punitive nature of punishment to a more treatment-oriented approach. The "crime" of being a drug addict is re-conceptualized as an illness that can be treated and the offender re-integrated into society.

For us to assess the utility of drug court programs, we need to explore the effectiveness of these courts in reducing offending, providing financial benefits in comparison to more traditional methods of dealing with drug offenders, and look at the evidence that drug courts give effective treatment for drug offenders. We will make this assessment through an analysis of several measures that gauge the success of drug courts, including rates of rearrest for drug court participants, gauging the financial benefits of drug courts, and an examination of rates of retention in treatment for drug court participants.

Evidence Supporting the Effectiveness of Drug Courts

To begin research on a national, state, and local level demonstrating the effectiveness of drug courts in reducing recidivism is one of the most beneficial aspects of drug courts. For example, a 2003 study by the National Institute of Justice (NIJ) found that from a nationwide sample of 17,000 drug court graduates, only 16.4% were rearrested for a felony offense within one year of graduation (Roman, Townsend, & Bhati, 2003). Several meta-analyses have examined the connection between drug courts and recidivism, generally providing evidence for the NIJ's (2003) study. For example, Wilson and colleagues' (2006) meta-analysis looked at 55 independent drug court program samples, including those with both quasi-experimental and experimental designs. The results of Wilson et al.'s (2006) study found that the average recidivism rate dropped between 14 and 26% for drug court program participants. In another study, supporting the potential for drug courts to reduce recidivism, Mitchell and colleagues (2012) conducted a meta-analysis of 92 evaluations of adult drug court programs and found the typical drop during a three-year follow-up period was between and found the decrease in recidivism from 50% to 35%. More recently, Logan and Link (2019) reviewed the drug court literature to see if there was still evidence-based support regarding drug court's effectiveness. Their assessment results supported the general view that drug courts reduce recidivism.

Research on both a state and local level has also found similar results to those cited above and generally supports the utility of drug court programs in reducing recidivism. The Center for Court Innovation (CCI) released a report (Rempel et al., 2003) that was one of the most extensive statewide studies on drug courts to date, which analyzed the impact of the New York State's drug court system. The study found that the re-conviction rate of participants in the state's six drug courts was, on average, 29% lower over three years than for the same type of offenders who did not enter drug court (Rempel et al., 2003). Goldkamp and Weiland (1993) found a 33% rearrest rate for participants in the Dade County, Florida, drug court, compared to a 48% rearrest rate for the control group. Goldkamp et al. (2001) found that drug court participants in Las Vegas and to a lesser degree, Portland have lower rates of rearrest. Gottfredson et al. (2003) found that members of their sample who were in drug treatment had 30% fewer rearrests than members of the control group over a two-year period. In another study, Carey and Waller (2011) examined 24 Oregon drug court programs, finding they had an average 44% reduction in the number of rearrests and a 23% reduction in recidivism rate compared to offenders who do not participate in drug court programs. More recently, Cheesman et al. (2016) examined drug courts in the state of Virginia and found that programs integrating Moral Recognition Therapy (MRT) had a lower likelihood of recidivism. On a local level, in Chester County, Pennsylvania, drug court graduates had a 5.4% rearrest rate compared to a 21.5% rearrest rate for the control group (Brewster, 2001). Research on a national, state, and local level all supports the effectiveness of drug courts in reducing recidivism rates; this is the first and most important area we want to consider when considering the effectiveness of drug courts. After all, having less future drug crime not only helps the program participants but also provides a sense of safety to the public and supports using their tax dollars for treatment through drug courts instead of incarceration. It should be noted that while there is significant evidence supporting the ability of drug courts to reduce recidivism for adults, the evidence for juveniles is less supportive. A recent study by Hiller et al. (2021) concluded that there was not enough evidence to support the effectiveness of juvenile drug courts in reducing recidivism, suggesting that what may work for adults may not be as effective with youth populations.

The next area that should be examined is the financial benefits of drug courts. Research has shown (Rempel et al., 2003; Washington State Institute for Public Policy, 2003) that a state gains a high return on its investment in drug courts. A study by the Washington State Institute for Public Policy (2003) estimates that the average drug court participant produces over $6,500 in benefits that stem from the approximate 13.5% reduction in recidivism. These benefits consist of over $3,500 in avoided criminal justice system costs paid by taxpayers and approximately $3,000 in avoided costs to victims. Crumpton et al. (2004) examined the benefits of Baltimore County Drug Treatment Courts. They found that members of their sample cost taxpayers over $3,000 less than offenders processed through more conventional courts and almost $10,000 in savings to victims.

Further, on a state level, Carey and Finigan (2004) examined the cost benefits of drug courts in Multnomah County, Oregon. This study found that the drug court saved approximately $2,300 per client compared to traditional criminal justice processing. In addition, when costs to victims were included in the analysis, the savings increased to over $3,500 per participant. In total, the savings to the county were over $1.5 million per year (Carey & Finigan, 2004). More recently, Cheesman et al. (2016) examined the cost efficiency of Virginia's drug courts and found significant cost savings compared to the alternative; drug courts save taxpayers an average of $20,000 per participant.

The final area that should be explored to support the effectiveness of the drug court model is increased treatment retention rates. Research has shown (Belenko, 1998, 2001) that successful completion of treatment is key to effective substance abuse treatment. While coercive, drug courts work closely with offenders, often providing a support network for clients that continues even after graduation from the program (Butts & Roman, 2004). Using graduated sanctions, drug courts can increase retention rates in treatment (Goldkamp et al., 2002). Studies have found varying results of retention rates in drug court programs. Belenko's (2001) review of eight drug court evaluations found that, on average, 47% of the participants completed programs. The General Accounting Office (1997) reported that between 1989 and 1995, about 33% of all offenders enrolled in drug court programs completed those programs.

That completion rate ranged from 8% to 95%, during this time. Other studies have found this wide variation in program completion rates. For example, 31% in Baltimore City drug court (Gottfredson & Exum, 2002), almost 50% in Denver, Colorado's drug court (Harrison et al., 2001), 57% in the Riverside County, California, drug court (Sechrest & Shicor, 2001), and 66% of New York State drug courts (Cissner et al., 2013). These findings suggest mixed but promising results regarding the retention of drug court programs.

Based on the evidence cited above, it can be concluded that the drug courts should continue to be part of dealing with the drug problem on a national, state, and local level. Drug courts have been proven to provide substantial savings to taxpayers instead of more traditional criminal justice processes, reduce rates of recidivism, provide more effective treatment to offenders, and increase public safety. A treatment program that can accomplish all these goals, which provide benefits for the government, the offender, and the public, should be expanded. Increased use of drug court programs would allow these benefits to continue to grow on all levels, reducing crime rates, treating addiction in the offender population, and providing substantial savings to taxpayers. While the bulk of the evidence does support the effectiveness of drug courts, it is essential to explore evidence that challenges the effectiveness of these programs.

Evidence Challenging the Effectiveness of Drug Courts

The previous section examined several decades of evidence showing significant evidence of the effectiveness of drug court programs. In cost-effectiveness, lower rates of recidivism relative to more traditional processing, and program retention, we have seen drug courts can work. As with just about every other treatment and prevention program targeting criminal justice populations, there is also evidence to challenge the effectiveness of drug courts. In this section, we will examine some evidence that challenges the effectiveness of drug courts. To begin, while we may see a consensus (or as close to a consensus as we can get in social sciences) regarding the effectiveness of drug courts, there is less consistency regarding the findings of juvenile drug courts. The literature has found less support for JDCs relative to adult models (Logan & Link, 2019). Several meta-analytic studies of JDCs have determined that findings were inconsistent and inconclusive on general recidivism,

recidivism for drug law violations, and drug use (Mitchell et al., 2012; Tanner-Smith et al., 2016a, 2016b; Wilson et al., 2019). As with juvenile populations, there are studies such as Belenko and colleagues (1994) which have found drug courts programs may not be effective; in the case of Belenko et al. participants didn't have a different likelihood of rearrest relative to comparison group members. This finding challenges the evidence above, which supported the ability of drug courts to help reduce recidivism.

Turning our attention to other measures of drug court success, a study by Hepburn and Harvey (2007) used a quasi-experimental design to study the retention of two drug court programs. Their study used alternative measures of program retention, a single measure of program completion, and controls for sociodemographic and criminal history factors, finding no differences in program retention or completion in the two drug courts. Other studies highlight that drug court programs may have the opposite of the desired effects regarding recidivism. For example, Miethe and colleagues' (2000) study found that the overall recidivism rates of drug courts were 10% higher than comparison group members (26% for drug court participants and 16% for comparison group members, respectively). While not as substantial as the support for drug courts, we must be aware that these programs, while popular and generally supported, may still have limitations, and may only sometimes work as planned.

Future Research

Since drug courts began in 1989, there has been a consistent stream of studies examining their effectiveness in reducing drug offending, cost-effectiveness, and program retention rate. Numerous quantitative and qualitative studies have ultimately proved mixed, but leaning towards results that support the effectiveness of drug courts.

In the coming years, evaluations of drug court programs will likely continue to be an area of inquiry pursued by researchers. Process and outcome evaluations, studies exploring retention rates in programs, and cost effectiveness of these programs are all essential to gauge the ongoing effectiveness of drug courts for both adult and juvenile populations. In addition to these studies, a much-needed area is retrospective studies looking at the long-term influence of drug court participation over the life course. For example, a study looking at former participants who were in drug court programs in the 20s and 30s, at age 70 or older, could provide a valuable look at the influence of drug court programs over time. Would these studies find that the influence of drug courts wanes over time, or do the bonds and attachments built through drug court programs prompt lasting changes and relationships that help former drug court participants stay on a prosocial path?

The need for retrospective research examining the long-term influence of drug courts is just one of many areas of study that need to be explored. Other studies can examine the influence of drug court model modifications and variations, as well as the influence of the COVID-19 pandemic on the effectiveness of drug court programs. It is important to note that research in drug courts, like all treatment and prevention programs, needs to be ongoing. As culture and society shift and change, what may have worked in the past or present may not work in the future. The success of drug court programs cannot be taken for granted. Scholars, practitioners, researchers, and the public need to focus on drug courts to ensure they meet goals and provide the services needed to help clients, reduce recidivism, and provide cost-effective alternatives to incarceration.

Conclusions

Perhaps more than any other treatment court, drug courts have spread throughout the United States and have been popular with politicians, the public, practitioners, and participants. Like all treatment and prevention programs, these programs have mixed evidence regarding their effectiveness. Nonetheless, there is impressive evidence that they can "work" for some participants in helping address their underlying causes of substance use and criminal offending. Further, there is evidence of their benefits for the criminal justice system, including being more cost-effective than traditional criminal justice processing and incarceration, as well as addressing the issue of mass incarceration and the revolving door of prisons and jails.

Despite the benefits of drug courts, they are not without their critiques and limitations. From a philosophical level, using a court to provide treatment pushes judges and treatment court team members into roles they may not have the training, preparation, and experience to fulfill. The potential for net widening is also a considerable concern. Finally, the drug court model, which expanded into juvenile drug courts and has served as the template for seemingly endless variations of other treatment courts, may not be suited for some of the areas it is applied to. For example, should the structure and operations of drug courts be applied to issues like mental illness or intimate partner violence? Can what "works" in drug courts be successfully applied to prostitution? As we progress through the coming chapters, we will see some answers to these and other questions.

Treatment Court Success Story: Drug Courts

Name: Matthew Felt

Location: Toms River, NJ

Background: As this chapter demonstrates, there are a lot of potential benefits of drug court for participants. Once such person is Matthew Felt of Toms River, NJ. Like many across the United States Felt was struggling with addiction, in his case heroin addiction, which he started using in his late teens. Felt was arrested in 2014 and given the option to participate in a drug court program. Like many participants in drug courts, Matthew had a long history of drug arrests by the time he was 24, having been arrested on various drug charges 15 or 16 times.

What did the drug court help provide? Drug courts can help provide guidance, support, and direction for participants. Similar to many who struggle with addiction, Matthew wasn't sure of the direction his life should take and often felt hopeless. Drug Court, the second phase of the drug court he participated in, focused on employment, which prompted him to start his own business in November of 2016, High Power Capital, focusing connecting high-risk businesses in need of operating capital with groups of lenders. The rewards of successful employment and building a business with the support of the drug court help Matthew become a success story. The bonds and connections built through work with co-workers and clients help provide a network of support for drug court participants like Matthew, who don't want to let them down. A successful career like Matthew's also keeps someone too busy and engaged with prosocial activities and people to have the time to use and abuse drugs.

Drug Courts Can work! Giving people like Matthew Felt an option to be in a supportive environment which allows connections in the community to be maintained instead of incarceration gives participants in drug courts the chance to build a-new, address their addiction and related issues, and engage in prosocial behaviors which can lead to long-term successes and reaching major life goals such as starting a successful business.

Matthew Felt is a success story! After years of substance abuse, failures in treatment, arrests, and facing incarceration, drug court gave Felt the chance to change.

For more information on Matthew Felt see https://www.nj.com/healthfit/ 2021/03/he-gave-up-on-himself-but-after-drug-court-success-story-nj-man-started-his-own-business.html and High Power Capital Group at: https://highpowercapital.com/?_sp=a7d53217-c797-4ed8-997d-98b9e75eb6ec.1685632863365.

References

Andersen, D. (2015). Stories of change in drug treatment: A narrative analysis of "whats" and "hows" in institutional storytelling. *Sociology of Health & Illness, 37*, 668–682. https://doi.org/10.1111 /1467-9566.12228.

Belenko, S. (1998). Research on drug courts: A critical review. *National Drug Court Institute Review, I*(1), 1–42.

Belenko, S. (2001). Research on drug courts: A critical review: 2001 update. *National Drug Court Institute Review*, 1–64.

Belenko, S. (2019). The role of drug courts in promoting desistance and recovery: A merging of therapy and accountability. *Addiction Research & Theory, 27*(1), 315. https://doi.org/10.1080/16066359.20 18.1524882.

Belenko, S., & Dumanovsky, T. (1993). Program brief: Special drug courts. US Department of Justice, Bureau of Justice Statistics.

Belenko, S., Fagan, J. A., & Dumanovsky, T. (1994). The effects of the legal sanctions on recidivism in special drug courts. *Justice System Journal, 17*, 58–81. https://doi.org/10.1080/23277556.1994.10871193.

Berman, G., & Feinblatt, J. (2001). Problem-solving courts: A brief primer. *Law and Policy, 23*, 125–140. https://doi.org/10.1111 /1467-9930.00107.

Blomqvist, J. (2002). Recovery with and without treatment: A comparison of resolutions of alcohol and drug problems. *Addiction Research & Theory, 10,* 119–158. https://doi.org/10.1080/16066350290017248.

Brewster, M. P. (2001). An evaluation of the Chester County (PA) drug court program. *Journal of Drug Issues, 31*(1), 177–206. https://doi.org/10.1177/0022042601031001.

Bursik, R. J., & Grasmick, H. G. (1993). *Neighborhoods and crime: The dimensions of effective community control.* Macmillan.

Butts, J. A., & Roman, J. (Eds.). (2004). *Juvenile drug courts and teen substance abuse.* US Department of Justice.

Calvin, E. (2004). *Advocacy and training guide: Legal strategies to reduce unnecessary detention of children.* National Juvenile Defender Center. https://www.opd.wa.gov/documents/00553-2018_PLegal-Strategies-to-Reduce-Detention.pdf.

Carey, S. M., & Finigan, M.W. (2004). A detailed cost analysis in a mature drug court setting: A cost-benefit evaluation of the Multnomah County Drug Court. *Journal of Contemporary Criminal Justice, 20,* 315–338.

Carey, S. M., Finigan, M. W., & Pukstas, K. (2008). *Exploring the key components of drug courts: A comparative study of 18 drug courts on practices, outcomes, and costs.* NPC Research.

Carey, S., & Waller, M. (2011). *Oregon Drug Court cost study—Statewide costs and promising practices: Final report.* NPC Research. https://digital.osl.state.or.us/islandora/object/osl%3A6114.

Cheesman, F. L., Graves, S. E., Holt, K., Kunkel, T. L., Lee, C. G., & White, M. T. (2016). Drug court effectiveness and efficiency: Findings for Virginia. *Alcoholism Treatment Quarterly, 34*(2), 143–169. https://doi.org/10.1080/07347324.2016.1148486.

Cissner, A. B., Rempel, M., Walker Franklin, A., Roman, J. K., Bieler, S., Cohen, R., & Cadoret, C. R. (2013). *A statewide evaluation of New York's adult drug courts.* Center for Court Innovation. Urban Institute. https://bja.ojp.gov/sites/g/files/xyckuh186/files/Publications/CCI-UI-NYS_Adult_DC_Evaluation.pdf.

Cooper, C. (2001). *Juvenile drug court programs.* US Department of Justice, Office of Justice Programs, Office of Juvenile Justice and Delinquency Prevention.

Crumpton, C. D., Brekhus, J., Weller, J., & Finigan, M. (2004). *Cost analysis of Baltimore City, Maryland, drug treatment court: Includes out-*

come findings, cost analysis, summary and conclusions, only. www. npcresearch.com.

Curran, P. J., Muthen, B. O., & Hartford, T. C. (1998). The influence of changes in marital status on developmental trajectories of alcohol use in young adults. *Journal of Studies on Alcohol, 59*, 647–658. https://doi.org/10.15288/jsa.1998.59.647.

Dawson, D. A., Goldstein, R. B., Ruan, W. J., & Grant, B. F. (2012). Correlates of recovery from alcohol dependence: A prospective study over a 3-year follow up interval. *Alcoholism: Clinical and Experimental Research, 36*, 1268–1277. https://doi.org/10.1111/j.1530-0277 .2011.01729.x.

Elder, G. H. (1986). Military times and turning points in men's lives. *Developmental Psychology, 22*, 233–245. https://doi.org/10.1037/00 12-1649.22.2.233.

Friedman, A. S., Terras, A., & Glassman, K. (2000). Family structure versus family relations for predicting to substance use/abuse and illegal behavior. *Journal of Child & Adolescent Substance Abuse, 10*(1), 1–16. https://doi.org/10.1300/J029v10n01_01.

Garland, D. (2001). *The culture of control: Crime and social order in contemporary society*. University of Chicago Press.

General Accounting Office. (1997). *Drug courts: Overview of growth, characteristics, and results*.

Gilmore, A. S., Rodriguez, N., & Webb, V. J. (2005). Substance abuse and drug courts: The role of social bonds in juvenile drug courts. *Youth Violence and Juvenile Justice, 3*(4), 287–315. https://doi.org/10.1177/ 1541204005278803.

Goldkamp, J. S., & Weiland, D. (1993). *Assessing the impact of Dade County's felony drug court. Final report*. Crime and Justice Research Institute.

Goldkamp, J. S., White, M. D., & Robinson, J. B. (2001). Do drug courts work? Getting inside the drug court black box. *Journal of Drug Issues, 31*(1), 27–72. https://doi.org/10.1177/002204260103100104.

Goldkamp, J. S., White, M. D., & Robinson, J. B. (2002). An honest chance: Perspectives on drug courts. *Federal Sentencing Reporter, 14*, 369–372. https://doi.org/10.1525/fsr.2002.14.6.369.

Gottfredson, D., & Exum, M. (2002). The Baltimore City drug treatment court: One-year results from a randomized study. *Journal of Research in Crime and Delinquency, 39,* 337–356. https://doi.org/10.1177 /002242780203900304.

Gottfredson, D., Najaka S.S., & Kearley B. Effectiveness of drug courts: Evidence from a randomized trial. *Criminology & Public Policy, 2,* 171–196.

Harrison, L., Patrick, D., & English, K. (2001). An evaluation of the Denver drug court: The early years, 1995–1996. Colorado Department of Public Safety, Division of Criminal Justice.

Hart, H. L. A. (1958). Positivism and the separation of law and morals. *Harvard Law Review, 71*(4), 593–629.

Hepburn, J. R., & Harvey, A. N. (2007). The effect of the threat of legal sanction on program retention and completion: Is that why they stay in drug court? *Crime and Delinquency, 53*(2), 255–280. https:// doi.org/10.1177/0011128705283298.

Hicks, B. M., Iacono, W. G., & McGue, M. (2010). Consequences of an adolescent onset and persistent course of alcohol dependence in men: Adolescent risk factors and adult outcomes. *Alcoholism Clinical and Experimental Research, 34,* 819–833. https://doi. org/10.1111/j.1530-0277.2010.01154.x.

Hiller, M. L., Belenko, S., Dennis, M., Estrada, B., Cain, C., Mackin, J. R., Kagan, R., & Pappacena, L. (2021). The impact of Juvenile Drug Treatment Courts (JDTC) implementing federal evidence-based guidelines on recidivism and substance use: Multisite Randomized Controlled Trial (RCT) and Regression Discontinuity (RDD) Designs. *Health Justice, 9*(38), 1–15.

Hiller, M., Belenko, S., Taxman, F., Young, D., Perdoni, M., & Saum, C. (2010). Measuring drug court structure and operations: Key components and beyond. *Criminal Justice and Behavior, 37*(9), 933–950. https://doi.org/10.1177/0093854810373727.

Hirschi, T. (1969). *Causes of delinquency.* University of California Press.

Hoeve, M., McReynolds, L. S., & Wasserman, G. A. (2013). The influence of adolescent psychiatric disorder on young adult recidivism. *Criminal Justice and Behavior, 40,* 1368–1382. https://doi.org/10.11 77/0093854813488106.

Kandel, D., & Yamaguchi, K. (2002). Stages of drug involvement in the U.S. population. In D. Kandel (Ed.), *Stages and pathways of drug involvement: Examining the gateway hypothesis* (pp. 65–89). Cambridge University Press.

Kaplan, T., Miller, M. K., & Wood, E. F. (2018). Looking backward, looking forward: How the evolution of specialty courts can inform the courts of tomorrow. *Court Review: The Journal of The American Judges Association, 54,* 14–24.

Kaskutas, L. A. (1996). Pathways to self-help among women for sobriety. *American Journal of Drug and Alcohol Abuse, 22,* 259–280.

Kuehn, S., & Ridener, R. (2016). Inside the black box: A qualitative evaluation of participants' experiences of a drug treatment court. *The Qualitative Report, 21*(12), 2246–2267. https://doi.org/10.46743/21 60-3715/2016.2470.

Laub, J. H., Nagin, S., & Sampson, R. J. (1998). Trajectories of change in criminal offending: Good marriages and the desistance process. *American Sociological Review, 63,* 225–238. https://doi.org/10.2307/ 2657324.

Laub, J. H., & Sampson, R. J. (1993). Turning points in the life course: Why change matters to the study of crime. *Criminology, 31,* 301– 325. https://doi.org/10.1111/j.1745-9125.1993.tb01132.x.

Logan, M. W., & Link, N. W. (2019). Taking stock of drug courts: Do they work? *Victims & Offenders, 14*(3), 283–298. https://doi.org/10. 1080/15564886.2019.1595249.

Lurgio, A. J. (2008). The first 20 years of drug treatment courts: A brief description of the history and impact. *Federal Probation, 72*(1), 14–20.

Martinson, R. (1974). *What works?—Questions and answers about prison reform. The Public Interest, 42,* 22–54.

Messer, S., Patten, R., & Candela, K. (2016). Drug courts and the facilitation of turning points: An expansion of life course theory. *Contemporary Drug Problems, 43*(1), 6–24. https://doi.org/10.1177/0091 450916632545.

Miethe, T. D., Lu, H., & Reese, E. (2000). Reintegrative shaming and recidivism risks in drug court: Explanations for some unexpected findings. *Crime & Delinquency, 46,* 522–541. https://doi.org/10.117 7/0011128700046004006.

Mitchell, O., & Wilson, D. B., Eggers, A., & MacKenzie, D. L. (2012). Assessing the effectiveness of drug courts on recidivism: A meta-analytic review of traditional and nontraditional drug courts. *Journal of Criminal Justice, 40,* 60–71. https://doi.org/10.1016/j.jcrimjus.201 1.11.009.

Monitoring the Future. (2022a). Any illicit drug use: Trends in 12 month prevalence use grades 8, 10, and 12. http://monitoringthefuture.org/data/21data/AnyIllicit/Any Illicit_jsFigures.htm.

Monitoring the Future. (2022b). Marijuana: Trends in 12 month prevalence use grades 8, 10, and 12. http://monitoringthefuture.org/data/21data/MJ/MJ_jsFigur es.htm.

National Association of Drug Court Professionals. (1997). Defining drug courts: The key components. US Department of Justice, Office of Justice Programs, Bureau of Justice Assistance.

National Association of Drug Court Professionals. (2015). Adult drug court best practice standards. Vol. 2. http://www.nadcp.org/standards.

National Association on Addiction and Substance Abuse (CASA) at Columbia University. (2004). *Criminal neglect: Substance abuse, juvenile justice and the children left behind.* Columbia University. https://www.ojp.gov/ncjrs/virtuallibrary/abstracts/criminal -neglect-substance-abusejuvenile-justice-and-children-left.

National Drug Court Resource Center. (2021). Treatment courts across the United States (2020). University of North Carolina Wilmington. https://ndcrc.org/wpcontent/uploads/2021/08/2020_NDCRC_ TreatmentCourt _Count_Table_v8.pdf.

National Institute of Justice. (2021). Drug courts. https://www.ojp.gov/pdffiles1/nij/238527.pdf.

National Institute of Drug Abuse (NIDA). (2006). *Principles of drug abuse treatment for criminal justice populations: A research guide.* NIA Publication No. 065316. National Institute of Health. https://nida.nih.gov/sites/default/files/txcriminaljustice_0.pdf.

Office of Justice Programs. (1997). Defining drug courts: The key components. National Criminal Justice Reference No. 205621.

Office of Justice Programs. (2004). Defining drug courts: The key components. National Criminal Justice Reference No. 205621. (Original work published in 1997.)

Rempel, M., Fox-Kralstein, D., Cissner, A., Cohen, R., Labriola, M., Farole, D., Bader, A., & Magnani, M. (2003). The New York State Drug Court Evaluation: Policies, participants and impacts. Center for Court Innovation. Submitted to the New York State Unified Court System and the U.S. Bureau of Justice Assistance.

Rodriguez, N., & Webb, V. J. (2004). Multiple measures of juvenile drug courts effectiveness: Results from a quasi-experimental design. *Crime & Delinquency, 50*, 292–314. https://doi.org/10.1177/0011128703254991.

Roman, J., Townsend, W., & Bhati, A. S. (2003). Recidivism rates for drug court graduates: nationally based estimates. *The Urban Institute.*

Sabatine, E., Lippold, M., & Kainz, K. (2017). The unique and interactive effects of parent and school bonds on adolescent delinquency. *Journal of Applied Developmental Psychology, 53*, 54–63. https://doi.org/10.1016/j.appdev.2017.09.005.

Salvatore, C., Henderson, J., Hiller, M. L., White, E., & Samuelson, B. (2010). An observational study of team meetings and status hearings in a juvenile drug court. *Drug Court Review, 7*(10), 95–124.

Salvatore, C., Hiller, M. L., Samuelson, B., Henderson, J., & White, E. (2011). A systematic observational study of a juvenile drug court judge. *Juvenile and Family Court Journal, 62*(4), 19–36. https://doi.org/10.1111/j.1755-6988.2011.01066.x.

Sampson, R. J., & Laub, J. H. (1993). *Crime in the making: Pathways and turning points through life.* Harvard University Press.

Sampson, R. J., & Laub, J. H. (1994). Urban poverty and family context of delinquency. A new look at structure and process in a classic study. *Child Development, 65*, 523–540. https://doi.org/10.2307/1131400.

Scott, C. K., Dennis, M. L., Grella, C. E., Funk, R. R., & Lurigio, A. J. (2019). Juvenile justice systems of care: Results of a national survey of community supervision agencies and behavioral health providers on services provision and cross-system interactions. *Health & Justice, 7*(11), 1–18. https://doi.org/10.1186/s40352-019-0093-x.

Sechrest, D. K., & Shicor, D. (2001). Determinants of graduation from a day treatment drug court in California: A preliminary study. *Journal of Drug Issues, 31*, 129–148. https://doi.org/10.1177/002204260103100108.

Shaw, M., & Robinson, K. (1998). *Summary and analysis of the first juvenile drug court evaluations: The Santa Clara County drug treatment court and the Delaware Juvenile Drug Court Diversion Program.* National Drug Court Institute Review. https://ndcrc.org

/wp-content/uploads/2020/06/DCRVolume1-3_Summary_and_
Analysis_of_the_First_Juvenile_Drug_Court_Evaluations.pdf.

Stein, D. A., Homan, K. J., & Debard, S. (2015). The effectiveness of juvenile treatment drug courts: A meta-analytic review of literature.
Journal of Child & Adolescent Substance Abuse, 24, 80–93. https://
doi.org/10.1080/1067828X.2013.764371.

Steinberg, L., Fletcher, A., & Darling, N. (1994). Parental monitoring
and peer influences on adolescent substance use. *Pediatrics, 93,*
1060–1064.

Tanner-Smith, E. E., Lipsey, M. W., & Wilson, D. B. (2016a). *Meta-analysis of research on the effectiveness of juvenile drug courts.* Peabody
Research Institute, Vanderbilt University. NCJ 250439. https://www.
ojjdp.gov/JDTC/resources.html.

Tanner-Smith, E. E., Lipsey, M. W., & Wilson, D. B. (2016b). Juvenile
drug court effects on recidivism and drug use: A systematic review
and meta-analysis. *Journal of Experimental Criminology, 12*(4),
477–513.

Washington State Institute for Public Policy. (2003). Washington State's
drug courts for adult defendants: Outcome evaluation and cost benefit analysis. http://www.wsipp.wa.gov/ReportFile/827/Wsipp_
Washington-States-Drug-Courts-for-Adult-Defendants -Outcome
Evaluation-and-Cost-Benefit-Analysis_Full-Report.pdf.

Wilson, D. B., Mitchell, O., & MacKenzie, D. L. (2006). A systematic
review of drug court effects on recidivism. *Journal of Experimental
Criminology, 2,* 459–487.

Wilson, D. B., Olaghere, A., & Kimbrell, C. S. (2019). Implementing
juvenile drug treatment courts: A meta aggregation of process evaluations. *Journal of Research in Crime and Delinquency, 56*(4), 605–
645. https://doi.org/10.1177/0022427819826630.

CHAPTER 5

Mental Health Courts: Overview

One of the biggest challenges for the criminal justice system is to provide services for populations it was not designed to support. Researchers have continuously identified how the criminal justice system, including police and corrections, is often called upon to deal with public health issues, forcing these agencies to go beyond the boundaries of their perceived missions (Ratcliffe, 2021). During their day-to-day duties, the police come across a variety of vulnerable populations, including prostitutes, the homeless, victims of domestic abuse, and the mentally ill (Dijk & Crofts, 2017). The multitude of challenging issues facing police as well as other branches of the criminal justice system during their duties poses a variety of issues, not just for the criminal justice system but also its clients who may end up in jail or prison due to behavior brought about by mental illness, where they are far less likely to receive the same quality of care and support than they would in the community. This is a critical issue across the United States as many communities lack cohesive mental health services while the rate of mental health issues climbs across the country.

In this chapter, we have come to one of the most challenging issues facing the criminal justice system: the prevalence of mentally ill persons in jails and prisons. Severe mental illness in jails and prisons has become so commonplace that U.S. correctional institutions are known as "the new asylums" (Treatment Advocacy Center, 2016). Perhaps one of the most shocking statistics regarding mental illness in the criminal justice system is that in 44 states, there are more mentally ill persons in jails or prisons than in state psychiatric hospitals (Treatment Advocacy Center,

2016). Others have reported that 44% of inmates in prison have been diagnosed with a mental health issue, as have 43% of inmates in jail (Bronson & Berzofsky, 2017). These statistics demonstrate that mental illness is highly prevalent in correctional institutions, many of which are already overburdened by overcrowding, limited funding, and the need to provide services across a variety of areas including health, education, employment, and as discussed here, mental health.

As we might expect, those with mental illness may experience additional stress while incarcerated. With a reported 1 in 4 inmates experiencing severe psychological distress in jails (Bronson & Berzofsky, 2017), we can see that incarceration itself may exacerbate or lead to additional psychological stress; this can lead to a variety of issues and adverse outcomes, including more extended periods of incarceration for mentally ill inmates in jails. For example, in Florida's Orange County jail, the typical stay for inmates is 26 days. However, for mentally ill inmates, the typical stay is almost double, at 51 days. Similarly, the typical sentence at New York's Rikers Island is 42 days, but for mentally ill offenders, it is an astounding 215 days (Treatment Advocacy Center, 2016). The marked difference in the sentence length of a mentally ill offender not only may impact the mental health and well-being of the inmate, but increases the costs related to incarceration, another challenging area for the criminal justice system and in particular corrections, which routinely struggles with funding, staffing, and other resources.

Is it just the stress of incarceration that leads to these extended jail stays for mentally ill inmates, or are there other factors? According to the Treatment Advocacy Center (2016), the core reason we see the difference in length of stay in jails is that mentally ill offenders have more difficulty understanding and following the rules in correctional facilities. Ultimately, those with mental illness placed in jail or prison will be under stressful conditions in an environment that historically was unprepared to provide the treatment and services they need. There may be a better option than incarceration when it comes to mentally ill offenders: mental health courts, which represent a relatively new alternative, can divert this population from jail or prison into community-based treatment where they may be more likely to receive the treatment and service they need, less likely to deal with the psychological stresses and strains of incarceration, and more likely to reduce offending and find success in other areas like employment, education, and supporting their families.

As with other treatment courts, mental health courts are grounded in the drug court model. Mental health courts (MHCs) have been identified as a critical development in the synergistic relationship between the criminal justice and mental health systems (Petrila, 2003). MHCs have proven to be a popular treatment court, with 469 Adult MHCS and 43 Juvenile MHCs nationwide as of 2020 (National Drug Court Resource Center, 2020). While popular, MHCs are not without their criticisms; opponents have pointed out that the simple existence of courts focusing on mentally ill persons will make the problem worse rather than better for mentally ill populations involved in the criminal justice system. "Net widening" is the idea that police will cast a wider net and arrest more people who meet the criteria or perceived criteria of an MHC in order to get people treatment (Seltzer, 2005). As noted in previous chapters, "net widening" concerns other treatment court models, including drug courts. On the other hand, those who support specialty courts in general and MHCs argue that MHCs are an innovative and therapeutic approach to dealing with those who do not conform to the historically rigid model of the criminal justice system (Redlich et al., 2006, p. 348). In this chapter, we will examine the structure and critical characteristics of MHCs, look at examples of MHC phase structures, present the theoretical orientation of MHCs, consider evidence that supports and refutes their effectiveness, develop future areas of study, and finally provide concluding remarks.

Mental Health Court Program Model Example: Manhattan Mental Health Court

As with other treatment courts, there is no standardized MHC model, although there tends to be overlap in the phase structure and how programs are run. In order to provide a sense of what an MHC looks like in practice, we will examine the Manhattan Mental Health Court, which opened in March 2011 to provide supervision and treatment to non-violent felony offenders with mental illness (Farley, 2015). In order to be eligible for the Manhattan MHC potential clients need to be 18 years of age or older, have been arraigned with non-violent felony charges, and have been diagnosed with a severe mental illness. Eligible candidates may also be referred by mental health agencies, prosecutors, defense attorneys, and judges (Farley, 2015, p. 2).

Those defendants eligible for the Manhattan MHC must be able to enter a knowing and voluntary plea. Defendants have to plead guilty and agree to participate in the MHC program for a period of 2 to 12 months (Farley, 2015). The Manhattan MHC consists of a treatment court team, a dedicated judge, an assistant district attorney, a resource coordinator, case managers, and a team leader. Defense attorneys from the Legal Aid Society, New York County Defender Services, and Neighborhood Defender Services are provided for indigent defendants (Faley, 2015, p. 4).

The Manhattan MHC is in session once per week and usually starts with a pre-court meeting in the judge's chamber. Following the pre-court meeting, the session will occur, and a variety of court, clinical, and legal staff will be present, as well as resource coordinators, mental health services providers, defense attorneys and prosecutors, and other members of the courtroom workgroup. In addition, friends and family of clients of the program may be present. When a client's case is called, the client and defense attorney typically will sit at the defense table in front of the galley, across from the prosecutor. While it varies by case, others, such as the resources coordinator or case manager, may also be present and may speak during the court appearance. MHC court sessions may include various court appearance types, such as new cases, judicial status hearings, phase advances, graduations, and sentencing (Farley, 2015, pp. 4–5).

The Manhattan MHC consists of four phases which last between three to six months each. Phase One (Adjustment) is meant to help establish a connection between the participant and the treatment team, and requires participants to take any required medications and attend scheduled court sessions. The second phase (Engagement) is to help participants to make healthy lifestyle changes to create prosocial relationships and support in their lives. It is expected that participants will attend regularly scheduled court sessions during Phase Two. Next is Phase Three (Progress in Treatment), where participants should attend court sessions regularly and achieve emotional stability to the point where they have healthy coping strategies. Phase Four (Preparation for Graduation) is the last phase of the program, where participants continue with treatment and medications (if needed); during this phase, court attendance and case management are decreased (Farley, 2015, p. 6).

Movement from phase to phase relies on participants' compliance. Those participants who fail to comply may face sanctions from the judge. Noncompliant behaviors may include refusal to provide a urine sample, failure to take prescribed medications, missing appointments with case managers or treatment providers, missing court dates, or being arrested for new offenses. Sanctions for noncompliance may include verbal reprimands, writing an essay, increased appearance at court sessions, or a bench warrant/being returned to jail. For some infractions, the court may provide a "second chance" or a warning before giving the participant a sanction. The courtroom treatment team may also deal with problems by altering the treatment plan by adding elements such as detox, drug rehabilitation, or transfer to more or less restrictive treatment or housing (Farley, 2015, p. 6).

Participants who progress successfully through each phase may receive various positive incentives or rewards, which include reducing the number of required court appearances, cessation of drug testing, certificates, advancing to the next phase of the program, and ultimately graduation. For those who graduate, charges are either dismissed or reduced. For those who fail, the sentence identified in the plea agreement is imposed, and the participant typically goes to jail (Farley, 2015, p. 6). While MHCs have variance in their models, there are defining characteristics and elements critical to program structure and functioning.

Defining Mental Health Courts: Key Characteristics and Elements

Like other forms of treatment courts, some key characteristics and elements define mental health courts. Scholars (Goldkamp & Irons-Guynn, 2000; Redlich, 2005; Steadman et al., 2001) have identified six operational characteristics defining mental health courts. The first essential characteristic is that MHCs are criminal courts with a separate docket for people who are mentally ill. Some MHCs serve people with severe and persistent mental illness, while other MHCs have less rigid criteria and provide services for anyone who has demonstrated they have mental health issues. Further, the type of formal clinical screening processes varies by MHC. However, the core characteristic of having a separate docket for mentally ill clients and having a single judge presiding over the docket is at the center of MHCs (Redlich et al., 2006, p. 349).

The second characteristic of MHCs is the goal of diverting people with mental illness into community treatment instead of the criminal justice system, thereby reducing the potential harms of going in and out of the revolving doors of correctional facilities (Centers for Mental Health Services, 1995; Redlich et al., 2006, p. 349). Existing studies support MHCs successfully providing treatment and reducing recidivism, such as the Trupin and Richards (2003) study.

The following key characteristic identified is the mandatory nature of community mental health services. In other words, participants in MHCs must engage in the treatment process, including taking any prescribed medications, going to treatment sessions, and following any other components of treatment mandated by the MHC or related programs (Redlich et al., 2006). According to Redlich et al. (2006), it is common for MHCs to incentivize participants in MHCs in order to gain compliance so that a participant may be more likely to engage in treatment. For example, allowing an initial charge to be reduced, dropped, or vacated (as well as not going to jail or prison) with the successful completion of treatment (p. 349). Further, MHCs may have additional conditions such as maintaining employment, completing education, and addressing other challenging areas for participants such as familial relationships.

The fourth key characteristic of MHCs is providing continuing service through judicial status review hearings and direct supervision in the community. This characteristic reflects the foundation of all problem-oriented courts: the use of therapeutic jurisprudence to provide treatment and support for clients of the criminal justice system, instead of punishment. During judicial supervision hearings, participant compliance is monitored, and praise for meeting programmatic goals or accomplishments may be provided. Conversely, sanctions may be implemented if the participant fails to meet programmatic goals or violates the conditions of the MHC (Redlich et al., 2006, p. 349). Griffin and colleagues (2002) described three types of community supervision provided by MHCs: (1) those providing community supervision/treatment must provide supervision and report back to the MHC; (2) probation officers and related court personnel/staff; and (3) criminal justice and community treatment providers are jointly responsible (Redlich et al., 2006, p. 349).

Fifth, MHCs usually provide praise and support for compliance and sanctions or punishments for noncompliance. Most MHCs utilize therapeutic jurisprudence similarly to other treatment courts (Winick & Wexler, 2003). In general, participants in MHCs who have extended periods of stability and success will graduate from the MHC, where most programs drop or vacate the original charges that brought the participant to the MHC, with many programs ending supervision at this point. A variety of sanctions are imposed for those who fail to comply, including verbal reprimands, increased numbers of status hearings and levels of supervision, and returning people to jail. Those who continue to be noncompliant may be dismissed from the program and sent back to regular criminal court for processing or back to jail or prison to finish their sentence (Redlich et al., 2006, p. 349). The final key characteristic of MHCs is that participation is voluntary (like most treatment courts) (Redlich, 2005).

The above six characteristics of mental health courts provide a framework for us to consider the essential characteristics needed for MHCs to succeed in providing successful treatment and support for clients. In addition to these six characteristics, the Bureau of Justice Statistics awarded funding to the Council of State Governments Justice Center, which in 2007 prepared a report which identified ten essential elements of MHCs. Similar to the ten key components of drug courts, these ten essential elements will be presented in table format and defined. Each of these elements represents a component of MHC design and implementation needed for a successful program. It should be noted that while both adult and juvenile MHCs exist, these ten elements are conceptualized as pertaining to adult programs. There are two reasons for this: most MHCs were focused on adult populations, and there is a difference in the services provided for juveniles regarding mental health and criminal justice services relative to adults (Council of State Governments, 2007).

TABLE 5.1: 10 KEY ESSENTIAL ELEMENTS OF
MENTAL HEALTH COURTS

Element #1: Planning and Administration: The planning and administration of MHC programs should be guided by a group of diverse stakeholders from criminal justice, substance abuse treatment, mental health, and related systems.
Element #2: Target Population: MHCs' eligibility criteria need to incorporate both a community's treatment capacity and a public safety focus, as well as provide an alternative to pretrial detention for those defendants with mental health issues. Further, eligibility criteria have to consider the connection between the defendant's offense and their mental illness while factoring in each case's individual circumstances.
Element #3: Timely Participant Identification and Linkage to Services: Potential MHC clients are identified, provided referrals, accepted into MHCs, then connected to community-based services as soon as possible.
Element #4: Terms of Participation: MHC should have clear and direct terms of participation which incorporate a public safety function, help connect the defendant to treatment, are commensurate with the level of risk the defendant poses to the community, and provide beneficial outcomes for those who complete the MHC treatment program.
Element #5: Informed Choice: MHC programs must inform potential program participants about the requirements for the MHC to ensure they fully understand program requirements. Legal counsel is accessible to inform the decision to participate in the MHC and subsequent decisions about program involvement. There should also be procedures to address concerns about the defendant's competency to participate in the MHC.
Element #6: Treatment and Support Services: MHCs connect participants to individual community (ideally evidence-based) services utilizing an individualized treatment approach.
Element #7: Confidentiality: Any health or legal information collected or utilized by MHCs should be done so in a manner that protects the potential participant's confidentiality as a consumer of mental health support services, as well as their constitutional rights as a defendant. Any information collected by the MHC should be protected if the participant is transitioned back to traditional court processing.
Element #8: Court Team: A team of criminal justice professionals and mental health treatment providers should be provided ongoing training to assist MHC participants in reaching their treatment and criminal justice goals by reviewing court processes regularly.

Element #9: Monitoring Adherence to Court
Requirements: Mental health and criminal justice service providers work together to provide MHC participants monitoring to make sure they comply with program conditions; if not, individualized graduated sanctions are provided, and treatment modifications are made to ensure public safety and participant recovery.
Element #10: Sustainability: The impact of MHCs has to be measured via data collection and analysis, program performance must be assessed and modified as needed periodically, court processes should be institutionalized, and MHC support in the community encouraged and programs expanded.

Source: Council of State Governments Justice Center, 2007.

The Ten Key Essential Elements of Drug Courts provide insights into what can help guide MHC programs to best serve the joint goals of public safety and provide community services for participants. As with drug courts and other types of problem-oriented courts, guiding elements and principles help provide a framework for these programs to be developed and operate. As we look at different types of problem-oriented courts there are a variety of different models utilized, though most have the common features of a phase structure, the uses of rewards and sanctions, and the grounding in therapeutic jurisprudence. Before we turn our attention to other facets of MHCs, we will first take a brief look at an offshoot of adult MHCs: juvenile MHCs.

Juvenile MHCs

Mental health challenges are not only a problem in the adult criminal justice system, but also an increasingly more prevalent problem in the juvenile justice system (OJJDP, 2010). Research consistently shows that youth involved in the juvenile justice system have high rates (as high as 7 in 10 youths) of mental illness (Seiter, 2017). While having a mental illness in and of itself does not make someone delinquent or explain delinquency thoroughly (Seiter, 2017), research exploring the relationship between mental health disorders and offending has found that youth with one or more mental health disorders report committing a disproportionate amount of criminal or delinquent acts (Coker et al.,

2014). Like many issues in the juvenile or adult criminal justice systems, we may never know the full extent of the mental health needs of juvenile justice populations, as many standardized screening instruments used to diagnose these issues are utilized until juveniles are adjusted and placed in an out-of-home placement; as such we have at best, working estimates of the prevalence of mental health issues in the juvenile justice system (OJJDP, 2010).

Like adult MHCs (and many treatment courts in general), juvenile MHCs are grounded in therapeutic jurisprudence. This philosophical foundation is rooted in a non-adversarial, treatment-based approach to dealing with juvenile offenders while maintaining their rights to due process (Winick & Wexler, 2003). The primary focus of juvenile MHCs is to provide treatment and rehabilitation to youth clients (OJJDP, 2010). Providing youth successful treatment in juvenile MHCs is critical in helping them avoid not only further involvement in the juvenile justice system, but also transitioning into adult offenders and involvement in the adult criminal justice system.

As with adult MHCs, there needs to be more consistency regarding what a juvenile MHCs is and how it works regarding target populations, level of supervision, and types of offenses accepted (Council of State Governments, 2005; OJJDP, 2010). In order to help better understand the structure and focus of juvenile MHCs, the National Center for Mental Health and Juvenile Justice examined 11 juvenile MHCs (Cocozza & Shufelt, 2006). The study provided a survey of the everyday operation of mental health courts, which provides valuable insights into the various services and methods of how these programs function daily. The bulk of juvenile MHCs surveys allowed youth with various charges ranging from misdemeanors to felonies to participate in their program. Current charges were generally not an exclusionary factor. Conversely, mental health eligibility criteria were much stricter. About half of the MHCs took only youth with serious mental health issues, whereas other MHCs accepted youth with any identified mental health issues (Cocozza & Shufelt, 2006; OJJDP, 2010).

A variety of factors impacted the size of a court docket, including the size of the jurisdiction, available resources, and if the court provided direct services or referred youth to treatment providers. A key area where there was variety was the caseloads of the MHCs. Some had caseloads of less than 10; others served as many as 75 youths. For youth who completed the MHC programs, their time of involvement ranged between 3 to 6 months in one MHC to a 2-year minimum in other MHCs. The typical time in the MHCs was between 10 and 18 months (Cocozza & Shufelt, 2006; OJJDP, 2010).

Most programs provided services to youth via pre-existing community-based programs. As such, services provided to youth relied on the services available in the community. Various services were provided, including individual and group therapy, family therapy, medication and medication management, case management services, and evidence-based practices like Multisystemic Therapy (Cocozza & Shufelt, 2006; OJJDP, 2010, p. 2). As with juvenile drug courts, juvenile MHCs provide an important opportunity to provide diversion away from the juvenile justice system for youth offenders. Successful treatment through juvenile MHC participation can get a youth participant in an MHC the needed mental health services and support in related areas such as educational and employment support, to get them on a prosocial path, avoiding further delinquency, and the transition into adult offending and potential involvement in the adult criminal justice system, with its harsher, more punitive focus.

Mental Health Court
Theoretical Orientation

As with other treatment courts (e.g., drug courts), MHCs are grounded in therapeutic jurisprudence—the idea that judges and courts can be used as venues to provide treatment and support, instead of the more punitive focus of traditional courts. Scholars such as Scheff (1998) have argued that MHCs are also grounded in restorative justice. MHCs act to reintegrate offenders into communities via community-based programs in conjunction with a restorative justice model (Burns, 2006). Restorative justice is the belief that justice is accomplished for the offender and community impacted by crime (Davis & Cates, 2017, p. 252). It is defined by the Center for Justice & Reconciliation (2017) as a process to heal the harm and cultivate transformative change for all those involved in the crime incident. The critical issue of restorative justice is the view that crime is not just a violation of the criminal code; it involves much more, including harm to people, relationships, and the community. As such, a truly just response needs to factor in these harms and the crime itself (Center for Justice & Reconciliation, 2017). Restorative justice in treatment courts provides treatment options for an individual's issues (e.g., mental health counseling), which provides restoration for the offender as well as the opportunity for the offender to ameliorate the relationship with the victim. Working with treatment courts gives counselors and treatment providers a chance to provide individual therapy with vocational counseling, community service options, aftercare supervision, arbitration, and mediation with victims to focus on individual accountability (Haley, 2016). Utilizing a restorative justice approach, a participant in an MHC can work to address their own underlying mental health (and related) issues, as well as heal their relationship with any victims and the community. The use of both therapeutic jurisprudence and restorative justice orientations provides a philosophical and theoretical grounding for MHCs, and we will see in the next section how effective or ineffective MHCs are in addressing treatment and community needs.

Mental Health Courts: Do They Work?

Evidence Supporting the Effectiveness of Mental Health Courts

Mental health courts are a popular way to divert offenders with mental illness from the criminal justice system, where they may be subjected to victimization and lack of treatment. However, popularity does not always equate to effectiveness, so what does the research literature say about MHCs' effectiveness? Ultimately, the outcomes we are exploring are related to the effectiveness of problem-oriented courts, like MHCs, such as connecting clients to services, reducing recidivism, and successfully addressing issues like unemployment, which often are challenges for clients in problem-oriented courts. To date there is some evidence supporting these programs. MHCs have been shown to link clients to treatment effectively. For example, Boothroyd and colleagues (2003) looked at two MHCs in Florida and found they linked 82% and 73% of their clients to mental health services, respectively. After eight months, the second court dropped to only 57%. However, those in the MHCs still had a higher level of treatment relative to comparison groups being processed in misdemeanor court. In another study, Herinckx et al. (2005) examined a Clark County, Washington, MHC and found participants who were provided with more hours of case and medication management after MHC participation and went to outpatient services more often after participating in the MHC. A study finding similar results was a 2007 study by RAND of an MHC in Alleghany County, Pennsylvania, which revealed that participants in the MHC were more connected to mental health court programs than those in traditional jails (Ridgely et al., 2007); this was likely due to the MHC clients being connected to treatment services via the MHC program. In a related finding, many participants in MHC's participation view participation in the program as beneficial (Sarteschi et al., 2011). A 2010 study by Redlich and colleagues found that 91% of clients surveyed in Brooklyn and Washoe County programs cited advantages to participating in their respective MHCs; in regards to disadvantages, 46% and 59% of each respective MHC could not identify one.

Connecting MHC clients to services is a critical program function supported by the studies cited above. However, the unique nature of MHCs and the challenges their client populations face call on us to consider a variety of metrics and outcomes to consider success. The next for us to examine is the perspective of clients. In their 2013 study, Canada and Gunn examined the client from the MHC perspective. They found that participants identified the structure and accountability provided in MHCs, the supportive services, treatment access, and approaches used to motivate them as crucial factors in their recovery (Canada & Gunn, 2013). For example, a client of the MHC highlighted the supportive nature of the MHC by stating:

> It just feels like you have so many outlets when you are having problems. If I can't get a hold of my therapist, I can call the counselor. [Treatment providers] has a 24-hour hotline, and they have a house for people who are having problems. You know, if it is a crisis. So, I feel like I have no excuse. I have someone to call if I'm having some problems mentally or wanting to use drugs. That's how it feels, that I have a whole bunch of people who want to help me." (Canada & Gunn, 2013, p .10)

Another echoed a similar sentiment regarding their therapist:

> It's just being able to talk. If I have issues, if I have issues, if I notice I'm, you know, having—you know, if I'm acting impulsive, or thinking kind of shady, then I can go in there and discuss that with her, and leave out of there in an hour, you know, with a much more clear idea of what's going on, what's behind you, you know, why I'm doing what I'm doing. And I'm able to correct some of the things that I'm noticing myself. You know, she's able to help me recognize that, and I think that's—you can't put a price on that. (Canada & Gunn, 2013, p. 10)

In Canada and Gunn's (2013) study, participants discussed the role of informal peer support in the context of treatment as a critical component of client success. Like other treatment courts, social bonds and attachments are critical components of MHCs. In regard to group interaction, one participant stated the following:

> All of it kind of ties together because of these [people] related to your addiction, and I think it just gives me a chance to vent. It gives me a chance to hear my solution through what other people say. Sometimes what they say is a solution for me. It gave me a chance to communicate and gave me a chance to—I got connected with people. People would look forward to seeing me. It was, "Hey, [Name] how (are) you doing? And give you a hug, "I'm glad to see you," so just through that it was helpful, all of it. (Canada & Gunn, 2013, p. 11)

We have found similar sentiments of participants in MHCs reported in the mainstream media as well. For example, a 2019 article on the Sacramento County website quoted a participant in Sacramento County Mental Health Court echoing the findings of Canada and Gunn by stating:

> Court helped me keep a balance in my life and supplied me with positive people who wanted the best for me. It also helped me maintain a healthy lifestyle to not become an inmate again. I also appreciated the periodical support boost by the judge. (Sacramento County website, 2019)

As the above quotations support, MHCs are popular with their clients and can, like drug courts, provide the social support and guidance needed to be successful in the program. The above statements for participants also suggest that social bonding may be a component of MHC. Participants' perspectives are critical and help us to understand how these programs may "work" from the client perspective. Other outcomes such as reduction in recidivism also provide a way to gauge the effectiveness of these programs.

For any treatment program, be it a problem-oriented court like an MHC or a facility-based program like a therapeutic community, what many may focus on most is the effectiveness of the programs in reducing recidivism. Prior research has found that MHC participation reduces arrest (e.g., Herinckx et al., 2005), charges (e.g., McNiel & Binder, 2007), and the number of days in jail (Lowder et al., 2016). Turning our attention back to Sacramento County's MHC, it was reported that for those who participated in the MHC, the rate of re-arrest decreased by 25 percent. Further, those who participated in the MHC had lower reoffending rates after the program than they did before they participated in the MHC, and their average number of arrests was reduced. To expand our look at recidivism, Lowder and colleagues' (2018) meta-analysis exploring the effects of MHCs in reducing recidivism provides an insightful look at how MHC participation influences recidivism. Their analysis of 17 prior studies published from 2004 through 2015 found a minor influence of MHC participation relative to more traditional forms of criminal justice processing, but even a minor influence suggests that these programs may influence the reduction of recidivism in mentally ill offenders.

The final area which can help us gauge the effectiveness of MHCs is their cost-effectiveness. While MHCs show some level of influence on recidivism and access to treatment services and are viewed favorably by clients, cost-effectiveness may be a factor that attracts politicians, legislators, and members of the public concerned with cost savings in processing clients of the criminal justice system. Turning our attention to the Alleghany County, Pennsylvania, MHCs evaluation conducted by the RAND corporation mentioned above, Ridgely et al. (2007) reported that the court saved taxpayers $3.5 million over two years. In a more recent study, Kubiak and colleagues (2015) examined the costs of treatment, arrest, and confinement 12 months after participation in an MHC. Results found that the total outcome costs per person for the 12 months after participating in the MHC for those who completed the program was $16,964, significantly different than the $32,258 of those who did not complete the program, as well as being significantly different from the comparison groups, which cost $39,870 (Kubiak et al., 2015). While there is some evidence supporting the utility of MHCs, we will likely need more research in the coming years to help come to a consensus regarding their overall effectiveness. Cost savings, clients' perceptions, reductions in recidivism, and linking clients to services are all potential outcomes that suggest MHCs have the ability to successfully provide treatment to participants. However, for now, there is some level of evidence to support their effectiveness, and possibly more in the coming years as evaluation-based research examining MHCs continues.

Evidence Challenging the Effectiveness of Mental Health Courts

While MHCs have the above-discussed areas of strength and evidence to support their effectiveness, these programs are not without their disadvantages, limitations, and evidence of their ineffectiveness. MHCs may be popular, but as Sarteschi and colleagues (2011) found, these programs have some significant disadvantages.

To begin, MHCs are reactionary in nature. In other words, MHCs offer treatment and support services after a mentally ill offender has committed a crime and been brought to the attention of the criminal justice system through arrest and being charged with a crime (p. 13). In an ideal situation, clients of MHCs would be proactively provided services to avoid committing crimes and involvement in the criminal justice system. MHCs may be able to prevent additional offenses once a participant is part of the program, but as currently structured aren't focused on primary prevention. This does raise the question, could MHCs be modified so that those identified as at risk in the community could be referred to the MHC for treatment? On the other hand, the traditional "job" of the court is already being modified to provide treatment; providing primary prevention, while an intriguing idea, may be beyond the scope of what a MHC could provide. The second concern Sarteschi et al. (2011) raise is the voluntary nature of participation in MHC. The concern raised is there may be coercion in MHC programs:

some evidence suggests there may be confusion on the part of participants regarding the voluntary nature of these programs. For example, studies such as Redlich and colleagues (2010), examined 200 participants in an MHC to study the level of voluntary participation in the MHC and looked at participant's level of legal competence to agree to participate in the MHC, and how informed the participants were about MHC court procedures. The bulk of participants in the study stated they were not told the MHC program was voluntary, and the bulk did not understand the full scope of the court procedures but did understand the "basics" of the court program (Redlich et al., 2010). A third concern raised by Sarteschi et al. (2011) is the legal concerns around a guilty plea. Most participants in MHCs agree to plead guilty under the belief that their charges will be dropped, expunged, or dismissed after completion of the program (Bazelon Center of Mental Health Law, 2004). However, the Bazelon Center of Mental Health Law's (2004) review of 20 MHCs found charges were not always dismissed automatically, raising significant concerns about the effectiveness of MHCs in having guilty pleas removed from participants' criminal records in a timely fashion. Expungement has been traditionally one of the main benefits of participation in a problem-oriented court; if MHCs can't provide it (or provide it in a timely fashion) it may undermine their inherent effectiveness and the desirability of participating in these programs for potential participants.

These critical areas of concern are significant challenge areas for MHCs which remain areas of concern as of this writing. Suppose participants in MHCs were offered more consistent services, perhaps in concert with criminal justice agencies to ensure service delivery (such as "check ins" on those participating in community-based mental health services by community police officers or officers assigned to mental health units). In that case, we might be able to avoid the need to divert these individuals into MHCs in the first place, saving the criminal justice system the time and money associated with arrest and processing into the MHC, any potential victims of the trauma of being victimized, as well as the mentally ill offender the traumatizing experience of committing an offense and being arrested. It is also critical that participants in MHCs do so voluntarily with no coercion involved. While it may be challenging in practice to divert mentally ill offenders into treatment given the nature of some mental illnesses, it is nevertheless critical that participation in MHCs is informed and voluntary, otherwise the effectiveness of the treatment may be undermined by a lack of trust, trust which is needed for MHCs to be effective. Finally, and perhaps most importantly, is the need to ensure that the expungement of guilty pleas is accomplished; one of the key benefits of any treatment court is its ability to offer this reward to participants who successfully complete programs. Expungement, dismissing, and so forth provide the chance for participants in MHCs and other treatment courts a way to avoid the stigma (or additional stigma if they have prior convictions) of being a criminal offender, which, as mentioned throughout this book and the general criminological literature, is essential in maintaining prosocial behavior, attachments, and bonds.

MHCs also face some conceptual limitations; while this chapter identified MHCs as being grounded in therapeutic jurisprudence and restorative justice, others, such as Sarteschi et al. (2011), have pointed out that there needs to be a cohesive theoretical framework or orientation in MHCs. More recent studies, such as Hahn (2015), have identified other theoretical frameworks, such as risk-need-responsivity (RNR), which argue that intensive interventions should be used for the highest risk defendants and lower risk defendants should receive the least invasive interventions (Andrews & Bonta, 2010; Andrews & Dowden, 2006). While other treatment courts (see Chapter 4's discussion of social bonding, therapeutic jurisprudence, and life course theory as theoretical frameworks for drug courts) may have a grounding in a variety of theoretical orientations, and MHCs may be able to as well, it is essential to understand these conceptualizations and their grounding as well as how to relate to services provided for the outcomes of these programs. In other words, we need a clear understanding of how the services and treatment provided by MHCs connects to outcomes such as reductions in recidivism. As MHCs are a newer entry into treatment courts, these theoretically grounded goals will need to be accomplished in the coming years as research continues to expand and evaluate MHCs.

The final area of examination challenging the effectiveness of MHCs is an examination of the empirical literature. As with other treatment courts, recidivism is often viewed as the primary metric of success or failure of a treatment court program. Studies have found that participation in MHCs does not affect recidivism (e.g., Dirks-Linhorst & Linhorst, 2012). In their 2018 meta-analysis of 17 studies examining the effectiveness of MHCs in reducing recidivism, Lowder et al. (2018)

found a small effect of MHC participation relative to more traditional forms of criminal justice processing. In another meta-analytic study, Cross (2011) found that MHC participation did reduce recidivism (comparing participants with MHCs with those who did not participate). Cross (2011) also found that participation in MHCs had a negative effect on their mental health, an issue of critical concern given their focus on mental health.

Ultimately it is challenging to report on the effectiveness of MHCs as many studies noted issues with various methods of reporting recidivism, studies needing more comparison groups, or no outcome measures being reported. That being said, we can ultimately conclude that there is a need for additional research (discussed next) and some level of evidence suggests that MHCs have benefits. However, there are some significant areas of concern that need to be addressed to maximize the effectiveness of these programs.

Future Research

Mental health courts represent an essential and dynamic way for the criminal justice system to address clients with mental illness. As discussed above, a significant number of criminal justice clients have mental health issues; as such, there will likely remain a need for programs like MHCs. Research evidence regarding the effectiveness of MHCs (like many treatment courts) is mixed. There is a need for continued research to explore various key areas. First, there is a need for more qualitative studies in this area; a large portion of studies examining MHCs tend to be from a quantitative perspective. While quantitative perspectives dominate evaluation-based research, qualitative studies also provide valuable insights into many of quantitative studies' patterns, trends, and findings. Next, many MHCs have sanctions but tend not to use them. A greater understanding of these sanctions and why they aren't used may help guide programs to utilize more effective sanctioning approaches. Third, more research needs to be conducted to explore the long-term influence of mental health courts and the role of aftercare, as few mental health issues are resolved in the short term, and most require long-term management. The role MHCs play in the long-term mental health care of graduates of MHCs is key to understanding their long-term influence.

The fourth area of inquiry could be the impact of being part of a treatment group for MHCs. For example, a study exploring if judges in MHCs experience higher levels of stress relative to other types of courts may provide insights into how these programs should be staffed most effectively to minimize stress on members of the treatment workgroup. The final and perhaps most important area of inquiry for future research is to understand better how the existence of mental health courts, which, as explored here, have varying degrees of success and benefits to those with mental illness in the criminal justice system, have yet to solve or significantly reduce the number of persons incarcerated with mental illness. Researchers such as Prins (2014) have stated that there are still high numbers of the mentally ill in prisons; knowing how to more effectively and expansively divert those with mental illness into community-based treatment guided by MHCs is critical for not only saving money for the criminal justice system but providing solutions for mentally ill persons without further risking their safety and causing more trauma or exacerbating existing mental health challenges as incarceration frequently does.

Conclusions

One of the biggest challenges for the criminal justice system are mentally ill offenders. Many with mental illness in communities across the country find themselves undiagnosed, under treated, or lacking effective treatment options. Large numbers of those struggling with mental illness find themselves in encounters with police, arrested, and ending up in already overcrowded and under-sourced jails and prisons. When incarcerated, many of these individuals will struggle with their mental illness even more due to the stressful conditions of incarceration, which may ultimately lead to infractions while incarcerated, further degradation of their mental health, and a decreased likelihood of successful reintegration once released. Diversion programs like mental health courts are needed to not only provide these individuals the treatment and support services they need to prevent further offending behaviors, but also to reduce the stress and strain on police, courts, and the corrections systems.

Mental health courts represent one of the most innovative uses of the treatment court approach. The prevalence of people with mental illness who end up in the criminal justice system has been shown to be a consistent area of challenge in our society. Many people in the criminal justice system not only pose a danger to the general society and themselves but also face higher risks than others when they are placed in custody. Mental health courts allow the criminal justice system to provide treatment and support instead of punishment for those with mental illness. While the empirical evidence is yet to be entirely conclusive, there is evidence to suggest there are benefits of MHCs for clients of these programs, the criminal justice system, and the general public. If mental health courts could be found to be largely effective, they may provide an ideal diversion from the traditional adult and juvenile justice systems. MHCs could provide the treatment and support needed for those struggling with mental illness to get the help they need to manage their mental illness, while addressing other areas of need such as life skills, employment, and housing. MHCs may also provide the added benefit of reducing the stress and strain on the correctional system and provide cost savings as well.

Treatment Court Success Story: Mental Health Courts

Name: Jessie Fiero

Location: Woodland, CA

Background: As we have read in this chapter, mental health issues are highly prevalent in criminal justice populations. Many jails and prisons are filled with inmates struggling with challenges related to mental health issues, often posing a danger to themselves and other inmates and staff members in these facilities. Mental health courts may offer a better strategy for mentally ill persons, providing an opportunity for supervised treatment in the community and the support needed to get on track. An example of someone who has been helped by a mental health court is Jessie Fiero. Like many struggling with mental health issues, Jessie, who was diagnosed with depression and a teenage, spent over a decade living on the streets, frequently getting arrested for a variety of charges including shoplifting, burglary, assault, and having drug paraphernalia.

Eventually, Jessie Fiero found himself in the Yolo County, California, mental health court, a program which could offer him housing, treatment, and support, instead of more time in jail where he would likely receive no treatment at all.

What did the mental health court help provide? The Yolo County mental health court provided a variety of services; probably the most important was getting Jessie into a halfway house where he had a safe place to sleep, eat, and get treatment. He also got into a support group and got a sponsor who has mentored and supported Jessie.

Mental health courts can work! Jessie Fiero is a success story! After years of homelessness, substance abuse, and arrests, mental health court gave Fiero the chance to change. Jessie has reached many life goals, including taking college classes and getting his class A driver's license and his fork-lift certificate.

For more information on Jesse Fiero see: https://www.davisenterprise.com/news/local/crime-fire-courts/yolos-mental-health-court-sets-defendants-back-on-track/.

References

Andrews, D. A., & Bonta, J. (2006). *The psychology of criminal conduct.* (4th ed.). LexisNexis/Matthew Bender.

Andrews, D. A., & Dowden, C. (2006). Risk principle of case classification in correctional treatment. *International Journal of Offender Therapy and Comparative Criminology, 50,* 88–100. https://doi.org/10.1177/0306624X05282556.

Bazelon Center for Mental Health Law. (2004). The role of mental health courts in system reform. http://www.bazelon.org/wpcontent/uploads /2018/03/Role-of-Mental-HealthCourts.pdf.

Boothroyd, R., Poythress, N., McGaha, A., & Petrila, J. (2003). The Broward mental health court: Process, outcomes, and service utilization. *International Journal of Law and Psychiatry, 25,* 55–71. https://doi.org/10.1016/S0160-2527(02)00203-0.

Bronson, J., & Berzofsky, M. (2017). *Indicators of mental health problems reported by prisoners and jail inmates, 2011–12.* NCJ 250612. US Department of Justice, Office of Justice Programs, Bureau of Justice Statistics. https://bjs.ojp.gov/content/pub/pdf/imhprpji1112.pdf.

Burns, J. (2006). A restorative justice model for mental health courts. *Review of Law and Social Justice, 23*(3), 428–455.

Canada, K. E., & Gunn, A. J. (2013). What factors work in mental health court? A consumer perspective. *Journal of Offender Rehabilitation, 25*(5), 311–377. https://doi.org/10.1080/10509674.2013.801387.

Center for Justice & Reconciliation. (2017). Lesson 1: What is restorative justice? http://www.centerforrestorativeprocess.com/lesson-1.html.

Center for Mental Health Services (CMHS). (1995). *Double jeopardy: Persons with mental illness in the criminal justice system. A report to Congress.* US Department of Health and Human Services, Substance Abuse and Mental Health Services Administration.

Cocozza, J., & Shufelt, J. H. (2006). *Juvenile mental health courts: An emerging strategy.* N.Y. Council of State Governments.

Coker, K. L., Smith, P. H., Westphal, A., Zonana, H. V., & McKee, S. A. (2014). Crime and psychiatric disorders among youth in the U.S. population: An analysis of the National Comorbidity Survey-Adolescent Supplement. *Journal of the American Academy of Child and Adolescent Psychiatry, 53*(8), 888. https://doi.org/10.1016/j.jaac.2014.05.007.

Council of State Governments. (2005). *A guide to mental health court design and implementation.*

Council of State Governments Justice Center. (2007). *Improving responses to people with mental illness: The essential elements of a mental health court.* https://bja.ojp.gov/sites/g/files/xyckuh186/files/Publications/MHC_Essential_Elements.pdf.

Cross, B. (2011). *Mental health courts effectiveness in reducing recidivism and improving clinical outcomes: A meta-analysis.* US Department of Justice, Office of Justice Programs. https://www.ojp.gov/ncjrs/virtual-library/abstracts/mental-health-courts-effectiveness-reducing-recidivism-and.

Davis, T. O., & Cates, K. A. (2017). Mental health counseling and specialty courts. *The Professional Counselor, 7*(3), 251–258.

Dijk, A. V., & Crofts, N. (2017). Law enforcement and public health as an emerging field. *Policing and Society, 27*(3), 261–275. https://doi.org/10.1080/10439463.2016.1219735.

Dirks-Linhorst, P. A. M., & Linhorst, D. M. (2012). Recidivism outcomes for suburban mental health courts defendants. *American Journal of Criminal Justice, 37*, 76–91.

Farley, E. J. (2015). A process evaluation of the Manhattan mental health court. Center for Court Innovation. https://www.courtinnovation.

org/sites/default/files/documents/MMHC%20Process%20Evaluation%20Final.pdf.

Goldkamp, J., & Irons-Guynn, C. (2000). *Emerging judicial strategies for the mentally ill in the criminal caseload: Mental health courts in Fort Lauderdale, Seattle, San Bernardino, and Anchorage.* NCJ 182504. US Department of Justice, Office of Justice Programs, Bureau of Justice Assistance.

Griffin, P., Steadman, H. J., & Petrila, J. (2002). The use of criminal charges and sanctions in mental health courts. *Psychiatric Services, 53,* 1285–1289. https://doi.org/10.1176/appi.ps.53.10.1285

Haley, M. J. (2016). Drug courts: The criminal justice system rolls the rock. *Loyola Journal of Public Interest Law, 17,* 183–214.

Hahn, J. W. (2015). *New York State mental health courts: A policy study.* https://www.courtinnovation.org/sites/default/files/documents/MHC%20Policy%20Study%20Report_Final.pdf.

Herinckx, H. A., Swart, S. C., Ama, S. M., Dolezal, C. D., & King, S. (2005). Rearrest and linkage to mental health services among clients of the Clark County mental health court program. *Psychiatric Services, 7,* 853–857. https://doi.org/10.1176/appi.ps.56.7.853.

Kubiak, S., Roddy, J., Comartin, E., & Tillander, E. (2015). Cost analysis of long-term outcomes of an urban mental health court. *Evaluation and Program Planning, 52,* 96–106. https://doi.org/10.1016/j.evalprogplan.2015.04.002.

Lowder, E. M., Desmarais, S. L., & Baucom, D. J. (2016). Recidivism following mental health court exit: Between and within-group comparison. *Law and Human Behavior, 40,* 118–127. https://doi.org/10.1037/lhb0000168.

Lowder, E. M., Rade, C., & Desmarais, S. (2018). Effectiveness of mental health courts in reducing recidivism: A meta-analysis. *Psychiatric Services, 69*(1), 15–22. https://doi.org/10.1176/appi.ps.201700107.

McNiel, D. E., & Binder, R. L. (2007). Effectiveness of a mental health court in reducing criminal recidivism and violence. *American Journal of Psychiatry, 164,* 1395–1403.

National Drug Court Resource Center. (2020). *Treatment courts across the United States (2020).* https://ndcrc.org/wpcontent/uploads/2021/08/2020_NDCRC_TreatmentCourt_Count_Table_v8.pdf.

Office of Juvenile Justice and Delinquency Prevention (OJJDP). (2010). Literature review: Mental health courts. https://ojjdp.ojp.gov/model-programs-guide/literaturereviews/mental_health_courts.pdf.

Petrila, J. (2003). An introduction to special jurisdiction courts. *International Journal of Law and Psychiatry, 26*, 3–12. https://doi.org/10.1016/s0160-2527(02)00206-6.

Prins, S. J. (2014). The prevalence of mental illness in U.S. state prisons: A systematic review. *Psychiatric Services, 65*(7), 862–872. https://doi.org/10.1176/appi.ps.201300166.

Ratcliffe, J. (2021). Policing and public health calls for service in Philadelphia. *Crime Science, 10*(5), 1–6.

Redlich, A. D. (2005). Voluntary, but knowing and intelligent? Comprehensive mental health courts. *Psychology, Public Policy, and Law, 11*, 605–619. https://doi.org/10.1037/1076-8971.11.4.605.

Redlich, A. D., Hoover, S., Summers, A., & Steadman, H. J. (2010). Enrollment in mental health courts: Voluntariness, knowingness, and adjudicative competence. *Law and Human Behavior, 34*, 91–104. https://doi.org/10.1007/s10979-008-9170-8.

Redlich, A. D., Steadman, H. J., Monohan, J., Clark Robbins, P., & Petrila, J. (2006). Patterns and practice in mental health courts: A national survey. *Law and Human Behavior, 30*, 347–362. https://doi.org/10.1007/s10979-006-9036-x.

Ridgely, S. M., Engberg, J., Greenberg, M. D., Turner, S., DeMartini, C., & Dembosky, J. W. (2007). *Justice treatment and cost: Evaluation of the fiscal impact of Allegheny County Mental Health Court. Technical report sponsored by the Council of State Governments and conducted under the auspices of the Safety and Justice Program within RAND Infrastructure, Safety, and Environment* (ISE).

Sacramento County website. (2019, September 19). Mental health court case study on recidivism. SacCounty News. https://www.saccounty.gov/news/latest-news/Pages/Mental-Health-Court-Case-Study-on-Recidivism.aspx.

Sarteschi, C. M., Vaughn, M. G., & Kim, K. (2011). Assessing the effectiveness of mental health courts: A quantitative review. *Journal of Criminal Justice, 39*, 12–20. https://doi.org/10.1016/j.jcrimjus.2010.11.003.

Scheff, T. J. (1998). Community conferences: Shame and anger in therapeutic jurisprudence. *Revista Juridica Universidad de Puerto Rico*,
67(1), 97–120.

Seiter, L. (2017). *Mental health and juvenile justice: A review of preva-
lence, promising practices, and areas for improvement*. National
Technical Assistance Center for the Education of Neglected or
Delinquent Children and Youth.

Seltzer, T. (2005). Mental health courts: A misguided attempt to address
the criminal justice system's unfair treatment of people with mental
illness. *Psychology, Public Policy, and Law, 11*, 570–586. https://doi.
org/10.1037/1076-8971.11.4.570.

Steadman, H., Davidson, S., & Brown, C. (2001). Mental health courts.
Their promise and unanswered questions. *Psychiatric Services, 52*,
457–458. https://doi.org/10.1176/appi.ps.52.4.457.

Treatment Advocacy Center. (2016). *Serious mental illness (SMI) prevalence in jails and prisons*. https://www.treatmentadvocacycenter.
org/storage/documents/backgrounders/smi-in-jails-and-prisons.
pdf.

Trupin, E., & Richards, H. (2003). Seattle's mental health courts: Early
indicators of effectiveness. *International Journal of Law and Psychiatry, 26*, 33–53. https://doi.org/10.1016/S0160-2527(02)00202-9.

Winick, B. J., & Wexler, D. B. (2003). *Judging in a therapeutic key: Therapeutic jurisprudence and the courts*. Carolina Academic Press.

CHAPTER 6

Domestic Violence Courts: Overview

Many issues the criminal justice system is tasked with addressing occur in a variety of circumstances. For example, larceny or shoplifting may occur in a retail establishment, or vandalism may happen in a public building like a high school or church. Some crimes occur in the privacy of the home, an arena which historically the criminal justice system didn't address. One type of crime that frequently occurs in private spaces like the home is domestic violence or intimate partner violence. Domestic violence is a significant and prevalent problem throughout the United States, impacting approximately 10 million people yearly (Huecker et al., 2022). While the full scope of domestic violence may never be known, according to the Centers for Disease Control and Prevention (2022) National Intimate Partner and Sexual Violence Survey (NISVS), it is estimated that 26% of men and 41% of women have had an experience with sexual violence, physical violence, and/or stalking by an intimate partner. Psychological aggression from intimate partners is another form of highly prevalent abuse, which the CDC estimates that 53 million men and 61 million women experience at some point during their lives (CDC, 2022). Typical impacts of domestic violence reported include missing a day or more of work, fear, and safety concerns, getting help from law enforcement, injury, and experiencing post-traumatic stress disorder (CDC, 2022). As the above-mentioned information supports, domestic violence is a prevalent crime that can have lasting impacts on victims across multiple life domains.

Historically, responses from the criminal justice system have been essentially non-existent as crimes committed within the context of the home or personal relationships were viewed as private. However, we have seen a shift in responses from police over the last few decades, with the criminal justice system taking a more active role in dealing with domestic violence offenses (Tsai, 2000; Wolff, 2013). One such response from the criminal justice system has been domestic violence courts, a variant of the problem-oriented or treatment court approach that emerged in the 1990s to respond to legal and social pressures for innovation in dealing with domestic violence cases being brought to the criminal justice system in increasingly higher numbers for prosecution (Moore, 2009; Wolff, 2013). Domestic violence courts, along with other criminal justice system responses to domestic violence such as mandatory arrest policies and domestic violence units in policing, provide a more "hands-on" approach in dealing with domestic violence relative to the historic "hands off" approach the criminal justice system took in the past (Moore, 2009; Gutierrez et al., 2017).

The call for more formal responses from the criminal justice system regarding domestic violence is rooted in the victim's rights and feminist movements of the 1970s; by the end of that decade, battered women's groups, victims, and feminists were calling for a change in domestic violence policy and arguing that domestic violence needed to be viewed as a criminal instead of private matter (Epstein, 1999; Moore, 2009). These, combined with systemic pressures, led to the passage of several pieces of legislation, such as the Violence Against Women Act of 1994, the Victims of Domestic Violence Act in 1995, and the Protection Against Family Violence Act in 1999, increased funding for victim services, special prosecution units, and the use of the aforementioned mandatory arrest policies (Buzawa & Buzawa, 1996; Gutierrez et al., 2017). These innovations brought about an influx of cases into the courts, resulting in a significant backlogging of cases which were also impacted by other types of criminal justice policy changes, such as harsher drug laws during that era (Mauer & King, 2007).

While the call mentioned above for change regarding domestic violence, which led to legislative and policy changes, was occurring, we also saw the development of problem-oriented courts, starting with the Miami-Dade County Drug Treatment Court, which started in 1989 (National Institute of Justice, 2021). The first domestic violence court was established several years later, in 1993, in Miami, Florida (Karan et al., 1999). The Miami Domestic Violence Court wanted to provide better responses from the judiciary through special intake units, specialized judges, a dedicated calendar, and a fully integrated domestic violence court (Gover et al., 2003, p. 111). A process evaluation of the Miami court conducted by Goldkamp and colleagues in 1996 found misdemeanor cases having a 37% lower rate of dismissal compared to cases before the implementation of the court. Further, Goldkamp et al. (1996) found that a large number (between 40% and 50% of offenders) processed through the domestic violence court had been using alcohol or drugs at the time of the domestic violence event. The Miami Domestic Violence Court program successfully enrolled and retained participants in treatment relative to a comparison group. Perhaps the key finding of the Goldkamp et al. (1996) study was that participants in the integrated treatment program had a lower rate of recidivism against the same victim relative to the control group (6% compared to 15%).

A challenging Issue with domestic violence court programs is the complexity and overlap between the civil and criminal justice systems in cases. A single case may call for numerous responses from the criminal and civil justice systems, needing a separate set of requirements and procedures to address them (MacDowell, 2011). As discussed throughout this book, problem- or treatment-oriented courts have taken on many areas of focus, including drugs, reentry, teens, mental health, and domestic violence. Similar to other treatment courts, domestic violence courts (DVCs) provide an opportunity for offenders accused of domestic abuse to be placed in a diversion program instead of the traditional criminal justice process. The DCV model is rooted in therapeutic jurisprudence, which aims to provide treatment and support services through the coordination of a variety of services and agents, including the victim, judges, police, mental health workers, drug treatment providers, and others to restore the harm caused to the victim (Ostrom, 2003; Wexler & Winik, 1996). DVCs are a popular strategy for dealing with domestic abuse, and an estimated 200 programs are operating in the United States (Burchett, 2022). Despite their popularity and widespread use, there are many questions about the effectiveness of DVCs as there have been fewer empirical evaluations of their impact relative to other types of treatment courts (Gutierrez et al., 2017). In this chapter, we will examine the requirements of a domestic violence court and how programs are structured; we will then examine theoretical orientations of DVCs, the critical factors needed for DVCs to operate, evidence supporting and refuting their effectiveness, and finally a look at future areas of research and conclusions.

Domestic Violence Courts Requirements, Goals, and Program Structure

Like other types of treatment courts, DVCs have requirements for participation, goals, and distinct program structures. To begin with DVC requirements, offenders are usually offered a diversion to DVC at the pretrial stage or after their initial court appearance. Most DVCs mandate candidates to plead guilty to charges before they can join the DCV. Like most treatment- or problem-oriented courts, judicial monitoring is a central component. However, in some cases, offenders may be referred to other community-based services such as mental health agencies and substance abuse treatment programs, along with batterer intervention programs (Gutierrez et al., 2017) to help address the reasons why and factors that influenced their domestic abuse.

To examine specific DVC requirements, we will turn our attention to a recent report from the State of New York Supreme Court in Kings County New York, *Integrated Domestic Violence Court: Protocols for Sustainability 2021*. In addition to other sources discussed below, this report provides examples of program requirements that can provide a sense of how DVCs operate in practice. It is important to note that the New York State Integrated Domestic Violence Court Model (IDVC) is grounded in principles reflective of empirical research, best practices, practical experience, and analysis of the court system's current ways of dealing with domestic violence. The New York State IDVC model uses the "one family to one judge model," which works with families impacted by domestic violence to coordinate civil and criminal cases in front of a single judge (rather than multiple judges) to provide information about any family issues and challenges to assist in judicial decision making. The court utilizes its consolidated resources to provide services to the families they serve (State of New York, 2021, p. 1). When looking at the goals of DVCs, we will be discussing DVCs on a national level and provide a local-level court as a point of reference to see how the goals identified at a national level are reflected in the program. Finally, we will turn to a process evaluation of the Brooklyn Youthful Offender Domestic

Violence Court to look at the program structure of a DVC. Since there are various approaches and models to domestic violence courts, we are looking at several examples of these programs to help get a sense of how they differ in practice, though they still have similar missions.

Program Requirements

Cases come to the attention of the New York State IDVC court when an arrest for domestic violence crime is made. In order to have cases transferred to the IDVC, families have to meet two requirements: (1) a misdemeanor or felony case commenced in the criminal court based on allegations between two intimate partners of domestic violence, and (2) a family offense petition has been filed between intimate partners such as domestic civil violence, a custody/visitation or paternity issue between the same parties in family court, or there is an ongoing matrimonial case such as divorce, and ancillary relief started in the New York Supreme Court (or all three) (State of New York, p. 3).

Upon approval from the IDVC Coordinator to transfer the case to the IDVC, the family is notified. The judge is provided with documentation of the Criminal Court accusatory instrument and the matrimonial file or family Court petition. A key area of consideration when deciding if a case should be transferred to the NY State IDVC is if the case has gone beyond the stage in the original court proceedings where transferring it to another court would not be an effective method of processing the case (State of New York, p. 3).

Once the case has been deemed eligible for the IDVC and it is established the issues in the case are appropriate to be transferred to the IDVC, the IDVC Coordinator generates an order for the judge to sign. The IDVC judge is the final deciding authority on the transfer of the case to the IDVC, and if the judge does decide the case should be transferred to the IDVC executes a Supreme Court Order Transfer order to bring all court proceedings fitting into the services of the IDVC (State of New York, p. 3). The transfer order instructs any Matrimonial, Family, or Criminal Court issues to be transferred to the IDVC and provides the initial appearance date. At this stage, the consolidated proceeding is given a distinct IDVC Family Docket Number (State of New York, p. 3).

Once the IDVC Coordinator receives the signed transfer order, it is forwarded to the original courts. If the next court appearance were scheduled for the originating court the parties would be notified that it has been transferred to the IDVC Court and informed of their court appearance date. The IDVC coordinator would notify other parties involved, including judges, attorneys, and service providers. The New York State IDVC tries to stick with the original Court session dates to minimize confusion (State of New York, p. 3). The process described here of the New York State IDVC provides an idea of how these programs may operate in progress. We can now examine the role of goals of these programs.

Goals

Turning our attention to the goals of DVCs, we can look at the findings of one of the most comprehensive national examinations of DVCs, a 2010 report from the National Center for Court Innovation authored by Labriola and colleagues. Targeting over 300 DVCs across the United States, Labriola et al. (2010) utilized site visits, national surveys, and phone interviews to help provide a practical understanding of DVCs. One of the report's critical areas was identifying DVC goals. Results of Labriola et al. (2010) identified three DVC goals:

1. Victim Safety: A large portion of DVC survey respondents (83%) identified increasing victim safety as "extremely important." The focus on victim safety was reflected in the site visits where stakeholders link victim safety to victim services, safe areas for victims to wait in courthouses, and orders of protection (Labriola et al. 2010, p. v).

2. Offender Accountability: 79% of DVC respondents identified offending accountability for illegal actions as "extremely important." Likewise, in site visit interviews, it was frequently expressed that accountability was reached by providing offender supervision, mandated participation in batterer programs, and strategies to increase offender compliance with protection orders. It was noted that stakeholders did not typically focus on the severity of sentencing to make offenders more accountable (Labriola et al., 2010 p. v).

3. Other Goals: This includes responses to the DVC survey who did not get to a high enough level of agreement as to

how they were related to other goals they were asked to evaluate (Labriola et al., 2010 p. vi):

- Deterrence: Deterring recidivism (68%) and punishing non-compliant offenders (60%) were rated high by the bulk of survey respondents (Labriola et al., 2010, p. vi).
- Rehabilitation: A little over a quarter of survey respondents (27%) identified offender rehabilitation as extremely important. These results may have been influenced by the responses from DVC in New York State (where many DVC programs are housed). Programs outside of New York State rated rehabilitation much higher (53%) than New York State respondents (19%) (Labriola et al., 2010 p. vi).

Another example program of DVC goals we will look at are those identified in the Center for Court Innovation for the Youthful Offender Domestic Violence Court in Brooklyn, New York, (Cissner, 2005, p. 11) listed below:

- Community Connections: Connection with schools in the area who help identify problem cases and bring them to the court, as well as act as partners in creating programs to prevent violence.
- Awareness of Prevention: Provide an overall focus on violence prevention, increase community awareness about youth dating violence, and address the harmful dating practices of teens before they reach adulthood.
- Accountability: Provide a swift, specific, and consistent response to youth dating violence.
- Developmentally Appropriate Batterer Programming: Develop programs appropriate for the distinct needs of youth batterers.
- Monitoring: Given intensive monitoring and judicial supervision of orders of protection.
- Victim Services: Provide victims access to services such as counseling and related social services, as well as information about court procedures.

These above goals, like those of the New York State IDVC, are an example of a youth-focused DVC program which we will explore more in the following section (Cissner, 2005, p. 11).

The final example of program goals is the domestic violence court in Lexington County, South Carolina, established in November 1999. The goals of this program are reflective of those listed above and include providing investigation and prosecution of domestic violence cases using increased resources, more collaborations, and a progression of court approval. The ultimate goal of the DVC in Lexington County is to increase victim safety, make defendants accountable for their actions, and decrease recidivism (Gover et al., 2003, p. 114).

Program Structure

To provide an example of how DVCs operate in practice, we will look at The Brooklyn Youthful Offender Domestic Violence Court (YODVC), which started in December 2003 as a collaboration between the Center for Court Innovation (CCI) and the New York State Unified Court system to provide a focus on teen dating violence. The YODVC operated similarly to adult DVCs but also provided a focus on issues and services specific to the needs of youth offenders and victims (Cissner, 2005, p. i). The Brooklyn YODVC partnered with a local community organization, STEPS to End Family Violence, to offer a free 12-week program to adolescent perpetrators of relationship violence. The program meets once a week with Youth Dating Violence victims for an hour and a half. The location is relatively close, approximately one block from the courthouse and has rolling admission with a coordinator on-site to provide quick intake screenings during YODVC operating hours (Herman, 2004). The STEPS program is different from adult batterer programs in that it provides developmentally appropriate strategies such as interactive and engaging activities designed to provide better communication skills, give information on gender roles, the dynamics of power in relationships, and an understanding of the impact of domestic violence (Herman, 2004, p. 4). The court also had a resource coordinator responsible for getting reports about defendants' program compliance and providing them to the judge (Herman, 2004, p. 4). Once participants are processed through screening and intake proceeds for the YODVC, the actual court experience occurs.

The YODVC had one judge (and a backup judge) who presided over misdemeanor domestic violence cases with youth offenders between the ages of 16 and 19. Like other treatment courts, the YODVC also utilized other members of the treatment court workgroup, including a nonrotating prosecutor and a victim advocate, provided case monitoring and staff training, and utilized a community-based treatment program (STEPS, discussed above) (Herman, 2004, p. 3). Meeting about once a week, after the court's lunch recess on Thursday afternoons, the YODVC sessions start; periodically, non-YODVC-eligible domestic violence cases that were not heard during the earlier sessions are heard along with cases for YODVC cases on the docket. However, the bulk of cases a year during YODVC sessions are spent on YODVC cases (Cissner, 2005, p. 20). The results of the process evaluation of the YODVC found that those in the YODVC program appear on average in front of the court every 27.9 days for those in the STEPS program; it was 18.5 days or about once per month for each group. Cissner's findings revealed that most YODVC did not go to trial when they were typically scheduled on a day when the calendar for the YODVC had relatively few other cases being heard, with trials occurring after the last case on the calendar had been finished. Sometimes trials were also scheduled during morning sessions of the domestic violence court adult program (Cissner, 2005, p. 27).

Sanctions were part of the YODVC for youth both in the STEP program and in the regular YODVC, such as the use of jail for those who did not complete the program. Judges also provided negative feedback to participants who failed to meet program requirements. Additionally, the judge used rewards such as positive reinforcement through compliments in the program. Upon completing 12 STEPS classes, defendants completed the STEP program requirements (Cissner, 2005, p. 27). As we explore in later sections of this chapter, we will see the promise the Brooklyn YODVC holds towards addressing teen abuse during dating.

Theoretical Orientation

As discussed above, attitudes towards domestic violence have changed over time, as theoretical conceptualizations explaining domestic violence have also done. Historically, domestic abuse, such as men hitting their wives, was acceptable or even expected in society (Campbell & Samuelson, 2005). In recent decades, we have seen a societal shift away from acceptance of violence against women in the home, with attitudes shifting toward viewing domestic abuse towards women as morally wrong and unacceptable (Herman, 1992; Jones, 2006). For almost twenty years, most explanations and treatment models for partner abuse were grounded in feminist and social learning theories (Lawson, 2003; Jones, 2006). These theoretical models primarily focused on male-to-female violence with defensive justifications used for female-to-male violence (Strauss, 1990). Using the lens of social learning theory, partner abuse is learned by observation—seeing that relationship violence is an effective tool for conflict resolution and maintaining control in a relationship (Bandura, 1979; Jones, 2006).

By the late 1980s, theories of domestic violence were going in the direction of feminist and social constructionist theory (Jones, 2006, p. 9); this was exemplified by Knudten (1989), who tied together critical issues related to the experiences of battered women. Knudten (1989) had three key conclusions: (1) all violations can be defined in terms of power over another, (2) victims should not be blamed for their victimization because they are culturally weak or are easy targets for offenders, and (3) emotional growth and healing are required to avoid victim blaming, and this occurs over time and will be different for each victim. Various interventions were developed within the criminal justice field to prevent abuse and provide treatment services for perpetrators to reduce recidivism (Wingfield & Blocker, 1998); one such intervention strategy has been treatment courts, such as domestic violence courts.

Domestic violence courts represent the changing attitudes toward domestic violence, with it now being viewed as a social problem in need of being addressed by the criminal justice system instead of being ignored; similar to other problem-oriented courts such as mental health and drug courts, domestic violence courts are grounded in therapeutic jurisprudence, focusing on offender accountability and providing victims safety by offering a variety of treatment and support services to support the victim, as well as address the causes of the offender's abusive behaviors in order to reduce reoffending (Gover et al., 2003).

The therapeutic jurisprudence model views legal rules, court processes, law enforcement, probation workers, treatment staff, and members of the courtroom workgroup as tools to direct the therapeutic outcomes of the court as they act as a team to address the issues that caused the domestic violence incident that brought the defendant into the DVC (Mirchandani, 2005). This treatment-focused approach provides those within the DVC and with it to utilize the law for treatment while directing DVCs to build and maintain effective relations with programs and organizations in the community that provide services to victims and offenders (Rottman & Casey, 1999). Studies have found that victims and offenders have identified therapeutic benefits associated with their cases being processed by a DVC, including being given a chance to change their stories, respectful and dignified treatment, and being taken seriously by the judge or hearing officer (Rotman & Casey, 1999; Gover et al., 2021, p. 369).

The expertise of the DVC treatment team brings to the attention of all of those involved in the DVC treatment process, especially DVC judges, the various manipulative tactics employed by defendants to try and sway the court and victim, including trying to steer perceptions of the victim as suffering from mental illness and filing cross complaints (Gover et al., 2021). Like other problem-oriented courts, judges play a pivotal role in DVCs and have been identified throughout the DVC literature as being critical actors in these programs, reflecting the therapeutic justice grounding of DVCs (as well as most other forms of treatment courts).

Critical Factors Needed for DVCs to Work

Like many treatment courts, DVCs have been a popular strategy since their inception. However, this popularity has yet to translate into research that identifies DVCs as an effective strategy. The primary challenge with this is insufficient evaluation-based research in DVCs (Gover et al., 2021). However, some critical components of a successful strategy that helped make DVCs work in New York State were identified by Mazur and Aldrich (2003) and are listed below. These criteria are grouped by specific domains and help give us a sense of what is needed for DVC programs to be effective:

Victims Services: Victims in domestic violence cases have distinct needs and challenges. Many are economically reliant upon abusers, may live with them, and have children in common. Due to these factors, the typical domestic violence case is more complicated than the typical assault case. The strategies identified below help ensure maximum safety and security for victims (Mazur & Aldrich, 2003, p. 7).

- Connect Victims to Advocates Quickly: Connecting victims to services that can provide access to long-term services, counseling, child services, job training, and other programs is critical to victim safety and well-being (Mazur & Aldrich, 2003, p. 6).
- Frontload Social Services: Advocates need to link to critical services for victims, including shelters, civil legal services, food, and social service agencies. These services can help promote more follow through on the part of victims (Mazur & Aldrich, 2003, p. 7).
- Keep Victims Informed: Make sure victims have current information regarding the case; this cuts down the burden on the victims when it comes to reappearance in court to find out the status of their cases and helps provide the victim a sense of safety and that the system is invested in their safety (Mazur & Aldrich, 2003, p. 8).
- Schedule Case Promptly: Getting cases scheduled quickly helps increase victim safety as they must wait for less for services and get protection orders processed faster (Mazur & Aldrich, 2003, p. 8).
- Create "Safe Spaces" in Courthouses: Having a safe space for victims to speak with advocates and separate waiting areas for victims is critical in providing a sense of safety for victims and increasing security (Mazur & Aldrich, 2003, p. 8).

Judicial Monitoring: Like any court, judges act as a symbol of authority and a representative of the criminal justice system. Judges are critical in treatment courts, as they are a vital part of DVCs, providing the supervision and authority needed to provide treatment and support services to the victims and batterers and ensure there is no future violence (Mazur & Aldrich, 2003, p. 7). The criteria below provide strategies to ensure judicial authority and monitoring will effectively address domestic violence.

- Assigning a Permanent Judge: Having one judge handling the criminal domestic violence cases from start to finish helps provide consistency in processing. It helps increase the judge's knowledge and expertise in dealing with the many issues common in domestic violence cases (Mazur & Aldrich, 2003, p. 8).
- Supervise Defendants Continuously: Intensive judicial supervision from arraignment through disposition is key. This ensures the defendant follows through on any treatment required, provides a check to ensure defendants are not contacting the victim, and gives judges the opportunity to respond to any violations in an expedient manner (Mazur & Aldrich, 2003, p. 8).
- Explore New Methods of Judicial Monitoring: Being mindful of new ways to provide supervision, such as curfews and ankle monitors, may offer easy ways to expand the judge's supervisory role and make the judge's supervision more effective (Mazur & Aldrich, 2003, p. 8).
- Dedicated Staff and Resources for Monitoring: Judges can't provide supervision on their own. Case managers and other staff are needed to provide supervision and to ensure compliance with court orders (Mazur & Aldrich, 2003, p. 8).
- Create a Separate Court Docket if There Is High Volume: Many courts have high caseloads given the number of cases in the criminal justice system at any given time. Creating a "compliance courtroom" where the judge is assigned to monitor offenders' compliance after sentence imposition can help ensure cases are addressed appropriately (Mazur & Aldrich, 2003, p. 8).

Accountability: DVCs need to help government agencies and community services with accountability for service to both the victim and offender (via monitoring and treatment) in the most efficient way possible (Mazur & Aldrich, 2003, p. 9).

- Build Strong Relationships with Service Providers: Service providers are critical in providing services to batterers and victims. Strong relationships can ensure effective communication to ensure DVCs are notified when an offender is not compliant (Mazur & Aldrich, 2003, p. 9).
- Hold Batter Programs Accountable: DVC judges and staff need to research batterer treatment programs to make sure the programs are effective and will work with the court to enforce program conditions and messages (Mazur & Aldrich, 2003, p. 9).
- Think Creatively: For DVCs to provide supervision, they may need to creatively work with existing programs/agencies and utilize these programs/agencies creatively. For example, probation and parole officers can be utilized to provide supervision of DVC offenders (Mazur & Aldrich, 2003, p. 9).
- Use Technology to Enhance Access to Information: Computer technology should be utilized to process and store information and facilitate communication. DVCs can use technology to present contradictory rulings and make informed decisions about the sentences for offenders (Mazur & Aldrich, 2003, p. 9).

Coordinated Community Response: To comprehensively address domestic violence, a variety of community components and service providers need to work together to convey the message that domestic violence is unacceptable in our society. DVCs are particularly critical in raising awareness and communicating with the community about domestic violence. Building partnerships in the community is key to effectively communicating these messages (Mazur & Aldrich, 2003, p. 9).

- Create Strong Linkages with a Wide Range of Partners: Since domestic violence is a complicated issue and often involves a variety of local services and agencies, communication with these is critical, as building solid relationships to ensure the messaging that domestic violence is unacceptable in the community is critical (Mazur & Aldrich, 2003, p. 9).
- Convening Regular Meetings with Criminal Justice and Social Service Partners: Interagency relationships are critical

in accomplishing the mission of DVCs. Regular meetings help to keep all involved aware of challenges, issues, and successes with the program. Judges can be facilitators and provide leadership in building and directing the DVC's partner agencies/agencies, including court officers, victims' advocates, defense attorneys, and the prosecutor's office. Meetings with partners can also help provide outreach to communities in need (Mazur & Aldrich, 2003, p. 9).

- Provide Court Personnel and Partners with Domestic Violence Education and Training: DVCs must provide ongoing training and information to staff and partners. This can be done through regular meetings (Mazur & Aldrich, 2003, p. 8).

Obstacles: Like other problem-oriented or treatment courts, DVCs face obstacles and barriers. The above listed items identified factors that help DVCs be successful. However, before we move on to a discussion of DVC's effectiveness and ineffectiveness, knowing what factors have been identified as obstacles can help give us an understanding of what is needed to be overcome or dealt with for DVCs to work in practice. DVCs require buy-in from various agencies and actors, including judges, victim advocates, and treatment programs. Below are the critical areas identified by Mazur and Aldrich (2003).

- Defense Objections: Defense counsel may oppose the court's use of intensive judicial monitoring and predisposing conditions of release in domestic violence cases. To help address this, planners can include defense counsel in all decisions and ensure they are informed of any developments in the case (Mazur & Aldrich, 2003, p. 41).
- Judicial Objectives: Some judges may feel their objectivity is lost in DVCs because they identify too closely with the victim (Mazur & Aldrich, 2003, p. 41).
- Partner Objections: Criminal justice professionals/agencies may claim (legitimately) that they are spread too thin as is and do not have the resources to dedicate to the DVC (Mazur & Aldrich, 2003, p. 41).
- Burnout: As with any treatment court focused on one mission, there is the potential for burn-out with the judge and

related members of the courtroom workgroup (Mazur & Aldrich, 2003, p. 41).

The above list helps us understand what can help make a DVC work, but does this translate to DVCs working? Despite their popularity, there are far fewer evaluations of DVCs than other forms of problem-oriented courts (e.g., drug courts, mental health courts). What evidence does exist is mixed at best. In the following sections, we will examine the limited evidence supporting and refuting the effectiveness of DVCs.

Evidence Supporting the Effectiveness of Domestic Violence Courts

DVCs have been part of the treatment court lexicon for over 30 years, but as stated previously, relatively few empirical studies have been conducted looking at these courts. One of the first studies examining a DCV examined a DVC that started in Miami, Florida, in 1993. As discussed in the introduction of this chapter, Goldkamp et al. (1996) found some solid support for this program. Other studies find similar results with DVCs reducing arrests or the severity of offenses at a rearrest (Gover et al., 2021). In their 2019 study, Tutty and Babins-Wagner utilized a historical control group and reported recidivism rates up to almost 42% for DV offenders who went through traditional court processing. Those offenders processed through DVCs had a much lower recidivism rate of slightly over 8%, a marked difference demonstrating the potential effectiveness of DVCs in reducing recidivism.

Gover et al., (2021) identified two significant benefits of DVCs, which may be indicators of DVC success: expedited and efficient case processing. In their 2015 multisite study, Cissner and colleagues found a reduction in recidivism and that the 24 New York DVCS in their sample had much more efficient case processing, finding an average reduction of more than two months between arrest and disposition. In another study, Tutty and colleagues (2011) examined the Calgary DVC. They revealed a marked increase in the number of cases concluded before trial after the DVC was instated, with the case completion range jumping from 43% to 70% following the start of the DVC. Another study by Collins and colleagues (2019) found that expedited case processing may be a critical component of DVCs. Collins et al. (2019) found that offenders in cases that were processed more than 60 days were rearrested for domestic violence at a rate of 10.9% compared to those whose cases took less than 60 days to be processed with a rearrest rate for domestic violence of 6.2%.

The evidence discussed provides a sense of the potential benefit of DVCs and some evidence for their effectiveness. We now turn our attention to evidence that refutes the effectiveness of DVCs.

Evidence Challenging the Effectiveness of Domestic Violence Courts

As discussed previously, there are relatively few empirical evaluations of DVCs, making discussing the effectiveness and lack of it challenging. Perhaps the lack of effectiveness of DVCs may reflect the lack of effectiveness of domestic violence treatment programs in general. For example, in their 2015 study of 10 DVCs, Cissner et al. concluded that the evidence regarding the effectiveness of DVCs in reducing recidivism was unclear. This was reflected in a study by Babcock and colleagues (2004), who conducted a meta-analysis of 22 treatment programs, finding that these programs, which included psychoeducational and cognitive-behavioral treatment, had little effect on recidivism. Other studies provide more direct evidence of the ineffectiveness of DVCs. A more recent study by George (2010) also found the potential limitations of domestic violence programs; in this case, state-certified domestic violence treatment did not have significantly different recidivation rates when compared to offenders who received other punishments such as fines. Other studies suggest that DVC participants who attend treatment do not have different recidivism rates compared with those who do attend treatment, such as Pinchevsky's 2017 study.

The issue of ineffectiveness may not be addressed entirely or more comprehensively until more outcome evaluation studies have been conducted. There is a need not only for more studies but for more diversity in the setting, as many of the existing studies have been conducted in urban areas. Studies examining programs in suburban and rural areas may help provide a more comprehensive look at DVCs and help us understand what works and does not work with them.

Future Research

While DVCs and their variants (e.g., IDVCs and YODVCs) have proven popular, there are quite a few areas in which future research is warranted. First, DVCs need more evaluation-based research. Several studies are looking at the effectiveness of DVC models, but fewer focus on DVCs compared to other types of problem-oriented courts like drug courts. More evaluation-based studies will help policymakers, scholars, and practitioners understand the utility of these programs, identifying strengths and weaknesses which can be addressed to make the program more effective. Next, there is a need for more research focusing specifically on the role of the judge as a therapeutic agent in DVCs. Prior studies examining other treatment courts, such as Salvatore and colleagues (2020) which examined the role of judges in reentry courts, are finding they played a critical role in the success of reentry court participants. If judges are as critical in DVCs as they may be in reentry courts, then their role may be paramount in the DVC programs. More studies exploring the role of the judge in DVCs may help provide a better understanding of their role and provide ways judges can help maximize the potential of these programs.

The third area on which future studies should focus is the role of DVCs for use in special populations where domestic abuse has been found to be highly prevalent. The first population is the LGBTQA+ community which has been identified as high risk for domestic abuse. For example, prior studies such as that Stephenson and colleagues (2010) have reported that rates of domestic abuse in LGBTQA+ populations are relatively high. As of yet, there has been little evaluation-based research examining the use and effectiveness of DVCs for LGBTQA+. As a population with high rates of domestic violence, studies must focus on using DVCs to address this issue in LGBTQA+ populations. The second population where there is a need to better understand the use of and potential effectiveness of DVCs is the elderly within the context of romantic relationships and at the hands of caregivers. Studies such as that by Roberto and colleagues (2013) have identified these as challenging areas, especially when a spouse is providing care for an infirm partner. Future studies can identify if DVCs are appropriate for particular populations or need to be modified to meet specific needs.

The final area studies should examine which battering programs are most effective in promoting long-term desistance in perpetrators of domestic violence. As we have seen in this chapter, different DVCs and DVC models incorporate varying types of batterer treatment programs, such as the STEP program in the Brooklyn YODVC. Identifying the most effective batterer programs could guide police and the practice of DVC and make more effective and efficient decisions in batterer treatment programs.

Conclusions

Domestic violence is a highly prevalent and challenging area in the United States. Historically the criminal justice system primarily ignored domestic abuse as it was viewed as a private matter. With a variety of social movements, including the second wave of the feminist movement in the 1970s, along with the children's rights movement and victim's rights movement of the 1980s, we saw a loud call from the public to address domestic violence more formally. One such response was domestic violence courts. Like many other treatment- or problem-oriented courts, DVCs were based on the drug court model, utilizing therapeutic jurisprudence to provide treatment, supervision, and support to domestic abuse victims and perpetrators to reduce domestic violence.

Compared to other types of treatment courts, there are far fewer empirical evaluations of DVCs, though those existing give a sense of the overall strengths and weaknesses of these programs and what areas need improvement to make these programs more effective. Evidence suggests that, while not perfect, DVCs can be a valuable tool in addressing a serious social problem. Examining the role of specific actors such as judges may be a key next step in better understanding how to make DVCs a more effective type of program. Additionally, exploring the role of specific types of treatment and therapies for victims and offenders may help craft DVCs or modify existing ones so they may better provide services for their clients.

Treatment Court Spotlight: Tribal Domestic Violence Courts

Why are Tribal Domestic Courts Needed? Some of the highest rates of domestic violence and sexual assault occur in Native American communities across the United States. Over 30% of Native American women will be raped during their lives; almost 90% of the perpetrators of these rapes are not Native Americans (Amnesty International, n.d.). Almost 40% of Native Americans are victims of domestic violence during their lives (Amnesty International, ND). Native American populations, in particular Native American women, are at high risk for sexual assaults and domestic violence. Tribal Domestic Violence Courts are needed to support victims and hold offenders accountable (see http://docs.wixstatic.com/ugd/3fb-28d_0130a67ad6fc4051af0895b18e199441.pdf for more information).

Focus: Tribal Domestic Violence Courts are specialized treatment courts that work with American Indians and Alaskan Native populations to address domestic violence in these communities. The courts also provide a focus on batterer monitoring and accountability.

Potential Benefits of Tribal Domestic Violence Courts Having judges who are knowledgeable about tribal culture who can incorporate it into proceedings where appropriate.

- Judges having training in domestic violence and the criminal and civil jurisdiction laws associated with Native American communities.

- Stability in the court through having one judge presiding over cases who has expertise in domestic violence and tribal laws.

- Judges, prosecutors, defense attorneys, and related staff are trained in domestic violence.

- Enhancement of victim safety through the presence of tribal victim advocates, courtroom safety protocols, and using communication with other courts.

- Using a variety of disciplinary areas to connect family members with services in keeping with Native American traditions.

- Providing improved collaborations between treatment providers in keeping with the needs of each tribal community.

- Better community response to domestic violence though connecting the family court with criminal justice staff, tribal domestic violence advocates, and other related service providers in the community.

- Ensuring batterer accountability through continuing monitoring of compliance.

- Provide early identification of domestic violence and safety issues, connect participants to victim services, and integrate tribal traditions about how to have a healthy, safe family.

- Utilize consistent staff who have comprehensive training in the area of domestic violence and work collaboratively to meet the needs of the victim and their family.

- Stronger relationships between the criminal justice system, child welfare, victim advocates, and other service providers.

Adapted from: http://docs.wixstatic.com/ugd/3fb28d_0130a67ad6fc40 51af0895b18e199441.pdf.

For more information on Tribal Domestic Violence Courts see: https://www.tribal-institute.org/lists/dvcourts.htm.

References

Amnesty International. (ND). Rape of native women. https://bidenhumanrightspriorities.amnestyusa.org/rape-of-native-women/.

Babcock, J. C., Green, C. E., & Robie, C. (2004). Does batterers' treatment work? A meta-analytic review of domestic violence treatment. *Clinical Psychology Review*, *23*, 1023–1053. https://doi.org/10.1016/j.cpr.2002.07.001.

Bandura, A. (1979). The social learning perspective: Mechanisms of aggression. In A. Touch (Ed.), *Psychology of crime and criminal justice* (pp. 298–36). Holt, Rinehart & Winston.

Burchett, S. (2022). Professor evaluates the effects of domestic violence specialty courts. https://www.shsu.edu/today@sam/T@S/article/2022/effectiveness-of-domestic-violence-courts.

Buzawa, E., & Buzawa, C. (1996). *Domestic violence: The criminal justice response* (2nd ed.). SAGE Publications.

Campbell, C., & Samuelson, S. L. (2005). Screening for domestic violence: Recommendations based on a practice survey. *Professional Psychology: Research and Practice*, *36*(3), 276–282. https://doi.org/10.1037/0735-7028.36.3.276.

Centers for Disease Control and Prevention (CDC). (2022). Fast facts: Preventing intimate partner violence. Centers for Disease Control and Prevention National Center for Injury Prevention and Control.

https://www.cdc.gov/violenceprevention/intimatepartnerviolence/fastfact.html.

Cissner, A. B. (2005). Process evaluation of the Brooklyn youthful offender domestic violence court. Center for Court Innovation. https://www.courtinnovation.org/publications/process-evaluation-brooklyn-youthful-offender-domestic-violence-court.

Cissner, A. B., Labriola, M., & Rempel, M. (2015). Domestic violence courts: A multisite test of whether and how they change offender outcomes. *Violence Against Women, 21*(9), 1102–1122. https://doi.org/10.1177/1077801215589231.

Collins, A. M., Bouffard, L. A., & Wilkes, N. (2021). Predicting recidivism among defendants in an expedited domestic violence court. *Journal of Interpersonal Violence, 36*(13–14), NP6890–NP6903. https://doi.org/10.1177/0886260518822343.

Epstein, D. (1999). Effective intervention in domestic violence cases: Rethinking the roles of prosecutors, judges, and the court system. *Yale Journal of Law & Feminism, 11*, 3–150.

George, T. P. (2010). Domestic violence sentencing and conditions. Washington State Center for Court Research. https://ofm.wa.gov/sites/default/files/public/legacy/sac/pdf/nchip/DV_sentencing_conditions_recidivism.pdf.

Goldkamp, J. S., Weiland, D., Collins, M., & White, M. D. (1996). *The role of drug and alcohol abuse in domestic violence and its treatment: Dade county's domestic violence court experiment. Report to the National Institute of Justice.* Crime and Justice Research Institute. https://www.ojp.gov/ncjrs/virtual-library/abstracts/role-drug-and-alcohol-abuse-domestic-violence-and-its-treatment-0.

Gover, A. R., Macdonald, J. M., & Alpert, G. P. (2003). Combating domestic violence: Findings from an evaluation of a local domestic violence court. *Criminology & Public Policy, 3*(1), 109–132. https://doi.org/10.1111/j.1745-9133.2003.tb00028.x.

Gover, A. R., Paquette-Boots, D., & Harper, S. B. (2021). Courting justice: Tracing the evolution and future of domestic violence courts. *Feminist Criminology, 16*(3), 366–381. https://doi.org/10.1177/1557085120987638.

Gutierrez, L., Blais, J., & Bourgon, G. (2017). Do domestic violence courts work? A meta-analytic review examining treatment and study quality. *Justice Research and Policy, 17*(2), 75–99. https://doi. org/10.1177/152510711772501.

Herman, J. L. (1992). *Trauma and recovery. The aftermath of violence from domestic abuse to political terror.* Basic.

Herman, K. (2004). Youth dating violence: Can a court help break the cycle? Center for Court Innovation. https://www.courtinnovation. org/sites/default/files/youthd atingviolence.pdf.

Huecker, M. R., King, K. C., Jordan, G. A., & Smock, M. (2002). Domestic violence. StatPearls [Internet]. StatPearls Publishing. https:// www.ncbi.nlm.nih.gov/books/NBK499891/.

Jones, W. R. (2006). Domestic violence court intervention project. The College of Brockport, State University of New York. https://core. ac.uk/download/pdf/233569318.pdf.

Karan, A., Leilitz, S. L., & Denaro, S. (1999). Domestic violence courts: What are they and how should we manage them? *Juvenile and Family Court Journal, 50,* 75–86.

Knudten, D. (1989). Criminal implications of victimology theory. *Clinical Sociology Review, 7*(1), 111–126.

Labriola, M., Bradley, S., O'Sullivan, C. S., Rempel, M., & Moore, S. (2010). A national portrait of domestic violence courts. Center for Court Innovation. https://www.ojp.gov/pdffiles1/nij/grants/229659. pdf.

Lawson, D. M. (2003). Incidence, explanations, and treatment of partner violence. *Journal of Counseling and Development, 81*(1), 19–32. https://doi.org/10.1002/j.1556-6678.2003.tb00221.x.

MacDowell, E. L. (2011). When courts college: Integrated domestic violence courts and court pluralism. Scholarly Works. 682. https:// scholars.law.unlv.edu/facpub/682.

Mauer, M., & King. R., (2007). *A 25-year quagmire: The war on drugs and its impact on American society.* The Sentencing Project. https:// search.issuelab.org/resource/25-year-quagmire-thewar-on-drugs-and-its-impact-on-american-society.html.

Mazur, R., & Aldrich, L. (2003). What makes a domestic violence court work? Lessons from New York. *Judge's Journal, 2*(42), 5–9, 41–42.

Mirchandani, R. (2005). What's so special about specialized courts? The state and social change in Salt Lake City's domestic violence court. *Law & Society Review, 39*(2), 379–418.

Moore, S. (2009). Two decades of specialized domestic violence courts: A review of the literature. The Center for Court Innovation. https://www.courtinnovation.org/publications/twodecades-specialized-domestic-violence-courts-reviewliterature.

National Institute of Justice. (2021). Drug courts. https://www.ojp.gov/pdffiles1/nij/238527.pdf.

Ostrom, J. (2003). Domestic violence courts. *Criminology & Public Policy, 3*(1), 5–108. https://doi.org/10.1111/j.1745-9133.2003.tb00027.x.

Pinchevsky, G. M. (2017). Understanding decision making in specialized domestic violence courts: Can contemporary frameworks help guide these decisions? *Violence Against Women, 23*(6), 749–771.

Roberto, K. A., McCann, B. R., & Brossoie, N. (2013). Intimate partner violence in late life: An analysis of national news reports. *Journal of Elder Abuse and Neglect, 25*(3), 230–241. https://doi.org/10.1080/08946566.2012.751825.

Rottman, D., & Casey, P. (1999). Therapeutic jurisprudence and the emerging of problem-solving courts. *National Institute of Justice Journal, 240,* 12–20.

Salvatore, C., Michalsen, V., & Taylor, C. (2020). Reentry court judge: The key to the court. *Journal of Offender Rehabilitation, 59*(4), 198–222. https://doi.org/10.1080/10509674.2020.1733164.

State of New York. (2021). *Integrated Domestic Violence Court: Protocols for sustainability 2021.* State of New York Supreme Court Kings County. https://www.nycourts.gov/legacyPDFS/Admin/OPP/IDV-protocol.pdf.

Stephenson, R., Khosropour, C., & Sullivan. P. (2010). Reporting of intimate partner violence among men who have sex with men in an online survey. *Western Journal of Emerging Medicine, 11*(3), 242–246.

Strauss, M. A. (1990). How violent are American families? Estimates from the national violence resurvey and other studies. In M. A. Strauss & R. J. Gekkes (Eds.), *Physical violence in American families: Risk factors and adaptations to violence in 8,145 families.* NCJ 136606. Transaction Publishers.

Tsai, B. (2000). The trend toward specialized domestic violence court: Improvements on an effective innovation. *The Fordham Review, 68*(4), 345–370. https://ir.lawnet.fordham.edu/flr/vol68/iss4/8/.

Tutty, L. M., & Babins-Wagner, R. (2019). Outcomes and recidivism of mandated batterer intervention before and after introduction of a specialized domestic violence court. *Journal of Interpersonal Violence, 34*(5), 1039–1062. https://doi.org/10.1177/0886260516647005.

Tutty, L. M., Koshen, J. L., Jesso, D., Ogden, C., & Warrell, J. G. (2011). Evaluation of the Calgary specialized domestic violence trial court and monitoring the first appearance court: Final report. file:///C:/Users/salvatorec/Downloads/HomeFrontEvaluationFinalReport-March2011.pdf.

Wexler, D. B., & Winick, B. J. (Eds). (1996). *Law in a therapeutic key: Developments in therapeutic jurisprudence.* Carolina Academic Press.

Wingfield, D. A., & Blocker, L. S. (1998). Development of a certificate training curriculum for domestic violence counseling. *Journal of Addictions & Offender Counseling, 18*(2), 86–94. https://doi.org/10.1002/j.2161-1874.1998.tb00128.x.

Wolff, N. (2013). Domestic violence courts: The case of Lady Justice meets the serpents of Caduceus. In R. L. Wiener & E. M. Brank (Eds.), *Problem solving courts* (pp. 83–112). Springer Science Business Media, LLC.

CHAPTER 7

Veterans' Courts: Overview

Thus far, we have examined a variety of populations, including those with mental illness, substance abuse disorders, victims of intimate partner violence, and sex workers. Each of these populations has a distinct set of challenges and needs; however, of all the populations we have examined thus far, veterans face some of the most distinct needs and challenges, with research and news reports in the general media highlighting their involvement in the criminal justice system. In recent decades, there has been an increasing focus on the criminogenic risk factors and distinct needs of veterans involved in the criminal justice system (Douds et al., 2017). For example, in the summer of 2022 a news report on NBCNews.com by Kube captured the concerns around veteran populations, reporting that an astonishing 8% of inmates in the United States were veterans. While surprising to some, this finding is relatively reflective of data and reports looking at veteran populations. To further illustrate the crisis many veterans are in across the United States we can look at another article from November of 2022 on TIME.com by Hagel (2022). The article brought attention to the problem of our military veterans ending up in the corrections system, reporting of our 19 million veterans in the U.S., 1 in 3 reports being arrested or going to jail at least once. What these numbers tell us is that our nation's veterans are in crisis, and as in so many other areas of challenge in our society, like those suffering with substance abuse disorders and mental illness, veterans are ending up in the correctional system instead of receiving the support and treatment services they need in the community.

To help better understand the scope and characteristics of veteran populations in corrections, we turn to a 2016 U.S. Department of Justice report by Maruschak and colleagues (2021), which reported that almost 108,000 veterans were in state or federal correctional facilities in 2016 (p. 1). The bulk of the veterans in state and federal prisons were male, with an average age of 52 for those in state prison and 51 in federal prison (both were significantly older than nonveteran inmates, by 14 years for state prisons and 11 years for federal prisoners, respectively) (Maruschak et al., 2021, p. 1). The highest proportion in state prison (38%) and in federal prison (31%) have served less than three years (Maruschak et al., 2021, p. 2). In their report, Maruschak et al. (2021) reported other information which gives a sense of the background and history of these veterans. Most veterans in prisons had served in the Army (of veterans in state prisons 56% and in federal prisons 53%) (p. 1). Those in federal prisons had served in a variety of conflicts and geographic areas, including 21% in Afghanistan, 22% in Iraq, and 27% in the Persian Gulf; in state facilities, there were similar percentages, with 16% serving in Afghanistan, 28% serving in Iraq, and 19% in the Persian Gulf (Maruschak et al., 2021, p. 2). What these numbers tell us is that we have a population of those who have served our country in crisis. From multiple generations, veterans who served in conflicts across the world are now finding their way into our jails and prisons, instead of receiving the support and treatment they need.

Having a sense of the number and characteristics of our veterans in the correctional system, we need to consider why they are ending up there. Hagel (2022), a veteran of the Vietnam conflict who served as both a United States Senator and United States Secretary of Defense, gives some valuable insights into what leads so many of our veterans from the fields of combat to the cells of our jails and prisons. Hagel (2022) pointed to the transition from the regimented military life, with its common culture, a strong sense of pride and mission, and open and directly stated goals and expectations, to the far less structured civilian life as a key challenge area. As many go from military life to civilian life, they face going from an institutionalized lifestyle which is highly structured to one where they are expected to jump into an increasingly complex society, where they must think for themselves, find housing and employment, and face other life challenges often with little support or guidance. It is interesting to note that there are parallels between the experiences of those transitioning from the regimented military life to civilian roles and those reentering society after serving extended sentences in a correctional facility. In navigating the challenging waters of civilian life, Hagel (2022) discussed how many returning veterans struggle with post-traumatic stress disorder (PTSD), a challenge for many which may lead to self-medication with drugs and alcohol and engaging in other behaviors that may lead them to the criminal justice system.

Veterans have witnessed violence, death, and countless other stressors. It is no surprise that PTSD is common in veterans, with rates of PTSD varying by conflict and era. It is estimated 5% who served during the Vietnam Era are diagnosed with PTSD yearly. For the Persian Gulf War around 14% of those who served diagnosed with PTSD yearly, and about 15% of those who served in Operations Iraqi Freedom (OIF) and Enduring Freedom (OEF) are diagnosed with PTSD yearly (US Department of Veterans Affairs, n.d.). With relatively high numbers of veterans across various eras and conflicts found to be suffering from PTSD years, it is not surprising that studies such as Hagel (2022) find how PTSD, typically under or not treated, leaves many veterans to self-medicate and ultimately develop substance abuse disorders.

Veterans have dealt with a unique set of challenges and come from distinct cultures. Douds and Ahlin (2019) discussed the military subculture and "warrior ethos," which is a critical component of veterans' experiences. Since they have had a unique socialization experience, combined with training, veterans perceive themselves to be different from the rest of society. Having served in the military, for no matter how long or short of a period, builds a sense of camaraderie and brotherhood or sisterhood unlike any other. The training and service build within each service member a "warrior ethos" or code of conduct rooted in group loyalty and honor, which follows veterans into civilian life (Douds & Ahlin, 2019, p. 3).

Military life and operations require diligence and a strong sense of trust that transcends personal relationships. Individual goals never take precedence over the needs of the group. The "warrior ethos" is established during the intensive training provided across all branches of the military services, conveying the sense that those in the group are part of a larger family and subculture. With any subculture, the level at which individuals are vested may vary. What is critical and an issue we will come back to is that the "warrior ethos" is a key bond that informs not only military life, but also the functioning of veterans' treatment courts (VTC) (Douds & Ahlin, 2019, p. 3–4).

Veterans' treatment courts (VTC) are one of the newer problem-oriented treatment courts created to address the needs of veterans. A blend of drug courts and mental health courts (Pratt, 2010), with Alaska being the first state to start the development of a VTC (Smith, 2012), and the first long-running program starting in 2008 in Buffalo, New York (Russell, 2009), VTCs seek to provide treatment services to eligible offenders to divert them from the traditional criminal justice system. Services offered vary but typically include mental health and substance abuse treatment, employment assistance, and housing services to address the causes of the offending to reduce recidivism (Hartley & Baldwin, 2016). VTCs have proven popular; as of 2016, there were over 450 VTCs across the United States (US Department of Veterans Affairs, 2021). In the following chapter, we will look at the structure of a VTC, examine the theoretical underpinnings of VTCs, examine evidence that supports and refutes their effectiveness, discuss future research, and provide conclusions.

Veterans' Court Requirements and Program Structure

In practice, VTCs typically operate as a combination of mental health and drug court. Drug courts usually work with those with a diagnosed substance abuse disorder. However, they may work with individuals with co-occurring mental health issues; drug courts generally exclude those with serious mental illness. Conversely, mental health courts typically only work with those with a serious, diagnosed mental illness (Russell, 2009). To help provide a better sense of what a VTC looks like in practice, we will look at the VTC in Buffalo, New York, as described by Russell (2009). The Buffalo, New York, VTC addresses the needs of drug and mental illness courts by working with veterans with a clinical diagnosis of substance abuse dependency and those diagnosed with severe and persistent mental illness (Russell, 2009, p. 131). The Buffalo VTC follows the ten key components of drug courts by the National Association of Drug Court Professionals and the US Department of Justice, in concert with the Ten Essential Elements of Mental Health Courts

(NADCP, 1997; Thompson et al., 2008; Russell, 2009). The Buffalo, VTC made modifications to these essential elements and components to make them more effective in meeting the needs of veterans (Russell, 2009, p. 131).

As previously mentioned, many veterans adhere to a "warrior code" and are less apt to seek medical and mental health care than the rest of society (Russell, 2009, p. 131). Further, many veterans deal with various challenges such as homelessness, substance abuse, depression, mental health issues, and unemployment, which may further complicate access to treatment and prevention services for physical or mental health issues (Russell, 2009, p. 131). To help veterans, Buffalo, New York, worked with a coalition of professionals, including the VTC staff and treatment team, the Veterans Benefits Administration, the Western New York Veterans Project, the Veterans Administration Health Care Network, as well as a variety of volunteers and community health care providers (Russell, 2009, p. 131).

The mission of the Buffalo, VTC is to provide veterans with successful rehabilitation services (Russell, 2009, p. 131). The VTC gives participants the tools to cope with their psychological, dependency, and social issues and to lead productive, prosocial lives. Screening for the Buffalo VTC is conducted using evidence-based screening tools, and potential participants are offered the opportunity to join the VTC. Potential participants in the VTC have been assessed with a clinical diagnosis of substance dependency, a clinical diagnosis of a mental health disease, or in some cases, both conditions. These individuals have usually been charged with committing a nonviolent felony or misdemeanor offense and are diverted from the traditional criminal court to the VTC.

A key factor in the Buffalo VTC is the incorporation of mentors. These mentors consist of volunteers who are active-service members or other veterans who provide peer-to-peer mentoring voluntarily to participants in the VTC. These mentors have been part of several generations of major military conflicts, including Korea, Vietnam, Operation Desert Shield, Operation Desert Storm, Operation Enduring Freedom, and Operation Iraqi Freedom (Russell, 2009, pp. 131–132). The VTC treatment team believes using mentors in the VTC is a good approach as, in their experience, veterans tend to respond well to other veterans who have had similar experiences (Russell, 2009, p. 132). Other VTC

**TABLE 7.1: THE TEN KEY COMPONENTS OF
VETERANS' TREATMENT COURTS**

Key Component #1: VTCs incorporate substance abuse treatment and mental health services with criminal justice system case processing.
Key Component #2: Using a treatment-based approach, prosecution and defense counsel work together to promote public safety and protect the veteran participant's due process rights.
Key Component #3: VTCs work to identify eligible participants as soon as possible and get them into an appropriate VTC program.
Key Component #4: VTC needs to provide access to various services to address veterans' problems, including homelessness, unemployment, medical issues, and family problems.
Key Component #5: Drug and alcohol testing is conducted as part of drug treatment consistently.
Key Component #6: Create a coordinated response to veterans' needs, including a graduated system of rewards and sanctions to reward compliance and punish noncompliance.
Key Component #7: Provide and maintain judicial oversight for each participant in the VTC.
Key Component #8: Program progress is observed to measure progress and ensure participants meet VTC objectives.
Key Component #9: Ongoing interdisciplinary training is provided to VTC treatment team members to ensure VTC operations are effective in planning, implementation, and operations.
Key Component #10: VTCs should build partnerships with community organizations and treatment providers to maximize program effectiveness.

Adapted from Justice for Vets, *The 10 Key Components of Veterans' Treatment Courts*.

programs incorporate mentors, with some estimating that up to 50% of VTCs incorporate them (Douds et al., 2021).

The Buffalo VTC program typically ranges in length from 12 to 18 months for the average participant. Veterans in the VTC attend status hearings regularly, where treatment plans and treatment conditions are reviewed and adjusted as needed. Rewards are given to those who meet their treatment conditions and, in a corresponding manner, to those who fail to meet treatment goals, sanctions are given. According to

Russell (2015, p. 394), the VTC does not use a scale or chart for how many chances a participant is given before they are removed from the program but, instead, situations are evaluated on a case-by-case basis along with the participant's level of commitment to the program. Russell (2015) noted that veterans in the VTC are frequently going through challenges of mental health issues or addiction issues, and successful completion of the VTC requires patience and courage on behalf of all involved, as well as significant oversight (Russell, 2015, p. 394). Like most other forms of problem-solving courts, those who complete the VTC program will have their records expunged (Russell, 2015, p. 394).

Like drug courts, VTCs have ten key components adopted in 2008 by the Buffalo VTC. The Ten Key Components are reflective of the Ten Key Components of Drug Courts but also contain some minor modifications so they may more effectively serve as a theoretical and philosophical basis of VTC:

These ten key components provide a framework to help us understand the guiding principles that direct the day-to-to-today operations of VTCs and their philosophical underpinnings. These ideas are essential as we focus on the theoretical orientation of VTCs.

Theoretical Orientation

Like most treatment courts, VTCs are theoretically grounded in therapeutic jurisprudence. As the above-listed key components reflect, VTCs use judicial oversight and the support provided by the rest of the treatment team to give treatment and rehabilitation services for veterans. Judges and the treatment court team are critical in other problem-oriented courts and, of course, critical for VTCs. This section will look at several theoretical orientations that can be applied to VTCs, starting with peer mentors and social bonding, restorative justice, and finally, identity theory. Within the context of the VTC, substance abuse disorders, mental health, housing, unemployment, and other areas are addressed. Understanding the theoretical mechanisms through which these services are provided and how treatment is assisted by participants in VTCs will allow for deeper insights into these programs and a better understanding of what can be done to help veterans in crisis.

Peer Mentors in VTCs

A critical difference between VTCs and other treatment courts is the extensive use of peer mentors. As Douds et al. (2021) reported, up to 50% of VTCs incorporate peer mentors. Scholars such as Douds and Hummer (2019) have pointed out that the mechanism through which mentoring works has yet to be discovered, with few studies examining the interaction between mentors and mentees. The Buffalo, New York, VTC was the first program that utilized mentors (with detailed manuals and information on the program's website) (Russell, 2009). VTCs recognized the value of mentors for program participants, with the difficulties of a program participant being able to be better understood by a peer mentor with similar experiences compared with a member of the treatment court workgroup. Further, those who have served in the military may be less likely to follow the authority of someone who does not have the same background (Taylor et al., 2013).

In general, most VTCs do not define the role or expectations for mentors; further, there is little theoretical grounding for the mentoring role (Douds & Hummer, 2019, p. 328). To better understand the role of mentors, we need to understand the theory underlying how mentoring works in the military, veterans, and criminal justice settings. Mentoring is a critical part of military culture, providing support systems, cultural education, and organizational socialization, and it can also help provide the guidance needed for career advancement (Douds et al., 2021). The mentor-mentee relationship in the military, both formally and informally, is prevalent throughout the literature as it helps to build a cohesive culture, provide knowledge and expectations associated with military roles, and can resolve some of the negative aspects of military services, such as being cut off from relationships with others outside of the military (Johnson & Andersen, 2010; Steinberg & Nourizadeh, 2001).

There are pros and cons to mentoring in the military. McGuire (2007) stated that those getting formal or semiformal mentoring are given psychological and career-oriented counseling, compared with informal mentoring. Others, such as Johnson and Anderson (2010), find that required mentorships add more paperwork. Less formal mentoring may be beneficial as there are fewer "official" obligations, and it is therefore less stress-inducing for the mentor and mentee (Douds et al., 2021). Utilizing peer support systems has benefits for those receiving mentoring, including increased self-esteem, less social isolation, higher levels of social functioning for the provider and the recipient, less stigma for the receiver of the support, and a greater sense of hope (Repper & Carter, 2011; Solomon, 2004; Douds et al., 2021, p. 5).

Mentoring programs provide the conditions needed for support and understanding that may facilitate success for VTC participants. Buck (2018) suggested three core conditions of peer mentoring: caring, listening, and setting manageable goals. Each of these conditions helps give us an understanding of how peer mentoring works in the context of the criminal justice system. Care has been identified as a critical feature in supporting change in criminal justice system clients (Buck, 2018, p. 193). The idea is that those providing services in the criminal justice system care about their clients personally in a genuine manner. Despite the nature of the criminal justice system (as being generally adversarial), caring can be a component of successful desistance. The idea of care, especially for those providing volunteer-based services and support in the criminal justice system, reflects altruism and understanding. In the case of VTCs, mentors may be viewed as having an emotional understanding of the experience of their mentees and genuinely caring for them on an interpersonal, not just a "professional" level (Buck, 2018). This caring may help provide the support needed for clients in VTCs to succeed. The next component of mentoring discussed by Buck (2018) is listening. In the criminal justice system context, listening is not a new idea, but it is essential for developing knowledge of what is needed by the clients to be successful. Mentors need to be open to listening and understanding what mentees find essential and what may work for them in the situation (Buck, 2018).

Listening in the context of VTCs may help mentors find what they can do to provide individualized support for their mentees and give them an opportunity to vent about their problems and challenges (Buck, 2018). Venting about problems may allow mentors to help their mentees work through challenges and issues and develop success strategies (Buck, 2018). The final condition discussed by Buck (2018) is encouraging small steps. Mentors can help mentees reach small attainable goals, which can create and sustain motivation in the VTC. Buck (2018) highlighted the essential role of incremental motivation in helping to persist despite challenges and relapses that typically occur during probation (p. 202). Caring, listening, and small goals are all fundamental aspects of the mentoring process and help us understand how we would expect mentoring to work in VTCs. However, given the nature of mentoring, the underlying construct may be the bond or attachment forged between the mentor and mentee.

Peer Mentoring as a Form of Social Bonding/Attachment

Social bonding and attachments are critical components of desistance (Salvatore, 2013). Recall Hirschi's (1969) argument that having a more substantial stake in conformity or mainstream society can prevent delinquency and crime. Individuals are less likely to engage in crime if they have stronger attachments and bonds. Salvatore (2013) stated that social bonds are essential in preventing crime in youth populations. The strength of social bonds may help connect individuals to mainstream society, with the fear of losing these bonds preventing engaging in behaviors that would endanger them. Thinking in terms of VTCs, explicitly focusing on the mentor-mentee relationship, it could be hypothesized that the relationship between peer mentors and VTC participants would act as an attachment or bond that could facilitate desistance. Social bonding theory has been explored to a point in the VTC literature (e.g., Gallagher & Ashford, 2021), and there is evidence in studies that suggest social bonding is a critical component of the VTC process. For example, in Buck (2018), a mentee in a VTC described caring experiences as follows:

> I'd be crying my eyes out. She'd give me a few cuddles, I don't know if they should do that or not, but it was what I needed at the time and I was dead happy. I'd feel a whole new lease of life. (p. 194)

Others, such as Gallagher and Ashford (2021), have pointed out that VTCs often highlight to participants that they share a bond of being a veteran with mentors, members of the treatment court team, and others who are respected in the general society. Tyler and Huo (2002) also discussed the role of social bonds in their mediational model, which indicated that fair and respectful treatment incorporated social bonds, leading to increased pride and respect linked to social identity, which helped to support the legitimacy of legal authority and laws (Gallagher & Ashford, 2021, p. 154).

Gallagher and Ashford (2021) incorporated social bonding into their test of Tyler's (1990) procedural justice theory. The central idea of Tyler's theoretical model is that when treatment is viewed as fair and respectful, it will raise the value of the system's legitimacy, increasing compliance with laws and representatives of the legal system (Tyler, 1990; Gallagher & Ashford, p. 154). In other words, if participants view VTCs as legitimate, bonding with peer mentors and members of the VTC team could facilitate that; there could be more significant levels of compliance with the VTC. The results of Gallagher and Ashford's (2021) study found a positive association between social bonds and procedural justice. This research supports the role of social bonds and the potential of social bonding theory's application to VTCs.

Restorative Justice

Another theoretical framework applied to VTCs is restorative justice, which seeks to restore the relationships between the victim, offender, and the community. Braithwaite (1999) stated that restorative justice's critical idea is to repair the harm caused to the victim and community by avoiding causing pain (in this case, punishment to offenders). Reintegration of the offender into the community is a crucial aspect of restorative justice, as is the community-based focus of the restoration process to help offenders avoid future crimes (Morris & Young, 2000). There are several methods through which treatment can be provided to address offenders' issues, including substance abuse treatment and mental health care (Huskey, 2017); as discussed above, these are common challenge areas for clients of VTCs.

Restorative justice is a logical theoretical framework to apply to VTCs. The desire of VTCs to provide treatment instead of punishment, to use mentoring and support to restore or resolve the underlying issues that brought the veteran to the VTC, combined with preventing reoffending, all tie together well. Further, the value placed on community in restorative justice makes it especially important for VTCs (Huskey, 2017, p. 730). VTCs can view crime as a community responsibility since military service to the nation is seen as the primary factor in causing the offending behaviors (Huskey, 2017, p. 730). This conceptualization fits into the concept of the restorative justice value that communities are responsible for offending behaviors and solutions (Huskey, 2017, p. 730).

The focus on restoration is critical here and can be the foundation of the VTCs work to help heal and restore the offender and the community.

Identity Theory Approach

The final theoretical approach we will examine for VTCs is a sociological theory, identity theory, which is focused on how role identities are organized hierarchically. Identities are layered based on their importance to the self and the level of connection the individual has to them; this, in turn, is influenced by the way these identities are connected to specific individuals (Howard, 2000). For veterans involved in the criminal justice system, the "offender" identity may risk their "veteran" identity (Ahlin & Douds, 2020, p. 321). To put it another way, for most veterans, their "veteran" identity is paramount, the most important way they self-identify and want to be identified by others. By engaging in offending behaviors or substance abuse, they risk this identity by having a "criminal" or "deviant" identity. VTCs provide an opportunity for veterans involved in the criminal justice system to reconcile this dual identity when provided the chance to participate in the VTC.

VTCs provide a chance for the "veteran" and "offender" identities to be presented holistically to the court (Ahlin & Douds, 2020, p. 322). Participants in VTCs can have conflicting identities, and one identity may add or subtract the status related to the other identity (Howard, 2000). In other words, an individual can be both a veteran and a criminal, with the "criminal" identity detracting from the "veteran" identity. Since veterans have held relatively high status and public support in recent years, veteran identity likely provides positive experiences for the individual, whereas criminal identity will lead to negative self-perceptions (Howard, 2000; Ahlin & Douds, 2020, p. 322). The theoretical orientations explored here provide a better understanding of the underlying mechanisms that influence the operations of VTCs. Next, we need to consider their effectiveness.

Evidence Supporting the
Effectiveness of Veterans' Courts

VTCs have experienced rapid expansion across the United States with the potential to provide treatment and support services for veterans in crisis. It is understandable why VTCs have expanded so quickly. Unfortunately, the expansion of VTCs has yet to coincide with a corresponding level of evidence regarding their effectiveness in reducing recidivism. While there have been more evaluation-based studies of VTCs in recent years, many need more methodological limitations and generalizability (Hartley & Baldwin, 2016). Interestingly, some studies have found extremely low recidivism rates, some as low as 2% for participants in VTCs (Holbrook & Anderson, 2011; Russell, 2009); these findings, while wonderful to see on paper and certainly suggestive of the success of VTCs, need to be considered in the greater context of the overall findings regarding the effectiveness and ineffectiveness of VTCs. It is also worth noting that the program which found such a low recidivism rate had only been in operation for a brief period.

Over the last decade, more survey-based research examining the effectiveness of VTCs has been conducted that provides a better sense of the effectiveness of VTCs. In 2011, Holbrook and Anderson conducted a survey-based study with 14 program participants, with 11 programs responding to questions dealing with recidivism and graduation. Of those 11 VTC programs, there were 59 graduates, with only one who recidivated. While the sample size of the VTCs in the study is relatively small (given a large number of VTCs in the United States), these findings are overall promising and suggest the viability of VTCs in reducing recidivism. In another study with a national sample of 79 VTCs, Baldwin (2013) gathered data regarding terminations, drop-outs, and graduation from over 3,600 participants in VTCs. Baldwin (2013) did not directly measure recidivism, but only approximately 2% of participants returned to the VTC after participating in the program. While not directly measuring recidivism, Baldwin's (2013) findings suggest VTCs can help reduce recidivism. In 2013, McGuire, Clark, and Blue-Howells conducted a national telephone survey of 168 VTCs, finding that about 70% of total participants graduate VTCs and about 30% are terminated from the programs. McGuire et al.'s study (2013), while not focusing on recidivism, does provide a sense of how many national participants in VTCs graduate, an essential metric in and of itself, although data on recidivism, and in particular long-term trends in recidivism, is of most interest. In another national study, Tsai et al. (2016) looked at over 22,000 veterans, comparing those in VTC and other types of treatment courts, and those not in VTCs or other types of treatment courts. The results of their study found that VTC participants were more likely to have better housing and employment outcomes relative to other criminal justice-involved veterans. It should be noted, VTC participants were also more likely to have new incarcerations; this finding may have been the result of the increased monitoring in VTCs (Tsai et al., 2016).

Evidence Challenging the Effectiveness of Veterans' Courts

Like any treatment court, VTCs have successes and failures. As the above section demonstrates, there is evidence of the viability of VTCs to provide treatment and support for veterans in crisis. A challenge in discussing the effectiveness or ineffectiveness of VTCs is the overall lack of evaluation-based research on these programs, limitations on data and methods, and lack of generalizability of findings. Here we will turn our attention to studies identifying evidence of the ineffectiveness of VTCs.

Starting with some general findings regarding VTCs, we find they fairly reflect what we would expect from problem-oriented court programs. For example, veterans who were incarcerated before joining VTCs were more likely to be reincarcerated during the VTC program (Johnson et al., 2016). Homelessness before joining a VTC, being on active duty, being a student, probation or parole violations, getting arrested for a new offense, a history of substance use, and length of time in a VTC have all been found to be risk factors for incarceration for VTC participants (Johnson et al., 2016).

One of the most comprehensive looks at VTCs is Baldwin's (2013) National Survey of Veterans' Treatment Courts, which identifies evidence suggesting the limitations of these programs. One of the most critical issues is that approximately one in five veterans eligible for VTCs drop out or opt out because they find the program too challenging or do not want treatment. This finding may suggest that while VTCs generally have the best interests of the veteran at heart, they may need to focus on veterans' individual needs or perspectives. There were other reasons identified by Baldwin's (2013) study, including getting a better deal in criminal court, not wanting to plead guilty, transportation issues, and a change of residency. Baldwin (2013) also identified that 8% of the participants in the VTCs in the study were terminated for a variety of reasons, with the bulk (61%) being due to nonparticipation in the program, failure to appear in court (about 50%), and testing positive for drugs (about 33%). In a more recent study examining over 900 VTC participants in 115 VA sites who started on VTC program from 2011 to 2015, Tsai et al. (2018) found a variety of personal and criminal history factors that influenced failures in VTCs. Tsai et al.'s (2018) results revealed that when factoring in background characteristics those who had a history of incarceration had worse criminal justice-related outcomes, as well as housing and employment outcomes. VTC participants who had property offenses or probation/parole violations and those with substance use disorders were more likely to experience a new incarceration. VTC participants who had more mental health problems were more likely to be receiving VA benefits and had a lower likelihood of having a job when they left the VTC program (Tsai et al., 2018). These findings help provide a sense of why some fail in VTCs. Ultimately, there is a need for more national research on VTCs as well as qualitative research to help better understand the limitations of these programs and their effectiveness.

Future Research

Veterans' treatment courts represent one of the newer and most specialized areas of problem-oriented courts. As veterans face a variety of challenges, including addiction, PTSD and other mental health issues, physical health challenges, housing issues, and unemployment, amongst others. VTCs may provide an opportunity to provide treatment and support for those who have served their country. VTCs have proven to be popular, spreading across the United States, and some evidence suggests they are effective; there are a variety of areas that need to be addressed by future studies.

One of the most distinct components of VTCs is peer mentoring and support as part of the treatment process. This involves having the understanding and support of another veteran who can understand the distinct components of military culture, as well as the challenges faced once someone leaves the rigid and structured life of the armed forces for the civilian world. The role of peer mentoring in VTCs seems logical and intuitive. However, there needs to be more understanding of how peer mentoring works in VTCs. As discussed above, social bonding/attachment may be the underlying factor that allows mentoring to work. Having a relationship with a peer mentor would provide VTC clients with an understanding and supportive peer to help guide them through treatment and a social bond and attachment that may prevent them from engaging in crime and substance abuse. Fearing disappointment or letting down their peer mentor, VTC clients may work hard to succeed in treatment and get on and stay on a prosocial path. On the other hand, other factors or theoretical orientations may need to be explored to understand better what makes the mentor-mentee relationships in VTCs "work." Studies looking at the roles and relationships of mentors in VTCs are limited, with many having sampling issues that limit the generalizability of their findings (Ahlin & Douds, 2020). Future research could be conducted at multiple sites on a national level to evaluate the role of mentors in a more focused manner and perhaps shed light on their role in program development, process, and outcomes.

Another area where scholars can expand their understanding is the role of the "warrior code" as not only being a causative factor in some of the challenges of veterans in civilian life but also how it may be utilized and incorporated into treatment strategies employed by VTCs. Perhaps the "warrior code" could be used to appeal to those in need of VTC services or be used to inspire their performance. Next, we need to consider the role of program format, models, and content. As VTCs spread, they follow the format and structure of similar treatment courts like drug courts, but is this effective? A national survey examining the structure and format of VTCs could help better understand how programs look and operate and could help identify best practices that would be incorporated into a more standardized approach to VTCs or fine tune the treatment court model to better address the distinct needs of veteran populations. We also need to consider whether VTC programs could be structured in a manner that is more reflective of military culture. If so, would it facilitate success for participants or end up causing more problems, as participants in VTCs ultimately need to be able to navigate the day-to-day challenges of civilian life, where there tends to be little formal structure? Finally, we need to understand the long-term influence of VTCs. Do VTCs have a long-term influence on the behavior of participants? Perhaps the relationship between the mentor and mentee in maintained past the VTC program, providing a bond and source of support for the VTC participant that helps them succeed long term. All of these areas of future research would help better understand how VTCs can operate to be more effective in providing needed services to veteran populations.

Conclusions

Veterans' treatment courts are an exciting and unique addition to problem-oriented court programming. Veterans are a distinct population coming from an institutionalized environment, compounded with the stress and trauma associated with military service, leaving many veterans struggling once they have entered civilian life. As discussed throughout this chapter, many veterans find themselves homeless, unemployed, and struggling with mental health issues such as PTSD and drug or alcohol addictions. Having come from a distinct military subculture, referred to as the "warrior's code," many veterans may not feel their needs and challenges can be understood by those who do not have the same shared experiences. Many veterans end up in the criminal justice system, in state and federal prisons, where they may be less likely to get the treatment and support services needed to avoid recidivism.

VTCs evolved as a tool to help veterans struggling with mental health and substance abuse; rather than placing them in the correctional system, VTCs offer the opportunity to divert these individuals into treatment and support services, giving them a chance to get the help they need to resolve the underlying issues which led them to involvement in the criminal justice system. VTCs incorporate therapeutic jurisprudence; similar to drug courts and other treatment-oriented courts, VTCs provide participants with a non-adversarial, treatment-focused experience. What is unique to VTCs is the use of mentors, whose experience and influence may be a key component of success for veterans in VTCs.

As one of the newer types of treatment courts, VTCs have grown in popularity rapidly, which may be a problem as the full scope of the problems facing veterans in the modern era has yet to be fully known (Hartley & Baldwin, 2016). Further, the innovative use of mentors, which may seem like a logical and practical approach, has yet to yield satisfactory results regarding successful programmatic outcomes (Douds & Hummer, 2019).

What is clear is that veterans are a subpopulation in crisis, in desperate need of treatment and support services. Processing through the traditional criminal justice system will not resolve the challenges veterans face; VTCs may be the solution, providing the guidance and understanding needed to take these veterans from the challenges of addiction and mental illness into the successful roles many have held in the past. As research continues to examine the effects of VTCs, we will see if empirical evidence finds more support for the effectiveness of these programs, a better understanding of their theoretical underpinnings, as well as the role of distinct components of VTCs, including peer mentors and the influence of the "warriors' code."

Treatment Court Success Story: Veterans' Courts

Name: Timothy Wynn

Location: Philadelphia, PA

Background: Timothy Wynn joined the Marines in 1999 and was deployed to Iraq in 2003. When he returned to the United States, he was arrested for a series of crimes including charges of aggravated assault and spent a year in county jail. Like many returning from military service, Timothy Wynn struggled with substance abuse and eventually addressed his issues with alcohol use. However, just addressing his substance abuse wasn't enough to resolve the untreated trauma he experienced due to his service in Iraq.

Like many who served in the military Timothy suffered from post-traumatic stress disorder (PTSD), which many self-medicate with drugs and alcohol. The stress and trauma from military service impacts those who have served in a variety of other ways, such as by estranging them from friends and family. Timothy Wynn experienced problems with his relationship with his wife that left him absent from his daughter's life for several years. In 2013, Timothy was involved in what was described as a "road rage incident," which led to him joining a veterans' court in Philadelphia, Pennsylvania.

What did veterans' treatment court provide? Timothy was sentenced to nine months in veterans' court, which he completed three months early.

During his time in the veterans' court Timothy received a level of treatment and support from the program, along with behavioral health services from the VA, which led to his diagnosis with PTSD. He was provided treatment for PTSD along with group counseling with other veterans who experienced similar things as he did while serving, leading Timothy with a feeling of being supported and understood in a way he hadn't been in the past and a way he certainly would not have been through traditional criminal justice processing.

Veterans' treatment courts can work! Giving veterans such as Timothy Wynn the chance to be in a program that can address the trauma they experienced during military service, as well as related issues such as substance abuse, can help them get back on a prosocial path and provide the support and respect that those who have served our country deserve. As we saw in the case of Timothy Wynn.

Timothy Wynn is a success story! After years of substance abuse, struggles with PTSD, and involvement in the criminal justice system, Veterans' treatment court gave Timothy the support he needed to address mental health issues and become a success story.

For more information on Timothy Wynn see: http://buffaloveteranstreatmentcourt.org/success-stories/.

References

Ahlin, E. M., & Douds, A. S. (2020). If you build it, will vets come? An identity theory approach to expanding veterans' treatment court participation. *Criminal Justice Review, 45*(3), 319–336.

Baldwin, J. M. (2013). Executive summary: National survey of veterans treatment courts. https://ssrn.com/abstract=2274138.

Braithwaite, J. (1999). A future where punishment is marginalized: Realistic or utopian? *UCLA Law Review, 46*(6), 1727–1743.

Buck, G. (2018). The core conditions of peer mentoring. *Criminology & Criminal Justice, 18*(2), 190–206. https://doi.org/10.1177/1748895817699659.

Douds, A. S., & Ahlin, E. M. (2019). *The veteran's treatment court movement: Striving to serve those who served.* Routledge.

Douds, A. S., Ahlin, E. M., Atkins-Plunk, C., & Posteraro, M. (2021). Noble intent is not enough to run veterans court mentoring programs: A qualitative study of mentor's role orientation and responsibilities. *Journal of Qualitative Criminal Justice & Criminology*, *10*(2), 1–34. https://doi.org/10.21428/88de04a1.a897747a.

Douds, A. S., Ahlin, E. M., Howard, D., & Stigerwalt, S. (2017). Varieties of veteran's courts: A statewide assessment of veteran's treatment court components. *Criminal Justice Policy Review, 28*(8), 740–769. https://doi.org/10.1177/0887403415620633.

Douds, A. S., & Hummer, D. (2019). When a veteran's treatment court fails: Lessons learned from a qualitative evaluation. *Victims & Offenders, 14*(3), 322–343. https://doi.org/10.1080/15564886.2019.159 5248.

Gallagher, J. M., & Ashford, J. B. (2021). Perceptions of legal legitimacy in veterans treatment courts: A test of a modified version of procedural justice theory. *Law and Human Behavior, 45*(2), 152–164. https://doi.org/10.1037/lhb0000441.

Hagel, C. (2022, November 11). Too many U.S. veterans end up behind bars: It's time to break the cycle. TIME. https://time.com/6232785/us-veterans-criminal-justice/.

Hartley, R. D., & Baldwin, J. M. (2016). Waging war on recidivism among justice-involved veterans: An impact evaluation of a large urban treatment court. *Criminal Justice Policy Review* (online first), 1–27. https://doi.org/10.1177/0887403416650490.

Hirschi, T. (1969). *Causes of delinquency*. University of California Press.

Holbrook, J. G., & Anderson, S. (2011). Veterans courts: Early outcomes and key indicators of success. *Widener Law School Legal Studies Research Paper, 25*, 1–52. https://papers.ssrn.com/sol3/papers.cfm?abstract_id=1912655.

Howard, J. A. (2000). Social psychology of identities. *Annual Review of Sociology, 26*, 367–393. https://doi.org/10.1146/annurev.soc.26.1.367.

Huskey, K. A. (2017). Justice for veterans: Does theory matter? *Arizona Law Review, 59*, 697–796.

Johnson, R. S., Stolar, A. G., McGuire, J. F., Clark, S., Coonan, L. A., Hausknecht, P., & Graham, D. P. (2016). U.S. Veterans Court programs: An inventory and analysis of national survey data. *Community Mental Health Journal, 52*, 180–186. https://doi.org/10.1007/s10597-015-9972-3.

Johnson W. B., & Andersen, G. R. (2010). Formal mentoring in the U.S. military: Research evidence, lingering questions, and recommendations. *Naval War College Review, 63*(2), 113–126.

Justice for Vets. (n.d.). The ten key components of veteran's treatment courts. https://allrise.org/publications/ten-key-components-of-veterans-treatment-courts/.

Kube, C. (2022). Commission will study why veterans are more likely than nonveterans to get in trouble with the law. NBCNews.com. https://www.nbcnews.com/news/crimecourts/commission-will-study-veterans-are-likely-nonveterans-get-trouble-law-rcna44326.

Mcguire, M. A. (2007). A joint perspective on mentoring: A look by senior military officers across the services on the prevalence and contribution of mentoring relationships. *Dissertation Abstracts International: Section B: The Sciences and Engineering, 68*(4-B), 2698.

McGuire J., Clark S., Blue-Howells J., Coe C. (2013). *An inventory of VA involvement in veterans courts, dockets and tracks.* Retrieved from http://www.justiceforvets.org/studies-and-stats.html.

Morris, A., & Young, W. (2000). Reforming criminal justice: The potential of restorative justice. In J. Braithwaite & H. Strag (Eds.), *Restorative justice: Philosophy to practice.* Routledge.

National Association of Drug Court Professionals, Drug Court Standards Committee. (1997). Defining drug courts: The key components. US Department of Justice, Office of Justice Programs. http://www.ojp.usdoj.gov/BJA/grant/DrugCourts/DefiningDC.pdf.

Pratt, M. (2010). New courts on the block: Specialized criminal courts for veterans in the United States. *Appeal, 15,* 39–57.

Repper, J., & Cater, T. (2011). A review of the literature on peer support in mental health services. *Journal of Mental Health, 20*(4), 392–411. https://doi.org/10.3109/09638237.2011.583947.

Russell, R. T. (2009). *Veterans treatment courts developing throughout the nation. Improving outcomes and services in a tight economy.* (White Paper). Erie County Court. https://justiceforvets.org/wpcontent/up loads/Veterans_Treatment_Courts_Developing_Throughout_the_Nation%20%281%29.pdf.

Russell, R. T. (2015). Veterans treatment court. *Touro Law Review, 31*(3), 385–400.

Salvatore, C. (2013). *Arrested adolescents' offenders: A study of delayed transitions to adulthood.* LFB Publications.

Smith J. W. (2012). The Anchorage, Alaska Veterans Court and recidivism, July 6, 2004–December 31, 2010. *Alaska Law Review, 29,* 93–111.

Solomon, P. (2004). Peer support/peer provided services for underlying processes, benefits, and critical ingredients. *Psychiatric Rehabilitation Journal, 27*(4), 392–401. https://doi.org/10.2975/27.2004.392.401.

Steinberg, A. G., & Nourizadeh, S. M. (2001). Superior, peer and subordinate mentoring in the U.S. Army. In Annual Meeting of the American Psychological Association, August 2001, Chicago, IL.

Taylor, J., Burrowes, N., Disley, E., Liddle, M., Maguire, M., Rubin, J., & Wright, S. (2013). Intimidation outcomes of mentoring interventions: A rapid evidence assessment. https://assets.publishing.service.gov.uk/government/uploads/system/uploads/attachment_data/file/254452/Intermediate-outcomes-of-mentoring-interventions.pdf.

Thompson, M., Osher, F., & Tomasini-Joshi, D. (2008). Improving responses to people with mental illnesses: The essential elements of a mental health court. Council of State Governments, Justice Center Criminal Justice/Mental Health Consensus Project. https://csgjusticecenter.org/wp-content/uploads/2020/02/mhc-essential-elements.pdf.

Tsai, J., Finlay, A., Flatley, B., Kasprow, W. J., & Clark, S. (2018). A national study of veterans treatment court participants: Who benefits and who recidivates. *Administration and Policy in Mental Health, 45*(2), 236–244. https://doi.org/10.1007/s10488-017-0816-z.

Tsai, J., Flatley, B., Kasprow, W. J., Clark, S., & Finlay, A. (2016). Diversion of veterans with criminal justice involvement to treatment courts: Participant characteristics and outcomes. *Psychiatric Services, 68*(4), 375–383. https://doi.org/10.1176/appi.ps.201600233.

Tyler, T. R. (1990). *Why people obey the law.* Yale University Press.

Tyler, T. R., & Huo, Y. J. (2002). *Trust in the law: Encouraging public cooperation with the police and courts.* Russell Sage Foundation.

US Department of Veterans Affairs. (n.d.). PTSD: National Center for PTSD. https://www.ptsd.va.gov/understand/common/common_veterans.asp#:~:text=These%20types%20of%20events%20can,PTSD %20in%20a%20given%20year.

US Department of Veterans Affairs. (2021). Veterans treatment courts and other veteran-focused courts served by V.A. veterans justice outreach specialists. https://www.va.gov/HOMELESS/docs/VJO/VeteransTreatment-Court-Inventory-Update-Fact-Sheet-Jan2021.pdf.

CHAPTER 8

Reentry Courts: Overview

So far in this book, we have explored a variety of treatment courts whose primary goal is to divert participants from the criminal justice system. The focus of this chapter is a look at a treatment court that works with a different approach; instead of diversion, reentry courts work with those who have been incarcerated and are transitioning back to the community. Reentry courts were established to address the high rates of recidivism found after release from correctional institutions (Taylor, 2013a). While the overall number of people in the corrections system has recently dropped for the first time in decades, an estimated 5,500,600 persons were still under the supervision of adult correctional systems in the United States at year-end in 2020 (Klukcow & Zeng, 2022). As the number of persons incarcerated has decreased, there has been a corresponding decrease in the number of inmates being released from federal and state prisons; however, there were still approximately 600,000 individuals released from correctional institutions in 2020 (Carson, 2021). Once released from a correctional institution, recidivism has been a critical challenge for many, with estimates as high as three-quarters of those released being rearrested within five years (Durose et al., 2014). As such a large number released into the community from correctional institutions end up back in them within a relatively short period, it is critical to provide comprehensive strategies to assist these individuals with reintegration into mainstream society (Taylor, 2013a). Studies have consistently shown that former inmates face a variety of challenges and obstacles in areas such as housing, limited education and employment histories, lingering legal issues, mental and physical health issues, family challenges, and the stigma associated with being an ex-inmate and criminal offender (Lattimore & Visher, 2009; Petersilia, 2003; Salvatore et al., 2020). Reentry courts are a comprehensive approach to providing support in these challenging areas and connect participants to various community-based services while overseeing the treatment process through court oversight, case management, and probation or parole supervision (Carey et al., 2018).

Relative to the other types of treatment- or problem-oriented courts we have explored thus far, reentry courts are a reasonably new entry into the treatment court milieu, with programs like the Harlem Parole Reentry Court coming to evaluators' attention at the beginning of the twenty-first century (Farole, 2003). As reentry courts are still relatively new, research in the area has been limited and evidence mixed regarding their effectiveness. Some studies have found that reentry courts can decrease revocations (Taylor, 2013b). Other studies have found mixed results, such as the Judicial Council of California (2014), which found no reductions in revocations or rearrests but did find decreases in revocations and reincarceration, and Hamilton (2010), which found reductions in rearrests but not on revocations or reincarnation. Finally, some studies have found that reentry courts have no significant impact on recidivism (Farole, 2003). Below we will examine how reentry court programs are structured, the theoretical orientation of reentry courts, review evidence that demonstrates the effectiveness and limitations of these programs, consider areas of future research, and offer concluding remarks.

Reentry Court Requirements and Program Structure

While the population that reentry courts serve is distinct from other treatment courts, they still are grounded in therapeutic jurisprudence and rely heavily on social bonding (Salvatore et al., 2020). The support, supervision, and guidance provided by the judge and other members of the courtroom workgroup are critical to the success of reentry court programs. As these programs have become more popular, we have seen various models employed. For the most part, many reentry court programs, like many treatment courts, follow a similar phase structure to drug courts. Before we look at an example of a program model, we will briefly examine critical elements of reentry courts or their "active ingredients." Hamilton (2010) identified several critical "active ingredients" of the reentry court model, which help produce better results relative to traditional probation for those transitioning from prison into communities (presented below).

Active Ingredients of Reentry Courts

The following three "active ingredients" are reflected in the reentry court literature and help provide a sense of what about reentry court programs works to give participants the support they need to be successful:

- **Procedural Justice:** The first "ingredient" discussed by Hamilton (2010) is procedural justice; this refers to reentry court as an open or public forum instead of the typical, closed-door process typical of traditional parole; this may give the reentry court participant a sense of more fairness, which may assist participants in internalizing the requirements of parole and encourage more compliance (Tyler, 1988). In the reentry court model, judges provide an open and public discussion of program requirements, sanctions, and why they are used (Travis, 2005). As seen in drug courts, procedural justice argues that if offenders understand the reasoning behind the court's decision, they will have respect for the law and may be more likely to follow it in the future. Looking at procedural justice from the perspective of a reentry court participant, we would see clear communication from the judge as to what is going on in the treatment process, including the underlying rationale and goals. This communication may help participants understand the "why" of the reentry court process and goals the program has for them and their peers in the program, which may help promote more compliance.
- **Ceremony:** Like drug courts, reentry courts make extensive use of celebrations during court sessions to celebrate the programmatic successes of participants. Throughout programs, various milestones may warrant celebration, but the graduation ceremony is the peak celebration for reentry courts (like

drug courts). During these ceremonies, judges may hand out certificates, give graduates handshakes, and provide celebratory praise for graduates (Travis, 2005). These ceremonies may include family members, the reentry court program team, and staff having a graduation party with cake, snacks, and refreshments. The celebratory nature of reentry courts is in stark contrast to the sedate completion of traditional parole, which might be a simple handshake between the parole officer and the client (Hamilton, 2010). Having witnessed graduation ceremonies in several different treatment courts over the years, I can attest to their power and impact on participants, their families, and members of the treatment court workgroup. It is likely that from the viewpoint of participants in reentry courts, the affirmations provided through these celebratory events help build esteem and a sense of community. These can help foster the desire to continue to succeed in the reentry court program and potentially participate as a peer mentor once the program is completed.

- **Judicial Authority**: As discussed in the introduction of this book (as well as various points throughout), the role of judges is critical in treatment courts due to their grounding in therapeutic jurisprudence. Unlike traditional courts, judges in reentry courts are involved in the supervision and support of reentry court participants. In reentry courts, the judge and parole officer work together to develop a treatment plan for the participant and any alterations, rewards, or sanctions needed during the treatment process (Hamilton, 2010). Travis (2005) clarified the role of reentry court judges, stating that compared to traditional parole, reentry court judges' influence is seen through formal court proceedings. Studies specifically focusing on the role of judges in reentry courts have found the influence of the judge and their critical role in addressing the reentry process for participants in these programs (Salvatore et al., 2020).

Program Requirements and Program Structure Example: ReNew Reentry Court, Newark, New Jersey

To help understand the structure and operations of a reentry court program, we will look at the ReNew reentry court program in Newark, New Jersey, referenced in the introduction to this book. Started in 2013, the ReNew program recruits participants from a pool of medium-to high-risk offenders who have served time in federal prison and are released on probation or supervised release in Essex County, New Jersey (where Newark is located). Potential participants have to be residents of Essex County either before or after incarceration and have been identified as at a moderate to high risk of recidivism. The ReNew program assesses the level of risk using a Risk Prediction Index (R.P.I.) score (Muller, 2009). Participation in the ReNew program is voluntary, and most who join the program require assistance in job training, employment, life skills, housing, mental health, parenting skills, and getting medical insurance and health care (Salvatore et al., 2020).

Potential participants referred to the ReNew program are reviewed by a senior probation officer and the chief of U.S. probation. Program participants appear as a group every two weeks in front of a federal magistrate or federal district judge to report their progress. The U.S. probation officer assigned to the ReNew court provides intensive supervision, which utilizes intermediate forms of community supervision that allow some offenders to serve their sentences outside of prison. Intensive supervision plans typically involve curfews, treatment for substance abuse disorders, finding and maintaining employment, and community service. The ReNew treatment court team consists of a district court judge and magistrate judge, the Federal Probation Office, U.S. Attorney's Office members, the Federal Public Defender's Office, volunteer attorneys, and occasionally interns from local colleges and universities. Those participants who complete 52 weeks in the program are then eligible for a reduction of their supervised release period for up to one year (Salvatore et al., 2020, p. 201).

ReNew participants appear before the reentry court treatment team every two weeks. There are pre-court session meetings where the treatment team meets. During these meetings, each participant's progress is discussed to inform the judge about any accomplishments or issues that have occurred since the last session; the judges are then prepared to discuss with each participant their progress and any awards or sanctions that may be applied. The ReNew program utilizes a series of graduated sanctions, ranging from verbal reprimand to incarceration and removal from the program (Salvatore et al., 2020, p. 202).

All participants in the reentry court program are present during the court sessions, along with the reentry court workgroup. Voluntary attorneys are usually in attendance to provide legal assistance with issues outside the bounds of the ReNew program, such as assistance with divorces, custody issues, and dealing out-of-state warrants or fines. Friends and relatives of participants and former participants (program mentors) can also attend these sessions. Once the session begins, the judge typically addresses the group for any challenges or issues across the group, such as enrolling in college courses or putting together a resume. Next, the judge usually discussed in open court successes, such as finding a job, and challenges that individual participants faced. If a program participant wishes to meet privately with the judge and treatment group, this occurs in the judge's chambers (Salvatore et al., 2020, p. 201).

During the session, the judges provide praise and encouragement where appropriate, such as when a participant finds a job, and provide encouragement and support for continued programmatic success. Suppose a participant faces a specific challenge, such as finding a job. In that case, the judge may provide a referral to a service provider or ask the reentry program coordinator to help determine an action plan to work through the challenging issue. Since the pre-court meeting informs the judges about participants' challenges, the judge is usually provided with an opportunity to prepare to discuss the challenge during the court session. During periodic graduation ceremonies, the judge provides a motion to the original sentencing judge to reduce supervision sentences up to 12 months (Title 18, U.S. Code, Section 3583(e) gives judges in the ReNew program the ability to reduce the defendant's term to supervisory release once they complete the ReNew Program) (Salvatore et al., 2020, p. 202).

Theoretical Orientation: Deterrence Theory and Risk-Need-Responsivity Model

As explored in previous chapters, there are several theoretical orientations in which treatment courts are grounded. The social bonding theory (discussed below) is one of the most prominent. However, there are two primary theoretical orientations in which reentry courts are grounded: deterrence theory and the risk-need-responsivity (RNR) model. Deterrence is that we are free to choose actions and choose our course of action rationally. In other words, people are rational and have free will. There are two types of deterrence: (1) specific, which targets the individual offender to deter them from committing the same behavior in the future, and (2) general deterrence, which looks at society as a whole: when the general society sees someone being punished for behaviors it sends a message to everyone in that society that this behavior will be punished, and therefore deters others from committing the crime (Vito & Holmes, 1994). Deterrence is most effective when punishments are applied swiftly, with certainty, and at a level equal to the crime (Nagin, 2013).

Research on reentry courts has found that the certainty of punishment has a deterrent effect on participants. For example, the findings of Project HOPE (Hawaii Opportunity Probation with Enforcement), which incorporated quick and specific punishments for parolees using drugs, found those who participated in the HOPE program had fewer parole violations, fewer positive drug tests, a reduction in arrests, and decreased chances of future time in prison, all fairly strong indicators of a successful reentry court program (Nagin, 2013). The findings from Project HOPE influenced the expansion of deterrence-based reentry courts throughout the country (Hamilton et al., 2016).

The second theoretical orientation frequently cited as the foundation of reentry courts is the risk-need-responsivity (RNR) model. The RNR model assesses inmates for various risk factors like education and employment history and prior substance use. Risk factors help identify the individual's needs once released into the community. Once identified, responsivity states that treatment should be on an individual level and target the offender's specific criminogenic needs (Andrews et al., 2011). A key component of RNR is that higher-risk individuals should be targeted for their specific criminogenic needs. In other words, RNR calls on a targeted treatment and support services to address a high-risk offender's needs to prevent future offending (Ndrecka, Listwan, & Latessa, 2017). By providing services commensurate with a reentry court participant's level of need, we can ensure that specific challenge areas are targeted, reducing the chances of violated program conditions and reducing recidivism.

The Role of Social Bonds

One of the core themes of this book is what "works" about treatment courts. Across various chapters, we have seen examples of the relationships between participants in the various types of problem-oriented or treatment courts and the members of the courtroom workgroup in these programs; some have noted the paramount role of the judge in these programs (e.g., Salvatore et al., 2020). As presented in the introductory chapter of this book, social bonds are critical in reentry courts for participants' success.

To briefly recap, Hirschi's (1969) social bond theory argues that social bonds connecting individuals to mainstream society through attachment and bonds built through education, employment, family, prosocial peers, and in this case, the attachment made by participation in a treatment court program, will prevent them from engaging in crime for fear of damaging or losing the bond. As studies (e.g., Salvatore et al., 2020) have found, reentry courts, like many other treatment courts, frequently utilize the bonds and relationships built during the treatment process to facilitate success in the program. As we have seen in previous chapters, the connections built between program participants and judges, parole officers, and others in the treatment court program help program participants build social capital (see below) and get the support and guidance they need to succeed in the community. In the example below, we see the distinct role of the judge in reentry court, specifically how the judge has a relationship and bond with participants and how that bond may transfer social capital to participants and provide support and guidance, making a substantial impact on participants:

> [The] judge's use of their own resources and time to help participants, that is life-changing for someone when a federal

judge is taking them to LensCrafters [for an eye exam and glasses]. [The] judges will call up their own family members… taking a chance on people. (Salvatore et al., 2020, p. 209)

In another example, we also see a judge utilize their own social network to help connect a reentry court participant with educational support and employment opportunity:

Judge [One] actually called a friend of theirs from Essex County College when I was really adamant about not getting a job, but [instead] continuing my education. I was probably like the first guy who's like, "I want to go to school,"…. I was so exhausted with the transition from the halfway house and then trying to get employment and [then] education, [this] was like my final, my final straw. So, [the judge] called on an acquaintance… [a] personal acquaintance of [the judge's] and then recommended I sit down with this person. The judge said [to their acquaintance], "Hey, I need you to give one of the [people] from my program as much assistance as you can with getting enrolled in school, or getting employment with the school [even something like] like [a] work-study or whatever [you can offer]. (Salvatore et al., 2020, p. 209)

Both of the above examples show the influence of the bond between judges and program participants. Instead of being punitive in their orientation, judges in reentry court programs provide guidance and support for program participants, often utilizing their own time, resources, and social networks to help support program participants. Several studies have noted that this type of support makes a critical difference for program participants and can help facilitate program success (Salvatore et al., 2020; Taylor, 2013a). Reentry courts may provide a critical opportunity for social bonds between participants and judges, other members of the treatment court workgroup, peer mentors, and engaged family members to support participants in reentry court in programmatic success.

The Role of Social Capital

As the above section examined, social bonds may be a critical component in reentry (and other treatment) courts. By building connections with members of the treatment court, particularly judges, participants may find the guidance and support needed to succeed in the community. However, another critical component of reentry court is the role of social capital. Throughout the evaluations of treatment courts, one of the distinct components discussed in reentry courts has been their ability to assist clients in building social capital. Social capital was defined by Clear (2007) as "the capacity of a person to call upon personal ties (typically within social networks) in order to advance some personal interest" (p. 80). Given Coleman's (1988) seminal work on social capital, this definition is perhaps ambiguous on purpose. Coleman clarified that "social capital is defined by its function" (p. S98). To put it another way, the type of social capital depends on what the goal being attempted is, such as finding employment (Taylor, 2013c). However, social capital has two key characteristics: it relies on "some aspect of social structures," and it "facilitates[s] certain actions of actors" (Coleman, 1988, p. S98). Focusing on the critical role of social ties in prompting action, Coleman (1988) stated that social capital "comes about through changes in the relations among persons that facilitate action" (p. S99). Similarly, Portes (1998) affirmed "the consensus is growing in the literature that social capital stands for the ability of actors to secure benefits by virtue of membership in social networks or other social structures" (p. 6).

In order to take advantage of the benefits of social capital, the individual needs social ties and networks (Taylor, 2013c). Social ties can be classified in groups or as social networks, defined by Clear (2007) as, "the array of relationships in which a person lives, works, and engages in recreation," (p. 77). In other words, social networks consist of our relationships with neighbors and other members of our communities, coworkers, and people we socialize with and engage in activities with, such as sports. From the perspective of reentry, these relationships are an essential part of developing social capital, and that social capital can, in turn, radically increase the chances of reentry success (Clear, 2007; Taylor, 2013c). For example, suppose an individual is released from prison and is engaged with neighbors, friends, and coworkers in a prosocial manner. In that case, they may be more likely to be referred to a job with favorable working conditions and a good wage than someone simply applying for a job. Through social networks, we can get insights into positions that may be private or not widely advertised.

Taylor (2013c) described two distinct processes through which recently released individuals can utilize social capital. First is the use of social capital to increase knowledge about opportunities. To put it another way, by utilizing one's social capital, one may be able to find out through one's social network about opportunities for employment or education that can provide advantages over others, such as grant funding for education or job opportunities that pay better than others and offer medical benefits. Take, for example, the case of a former prisoner with a sibling who works for an online retailer. The sibling may inform the former prisoner of a well-paying opportunity for a client relationships position that and offers tuition reimbursement and medical insurance. The former offender learned of the client relationship position via their tie to their sibling. This knowledge is a function of social capital (Taylor, 2013c, p. 6). Second, social capital can increase the chances of getting access to services or opportunities. It is often through our social networks that opportunities can be found. To build on the previous example, the former offender may ask their sibling to put in a good word for them with the hiring manager at the online retailer or to schedule an interview for the position. Suppose the former offender did not have the social capital built through connection to their sibling. In that case, they may not have found out about the client relations position or been able to get an interview.

The results of Taylor (2013c) demonstrate the critical role of social capital for participants in the STAR program in Philadelphia, Pennsylvania. Two critical groups provided social capital for STAR participants: family members and ex-offenders who had been through the STAR program. While the STAR program provided access to job opportunities and job placement programs, the relationships with family members, friends, and former participants in the STAR program allowed them to find stable employment. In a similar manner to the social bonding discussed above, reentry courts may provide or boost participants' social capital, providing access to employment, housing, education, and other areas critical to the success of reentry court participants. The benefits of social capital also encourage the use of mentoring in reentry court programs, as former program participants may be able to connect with current ones, offering guidance and support, as well as access to opportunities.

Evidence Supporting the Effectiveness of Reentry Courts

As you can probably tell from the introduction and this chapter, I am a fan of reentry courts. My colleagues and I have seen first-hand how they can assist those transitioning from prison into the community in various areas like finding a job, building a resume, getting an apartment, or getting into trade school or college. However, my first-hand experiences can only be generalized so far—so what does the literature say about reentry courts? Are they effective? In general, results have been mixed regarding the effectiveness of reentry court programs. However, those program evaluations which have found reentry courts have a positive effect on reducing recidivism tend to address issues across multiple life domains (e.g., education, employment, and health care) (Seiter & Kadela, 2003). For example, in their evaluation of the Key-Crest program, which modified the substance abuse and vocational training from prison, to work release, and eventually to parole, Inciardi and colleagues (1997) found recidivism decreased in program participants.

The best way to approach the effectiveness of reentry courts is to consider their primary object, reducing recidivism. One of the first reentry court programs was the Harlem Parole Reentry Court, which started in June 2001. Like most reentry courts, the Harlem Parole Reentry Court seeks to help return parolees during their reintegration into society by assisting with employment, finding stable housing, staying drug-free, and taking on responsibilities in their family and personal lives (Hamilton, 2010). Other studies such as Carey et al. (2018), Farrell and Wunderlich (2009, as cited in Vance, 2011), and Lowenkamp and Bechtel (2010, as cited in Vance, 2011) found an association between reentry court participation and decreases in new arrests or new charges (Taylor, 2020). While focusing on recidivism may seem logical, scholars have pointed out that other outcomes may measure the success of reentry courts (Taylor, 2020). Given the many areas of focus for reentry courts, it is essential to consider programmatic success beyond one recidivism outcome.

An area identified by Taylor's (2013a) evaluation of a federal reentry court found that participants were more likely to be employed at the end of the 18-month study period than a comparison group. Employment is a crucial goal of the reentry court, so success in this area is essential for participants' long-term success. In their evaluation of the Harlem Parole Reentry Court, Ayoub and Pooler's (2015) evaluation of the Harlem reentry court participants (relative to the comparison group) revealed promising findings in multiple areas, including "reentry court participants were more likely to be employed or enrolled in school, less likely to report using drugs, more likely to report higher values on family support and quality of family relationship measures, and more likely to report higher values on measures of procedural justice perceptions" (Taylor, 2020, p. 3). As reentry courts seek to address concerns across multiple life domains and areas, the findings of Ayoub and Pooler (2015) are particularly promising. They suggest that reentry courts can do more than reduce recidivism.

Evidence Refuting the Effectiveness of Reentry Courts

While the above section examined some of the studies which have found support regarding reentry courts, it is essential to discuss research that has found evidence that reentry courts are not effective or are only partially effective; there are the "mixed" results referred to earlier. For example, studies such as that of the Judicial Council of California (2014) have found some success for reentry with lower rates of reincarceration and revocation. However, there were no impacts on rearrests. In other words, the Judicial Council of California (2014) found some success with the reentry courts, but the success was only across some of the areas reentry courts are targeting. Also, finding similar reentry outcome limitations, Hamilton (2010) found a reduction of rearrests but not a reduction in reincarnation or revocations for the Harlem Parole Reentry Court. Some studies find programs are ineffective at reducing key outcomes, including Rauma (2016), evaluating five reentry courts where there were no effects on revocations or new felony arrests.

Another issue with reentry courts is the "supervision effect," which refers to how the increased level of supervision provided by reentry court programs may lead participants to higher rates of revocations for technical violations than those on parole. For example, Hamilton (2010) found lower reconviction rates and no differences in rearrest rates relative to a comparison group, but higher rates of technical violations for those in reentry courts (Hamilton, 2010). As Taylor (2020) mentions, some of the issues with reentry court research may be issues around study designs; ultimately, there is a need for more research to help come to a consensus regarding reentry courts' effectiveness.

Future Research

Reentry courts are an exciting innovation for problem solving or treatment courts. The ability to work with those being released from prison to help them address challenging areas like employment, education, housing, medical care, and legal issues, amongst others, may be the critical factor in determining the long-term success of those being released from prison. The prospect of successful reentry for those leaving prison offers a variety of benefits not only for the former individual inmate but also for society as a whole. Reduced recidivism translates to reduced harms of new crimes and not having to pay the costs of arresting, processing, and institutionalizing those who re-offend post-release.

Since reentry courts are relatively new, there is a need to study how they work in different populations and demographics. Programs like Project HOPE in Hawaii, Philadelphia's STAR Court, or Newark's ReNew have shown promise, as have many other programs nationwide. However, as a relatively new type of treatment court, evidence is limited about the effectiveness of these programs. Moving forward, future research will need to be conducted to closely examine the process of what is occurring in these courts—are they doing what they set out to do, the way they set out to do it? There is also a need for more studies to examine outcomes reflective of success such as finding employment, completion of education or training programs, getting health insurance, and getting regular health care, and of course, not getting rearrested and reincarcerated. We also need a more explicit focus on demographics; many studies tend to focus on male offenders of similar racial/ethnic backgrounds. More research examining the effectiveness of reentry courts for female offenders and a broader representation of racial/ethnic groups will help us understand the generalizability of reentry courts or identify modifications that need to be made to serve specific groups. For example, Salvatore et al.'s (2020) study sample only consisted of African American males. Do reentry courts work for women and other racial/ ethnic groups? Future research will need to address these questions. In addition, do reentry courts work across geographic and regional boundaries? Programs with noted success or potential, such as STAR Court, ReNew, and the Harlem Parole Reentry Court, are all programs on the East Coast of the United States. Would these work as well in Los Angeles, California, Seattle, Washington, or Albuquerque, New Mexico? Scholars and evaluators looking at reentry courts in the coming years can address these issues. If studies find the structure and format of these programs is effective across regions and populations this could lead to the development of a more standardized model for these types of treatment courts. On the other hand, if these program structures and formats are not found to work in other areas, modifications can be made that might allow for differences by region and population. Ultimately, retrospective research with former participants will be needed to show how being in a reentry program helped (or did not) with their long-term success or failure. Finally, additional theoretical research is needed to clarify which theoretical model most reflects current practice in reentry programs.

Conclusions

One of the most recent and promising entries into the lexicon of treatment courts, reentry courts offer participants the support and guidance necessary to succeed in the community once they are released from a facility. As discussed above, reentry is one of the most challenging issues for correctional officers. Reentry court programs may be a strategy to increase successful reintegration into communities post-incarceration. As recidivism is one of the biggest challenges facing the criminal justice system, in particular those being released from jails and prisons, it is critical to identify strategies that can help those leaving these institutions succeed once released. Reentry courts represent one of the potential approaches for reducing recidivism and are therefore of critical interest. This chapter looked at the limited literature on the success of reentry courts. While there are only a few studies in this area, and the research results are mixed, there is the promise of successful reentry for participants in these programs.

Reentry courts can give participants social capital and provide the social bonds necessary to succeed. With the support of a reentry court team and the guidance of an engaged judge, reentry courts can help participants develop a resume, find health insurance, get a driver's license, complete their education, resolve personal issues like divorce, and deal with lingering legal issues like fines and warrants. Studies have found that reentry courts can provide the "personal touch" that can make a massive difference for participants. The role of an engaged judge has been found to be of particular influence, as few clients of the correctional system have had a positive experience with representatives of the criminal justice system. Judicial interest in participants has been noted to be a critical factor for reentry court participants in driving their performance in reentry courts and successful outcomes (Salvatore et al., 2020. By providing the social bonding, mentoring, guidance, and support so many leaving correctional institutions never had in their lives (or at least from members of the criminal justice system), reentry courts may be a tool to help end the revolving door cycle in and out of prisons that has plagued our criminal justice system for so long.

Treatment Court Success Story: Reentry Courts

Name: "Kevin"

Location: New Haven, Connecticut

Background: Like many participants in reentry courts, "Kevin" had prior convictions. This led him to be viewed as a career offender under Sentencing Guidelines, which in turn led him to be sentenced to 26 years in prison for selling narcotics in 1991, when he was in his twenties. "Kevin" ended up spending the next several decades in nine federal prisons, occupying his time by doing a lot of reading a trying to keep himself busy.

Like many released from prison after serving an extended sentence, "Kevin" has come back to a markedly different world. Technology, such as mobile phones, has jumped in leaps and bounds from what it was in the early 1990s. However, some things haven't changed, like the types of criminal behaviors occurring in his community. Not wanting to fall into past behaviors that led him to prison in the first place, "Kevin's" probation officer advised he investigate reentry court.

While initially hesitant, "Kevin" considers the reentry court a "blessing" in his life.

What does the District of Connecticut reentry court provide its participants? Like many reentry courts the District of Connecticut reentry court meets bimonthly and provides participants intensive supervision. Those in the reentry court program go to a cognitive-thinking group known as Moral Reconation Therapy (MRT), which assists with moral reasoning.

The District of Connecticut reentry court provides a personal connection between members of the treatment court workgroup like the judge and prosecutor and the participants in the program. Successes like finding a job or apartment are discussed, as are challenges like the breakup of a romantic relationship. The reentry court environment is a supportive one for participants where building self-confidence is seen as a critical component of success.

Reentry court can work! Reentry court participants across the country like "Kevin" have benefitted from the support and guidance provided by reentry courts. Many participants in reentry courts have successfully found employment, located housing, mended relationships with their families, and now serve as mentors in their reentry court programs, helping those recently released from prison find a prosocial path in life and avoid reincarceration.

For more information on "Kevin" and the federal reentry court in the District of Connecticut see: https://judicature.duke.edu/articles/reflections-on-a-reentry-court/.

References

Andrews, D. A., Bonta, J. J., & Wormith, S. (2011). The risk-need-responsivity (RNR) model: Does adding the good lives model contribute to effective crime prevention? *Criminal Justice and Behavior, 38*(7), 735–755.

Ayoub, L. H., & Pooler, T. (2015). *Coming home to Harlem: A randomized controlled trial of the Harlem Parole Reentry Court.* Center for Court Innovation.

Carey, S. M., Rempel, M., Lindquist, C., Cissner, A., Hassuun-Ayoub, Kralstein, D., & Malsch, A. (2018). *Reentry court research: Overview of findings from the National Institute of Justice's Evaluation of Second Chance Act adult reentry court.* https://www.ojp.gov/pdffiles1/nij/grants/251496.pdf.

Carson, E. A. (2021). *Prisoners in 2020: Statistical tables*. NCJ 302776. US Department of Justice, Office of Justice Programs, Bureau of Justice Statistics. https://bjs.ojp.gov/content/pub/pdf/p20st.pdf.

Clear, T. (2007). *Imprisoning communities: How mass incarceration makes disadvantaged neighborhoods worse*. Oxford University Press.

Coleman, J. S. (1988). Social capital in the creation of human capital. *American Journal of Sociology, 94*, S95–S120. http://www.jstor.org/stable/2780243.

Durose, M. R., Cooper, A. D., & Snyder, H. N. (2014). *Recidivism of prisoners released in 30 states in 2005: Patterns from 2005 to 2010*. NCJ 244205. US Department of Justice, Bureau of Justice Statistics. https://bjs.ojp.gov/content/pub/pdf/rprts05p0510.pdf.

Farole, D. (2003). The Harlem parole reentry court evaluation. Implementation and preliminary impacts. https://www.courtinnovation.org/sites/default/files/harlem reentryeval.pdf.

Farrell, A., & Wunderlich, K. (2009). Evaluation of the Court Assisted Recovery Effort (C.A.R.E.) Program—United States District Court for the District of Massachusetts. As cited in Vance, S. E. (2011). Federal reentry court programs: A summary of recent evaluations. *Federal Probation, 75*(2), 64–73.

Hamilton, Z. (2010). Do reentry courts reduce recidivism? Results from the Harlem Parole reentry court. Center for Court Innovation. https://www.ojp.gov/ncjrs/virtual-library/abstracts/do-reentry-courts-reduce-recidivism-results-harlem-parole-reentry.

Hamilton, Z., Thompson Tollefsbo, E., Campagna, M., & van Wormer, J. (2016). Customizing criminal justice assessments. In F. Taxman (Ed.), *Handbook on risk need and assessment: Theory and practice*. Routledge Press.

Hirschi, T. (1969). *Causes of delinquency*. University of California Press.

Inciardi, J., Martin, S., Butzin, C., Hooper, R., & Harrison, L. (1997). Effective model of prison-based treatment for drug-involved offenders. *Journal of Drug Issues, 27*(2), 261–278. https://doi.org/10.1177/002204269702700206.

Judicial Council of California. (2014). Parolee reentry court program evaluation. https://www.courts.ca.gov/documents/lrcaparoleereentry-pc3015.pdf.

Klukcow, R., & Zeng, Z. (2022*). Correctional populations in the United States 2020: Statistical tables*. NCJ 303184. US Department of Justice, Office of Justice Programs, Bureau of Justice Statistics. https://bjs.ojp.gov/content/pub/pdf/cpus20st.pdf?utm_content=JUST-STATS&utm_medium=email&utm_source=govdelivery.

Lattimore, P. K., & Visher, C. (2009). *The multi-site evaluation of S.V.O.R.I.: Summary and synthesis*. Research Triangle Institute. https://www.ncjrs.gov/Pdffiles1/Nij/Grants/230421.pdf.

Lowenkamp, C., & Bechtel, K. (2010). An evaluation of the accelerated community entry court program. As cited in Vance, S. E. (2011). Federal reentry court programs: A summary of recent evaluations. *Federal Probation, 75*(2), 64–73.

Muller, J. (2009). Implementing pretrial services risk assessment with sex offense defendant population. *Federal Probation, 73*(2), 45–47.

Nagin, D. S. (2013). Deterrence in the twenty-first century. *Crime and Justice, 42*(1), 199–263. https://doi.org/10.1086/670398.

Ndrecka, M., Listwan, S. J., & Latessa, E. (2017) What works in reentry and how to improve outcomes. In S. Stojkovic (Ed). *Prisoner Reentry*, Palgrave Macmillan, New York, NY.

Petersilia, J. (2003). *When prisoners come home: Parole and prisoner reentry*. Oxford University Press.

Portes, A. (1998). Social capital: Its origins and applications in modern society. *Annual Review of Sociology, 24*, 1–24.

Rauma, D. (2016). *Evaluation of a federal reentry program model*. Federal Judicial Center.

Salvatore, C., Michalsen, V., & Taylor, C. (2020). Reentry court judge: The key to the court. *Journal of Offender Rehabilitation, 59*(4), 198–222. https://doi.org/10.1080/10509674.2020.1733164.

Seiter, R., & Kadela, K. (2003). Prisoner reentry: What works, what does not, and what is promising. *Crime & Delinquency, 49*(3), 360–388. https://doi.org/10.1177/0011128703049003002.

Taylor, C. (2013a). Tolerance of minor setbacks in challenging reentry experience: An evaluation of a federal reentry court. *Criminal Justice Policy Review, 21*(1), 49–70. https://doi.org/10.1177/0887403411427354.

Taylor, C. (2013b). Program evaluation of the Federal Reentry Court in the Eastern District of Philadelphia: Report on program effectiveness for the first 164 reentry court participants. Lasalle University Digital Commons. https://digitalcommons.lasalle.edu/cgi/viewcontent.cgi?article=1009&context=soc_crj_faculty.

Taylor, C. J. (2013c). The Supervision to Aid Reentry (STAR) program: Enhancing the social capital of ex-offenders. *Probation Journal, 60*(2), 119–135. https://doi.org/10.1177/0264550513478319.

Taylor, C. J. (2020). Beyond recidivism: An outcome evaluation of a federal reentry court and a critical discussion of outcomes that matter. *Justice Evaluation Journal.* https://doi.org/10.1080/24751979.2020.1721311.

Travis, J. (2005). *But they all come back: Facing the challenges of prisoner reentry.* Urban Institute Press.

Tyler, T. (1988). *The social psychology of procedural justice.* Plenum.

Vito, G., & Homes, R. M. (1994). *Criminology: Theory, research, and policy.* Wadsworth Publishing Company.

CHAPTER 9

Teen Courts: Overview

As we have moved through our topics, we have looked at a variety of diverse populations with distinct sets of needs. Youth populations are one of the most unique we will examine and perhaps the one most likely to engage in illegal behaviors. One of the most consistent findings in criminology has been the relationship between age and crime, with offending typically ramping up in adolescence and declining into adulthood (Shulman et al., 2013). One of the most popular explanations of the high rates of offending during the teenage years is grounded in brain development, which experts state isn't complete until the mid-twenties (Steinberg, 2008). Adolescent brains tend to be focused on short-term rewards and have a limited view of the future (Scott et al., 2018). In other words, teenage brains tend to focus on the moment and not consider the long-term consequences of their actions. As adolescents age through adulthood, self-regulation in the brain develops and may explain why we see a decrease in offending behaviors as many age (Steinberg, 2008). The workings of the teenage brain may be reflected in crime trends; statistics reveal crime peaks around age 17 or 18, then declines over time, especially after young adulthood (Barkan, 2001). To help understand trends in youth arrests, let us consider some trends for violent crimes. Peaking in 1994, youth arrests for violent crime reached new lows in 2020, 78% lower than the peak in 1994 and 50% less than in 2010 (Puzzanchera, 2022, p. 1). However, even with these historic drops in youth arrests for violent crimes, there were still approximately 424,000 arrests involving those under 18 in 2020. About 8% of these arrests were related to violent offenses, 5% to aggravated assault, 3% to robbery, and 1% to murder (Puzzanchera, 2022, p. 1). Studies have consistently found that even with minor variations in types of crime across data, time, and place, this pattern holds (e.g., Farrington, 1986), even across gender (Steffensmeier & Streifel, 1991). One of the few types of crime usually committed by older persons is white-collar crime, as those in their teens typically do not have opportunities to commit these crimes (Barkan, 2001).

Since youth represent one of the largest groups arrested in the United States, processing them in traditional criminal justice routes may lead juvenile offenders to various adverse outcomes. For example, confinement could cut off prosocial relationships with parents, other family members, and peers, as well as education, employment, or other opportunities for community engagement that could foster prosocial behavior and development (National Research Council, 2013). In addition to the previously mentioned adverse effects of incarceration for juvenile offenders, there may be psychological costs for incarcerated juveniles, such as the interruption of developmental processes and increased potential for involvement in the criminal justice system in the future (Gase et al., 2016). Even if youth are not incarcerated, just going through the proper processing of the criminal justice system can harm youth. Going through court processing creates a criminal record which can result in the stigma of being a criminal offender, which may hinder future educational and employment opportunities, and personal relationships, potentially putting youth on negative life trajectories that could have an increased chance of criminal justice system involvement, as well as poorer academic outcomes and health issues (Nellis, 2011).

Teen courts, also known as peer or youth courts, are specialized treatment courts that have evolved as an alternative to traditional criminal justice processing for youth offenders. Most juveniles referred to teen court are between the ages of 12 and 15 and have gotten into trouble for the first time, typically with offenses like vandalism, stealing, or nonviolent offenses (Butts & Ortiz, 2011). Teen courts started at a local level in the 1970s and had expanded throughout the U.S. by the 1990s, By 2015, they were operating in 49 states and the District of Columbia (Gase et al., 2016). Teen courts usually work with low-level and first-time offenders, have volunteer youth who take an active role in providing consequences to offenders (such as acting as attorney, jury, or judge), and have future teen court jury service as a potential sanction (Gase et al., 2016, p. 52). Teen courts offer a variety of sanctions focused on repairing the harms caused by the offense, including letters of apology to victims, essays, and community service (National Association of Youth Courts, n.d.). While there is no standard format or structure for teen courts, they do share a primary goal of fair and restorative justice in the processing and disposition of youth offenders (National Association of Youth Courts, n.d.).

Youths usually agree to participate in teen court programs to avoid more formal prosecution and adjudication in juvenile court. Youth who agree to participate in these programs but then refuse to comply face sanctions, which can include being returned to juvenile court to face their original charges (Butts & Ortiz, 2011). Studies have found benefits of teen courts such as high levels of satisfaction for parents and youth participants (Butts & Buck, 2000), improvements in psychological and social behaviors (Evans et al., 2016), more positive attitudes towards criminal justice authorities in general, and greater knowledge of legal processes (LoGalbo, 1998). Other studies have pointed out criticisms and limitations of teen courts, including the potential for net widening (Butts et al., 2002) and the potential negative outcomes of these programs (Povitsky, 2005). The goal of the juvenile justice system is to provide treatment (or at least the potential for treatment) in lieu of the more punitive adult criminal justice system. In order to discuss teen courts comprehensively, we must first understand the evolution of the juvenile justice system as a distinct branch of the criminal justice system and couch teen courts within that context.

Development of the Juvenile Justice System

One of the first major innovations of the American criminal justice system was developing a separate juvenile justice system. Before the development of the juvenile justice system, youth offenders were seen as "little adults" and generally punished as such. Children under the age of 7 were generally viewed as incapable of having criminal intent, and were typically not punished by the criminal justice system. Children between 7 and 10 were viewed in a somewhat less clear way when it came to criminal intent, with some occasions of children in this age range being viewed as being able to have criminal intent. Children over 14 were viewed as able to understand the consequences of their actions and commonly stood trial as adults would, facing adult punishments, including capital punishment (Sprauge, 1915).

Reformers in the area of juvenile justice took notice of the lack of specialized processing and treatment of juvenile offenders in the early 1800s (Thompson & Morris, 2016, p. 56), along with the increased understanding of children being less cognitively mature and developmentally different from adults led to several movements focusing on alternative strategies to deal with youth offenders. For example, in the 1820s, the Society for the Reformation of Juvenile Delinquency played a crucial role in lobbying the New York State Assembly to pass the 1824 legislation that established the New York House of Refuge. This "Reformatory" opened on January 1, 1925, and was the first such institution in the U.S. (Thompson & Morris, 2016, p. 57). The "Reform School" approach proved popular and expanded across the United States in the following years (Pickett, 1969).

Other therapeutic innovations in the early 1800s included the cottage system, which sought to make reform schools and related institutions like family units by building small cottage-type buildings. A "placing out" system involved putting children from highly impoverished urban communities who engage in delinquency into placements with rural people to live and work with another family. The use of Houses of Refuge and related facilities was innovative as they represented a better understanding of youth behavior and the different needs of youth relative to adults. At the same time, these institution-like facilities started to face many of the same challenges in adult institutions and prisons, such as abuse, overcrowding, and failing facilities (Pickett, 1969). The theoretical belief behind practices such as "placing out" seem to be rooted in the notion that a change of environment for youth could help change their behaviors, ignoring potential biological factors like developmental disabilities as factors that could influence delinquent behavior in youth (Thompson & Morris, 2016, p. 58).

The reform movement of the 1800s helped change policy and practices regarding juvenile delinquency. During this time, we also saw greater interest from the public in understanding the need for a different approach to dealing with juvenile offenders. In 1899, we saw the first juvenile court in the United States in Chicago, Cook County, Illinois. This innovation led to a change in society regarding the punishment of youth offenders (Thompson & Morris, 2016, p. 58). The new focus was targeting the protection and rehabilitation of youth rather than using the punitive approach of the past (Zimring, 2005). Juvenile courts proved popular, and by 1925 just about every state in the United States had a juvenile court system focused on rehabilitating youths who had participated in delinquency (Thompson & Morris, 2016). Another critical area of the development of juveniles has been a series of United States Supreme Court rulings that have expanded juvenile rights. These cases are briefly summarized next to provide a narrative of how juvenile rights have expanded over time (see Table 9.1).

TABLE 9.1: SUMMARY AND RULING OF KEY SUPREME COURT CASES IN THE DEVELOPMENT OF THE JUVENILE JUSTICE SYSTEM/JUVENILE RIGHTS

Kent v. United States (1966)	Morris A. Kent Jr., a 16-year-old male, who had been charged with rape and robbery after his fingerprints were found at the apartment of the female victim, had a history with the legal system that started when he was 14, prompted by a series of burglaries and thefts. Kent confessed to the rape and robbery and several similar crimes. However, he was found to be suffering from severe psychopathy during a psychiatric evaluation, where it was recommended that he be placed in inpatient psychiatric care. Due to the severe nature of the charges, Kent would be transferred to adult court to be tried as an adult. Kent's lawyer filed a motion for his case to remain in juvenile court, which incorporated the recommendation that he receive appropriate psychiatric care to be rehabilitated. Despite this motion, the court did not conduct a full investigative hearing and instead filed an order stating the investigation had been made, providing no verbal or written explanation of what was revealed, and transferring the case to adult criminal court. Kent was then found guilty and received a sentence of 30 to 90 years in jail. Kent's lawyer filed an appeal arguing the waiver to adult court wasn't valid, as the full investigation had not been made and as such Kent's constitution rights were violated because he was a minor. The case went to the U.S. Supreme Court, which deemed the waiver to adult court invalid (Thompson & Morris, 2016, pp. 59–60). The critical takeaway from this cause is that while *parens patriae* may protect youth in many cases, it had the opposite effect and reduced Kent's due process rights. Due process rights are critical for all defendants; in the case of Kent, *parens patriae* showed that the court did not act in the best interest of the youth and caused a loss of constitutional rights, putting him in jeopardy (in this case, being transferred to adult court) without the same level of due process (in this case a hearing) adults would have been provided (Thompson & Morris, 2016, pp. 59–60).

In re Gault (1967)	In this case, Gerald Gault, a 15-year-old male, was accused of making an obscene call to a female neighbor in June 1964. The neighbor, Mrs. Cook, filed a complaint, which resulted in Gault and a friend, Ronald Lewis, being arrested and put in a Children's Detention Home (Administrative Office of the US Courts, n.d.). Gault had been on probation at the time of the arrest; his parents weren't present, with both being at work. There was no note or other form of notice nor any effort to inform them of their son's location after the arrest. Gault's family was eventually informed of his location by Lewis's family. When Gault's mother went to the detention home, she was advised there would be a juvenile court hearing the following day. On the day of Gault's initial court hearing, the arresting officer filed a petition with the court, which was not served to Gault's parents. After the hearing, Gault was returned to the detention home, where he was held for several more days before being let go. On his release date, Gault's parents were informed there would be another hearing on June 15, 1964. Gault did not have a parent present on June 15, even though Mrs. Gault had requested she be present to see which of the two boys had spoken with the alleged victim. No record was made of the court session, and there were conflicting accounts of the admission of guilt by Gault. The adult punishment for the same crime was a maximum of a $50 fine and two months in jail. Again, no report was shared with Gault or his parents. At the end of the hearing, the judge committed Gault to a six-year term in juvenile detention (until he would be 21 years of age) (Administrative Office of the US Courts, n.d.). Gault's parents filed a writ of habeas corpus petition, later dismissed by the Superior Court of Arizona and the Arizona Supreme Court. The case next went to the U.S. Supreme Court, which agreed to hear the case to consider the procedural due process rights of a juvenile criminal defendant (Administrative Office of the US Courts, n.d.). The Supreme Court ruled *In re Gault*, if Gault had been 18 at the time of his arrest, he would have been afforded the procedural safeguards available to adults. In *Gault* the Supreme Court scrutinized the juvenile court system, finding that even though there are valid reasons for the different treatment of youth and adults, juveniles who are being subjecting to adjudication of delinquency and incarceration are "entitled to certain procedural safeguards under the Due Process Clause of the Fourteenth Amendment" (U.S. State Courts, n.d.).

In re Winship (1970)	Samuel Winship, a 12-year-old male, had been charged with stealing $112 from a woman's purse in a store. One of the store's employees stated they had seen Samuel running from the scene, though this statement was contradicted by other employees who stated the store employee in question could not have seen the act from their location at the time. Samuel had been adjudicated and put in a training school. The New York court stated they did not have to meet the same standards as adult courts and could instead rely on the preponderance of evidence to determine guilt (a lower standard relative to what is required in adult cases). Samuel's family appealed the ruling, with the Supreme Court ruling that juvenile courts must meet the standard of beyond a responsible doubt as the burden of proof (as is used in adult cases). Not meeting this standard was seen as a violation of the Fourteenth Amendment. The key ruling in juvenile cases must be held to the same standard of proof as adults, which is beyond a doubt (Thompson & Morris, 2016, p. 60).
Breed v. Jones (1975)	This case involved a 17-year-old male, Gary Steven Jones, who was charged with armed robbery in juvenile court, then adjudicated as a delinquent. The judge waived the jurisdiction of Jones to adult court at the disposition. Jones's counsel argued that the waiver to adult court violated the Double Jeopardy Clause, which was denied by the court, who argued that an adjudication hearing is not a trial. The Supreme Court ruled adjudication in adult court, following adjudication in juvenile court, was a violation of the Double Jeopardy Clause (Thompson & Morris, 2016, pp. 58–59).
Eddings v. Oklahoma (1982)	This case focused on the issue of a defendant's youth being a mitigating factor in deciding the application of capital punishment. Monty Lee Eddings, a 16-year-old male, had been transferred to adult court and charged with first-degree murder in Oklahoma, where he was found guilty and eligible for a death penalty sentencing. The Supreme Court ruled that age should be a mitigating factor when considering if someone should be put to death, and Eddings's case was reversed (Thompson & Morris, 2016, p. 61).
Schall v. Martin (1984)	This case examined the issue of pretrial detention for juveniles who pose a serious risk to the community's safety. Gregory Martin, a 14-year-old male, had been charged with possessing a weapon, assault, and robbery. At his adjudication hearing, he was detained because the court felt he was a serious risk of committing another offense. Martin's lawyer argued against this but could not prevent the pretrial detention. The Supreme Court found that pretrial detention is allowable if it provides protection for both the juvenile and society from other crimes that could be committed pretrial, as long as it is not intended as punishment (Thompson & Morris, 2016, p. 60).

Roper v. Simmons (2005)	Christopher Simmons, a 17-year-old male, had admitted to someone else that he committed premeditated murder, breaking into a woman's home, tying her hands, and throwing her off a bridge. Simmons was found guilty in a jury trial and received the death penalty. His case reached the U.S. Supreme Court, which cited research dealing with cognitive neuroscience, developmental psychology, and other social science that have found adolescent brains are not fully developed, which may impact various cognitive capabilities, including self-control and taking responsibility for one's actions. In other words, the Court found juveniles are less mature and have a lesser degree of reasoning, are more likely to be influenced by negative external influences, and are amenable to reformation compared to adults. The Court also acknowledges that society generally views juveniles as having a lesser degree of responsibility for their crimes; as such, being executed for crimes committed under the age of 18 would violate the Eighth Amendment (Thompson & Morris, 2016, p. 61).
Thompson v. Oklahoma (1988)	This case ruled that the imposition of the death penalty was a violation of the Eighth Amendment's protections against cruel and unusual punishment for those under the age of 15. William Wayne Thompson, a 15-year-old male, in concert with three adult males, kidnapped and beat a man who died. The victim, married to Thompson's sister, had allegedly committed acts of domestic violence and had been found in a river with various injuries, including gunshot wounds. All of the individuals in the crime were arrested. Thompson was given psychiatric evaluations, deemed eligible to stand trial as an adult, and sentenced to death at a jury trial. On appeal, the Supreme Court ruled that the execution of a juvenile violated the cruel and unusual punishment protections of the Eighth Amendment (Thompson & Morris, 2016, p. 61).
Graham v. Florida (2010)	In this case, Terrance Jamar Graham, a 16-year-old male, was arrested for armed robbery and subsequently pleaded guilty to a first-degree felony, which was punishable by life in prison. Graham was arrested for robbery again six months later while on probation. He did not admit guilt to this new alleged crime but did concede that he had violated his plea agreement for the prior felony. Consequently, he was sentenced to life in prison; since Florida had abolished the use of parole, it became a life-in-prison sentence without the chance of getting parole. The case eventually came before the Supreme Court, which ruled that juveniles cannot be sentenced to life in prison without parole in cases of non-homicide because this was a violation of the protections against cruel and unusual punishment provided by the Eighth Amendment (Thompson & Morris, 2016, p. 62).

Miller v. Alabama (2012)	Two youth offenders committed offenses that resulted in them being subjected to mandatory minimum sentencing, which removed the ability of the judge to use discretion to consider their juvenile status when considering sentencing factors that could make the punishment disproportionate to the offense. The Supreme Court ruled that the sentence (in this case, a mandatory life sentence without the possibility of parole) violated the Eighth Amendment. As such, judges have to consider a defendant's age when making sentencing decisions. In other words, the case integrates the notion of including proportionality, the idea that punishment has to not only be equal to the crime but should also factor in a juvenile's status (Thomson & Morris, 2016, p. 62).

Teen Court Characteristics

As with other treatment- or problem-oriented courts that have been examined thus far in this book, there may be similarities between teen courts and other types of treatment courts, including the focus on treatment instead of punishment. However, teen courts are distinct from other types of treatment courts as they are largely run by youth volunteers instead of more formally by members of the treatment court workgroup. However, adult court professionals are present and available during teen court proceedings. To help us better understand the variety of structures and procedures in teen courts, we turn to the 2016 meta-analysis by Gase et al., which looked at 17 studies examining teen courts. Of the studies examined, 17 looked at courts that accepted lower-level misdemeanor offenses such as drug or alcohol possession, burglary, and theft. Of these programs, four did not include violent crimes, and three did not accept some or any drug offenses. Four studies looked at courts that only took cases dealing with tobacco or alcohol possession, vehicle-related offenses, or school-based offenses. Turning to the age range of youth offenders served by the programs in the studies, 9 required youth to be between 11 or 12, or 17 or 18. Four of the studies took younger offenders, as young as age 7. Most of the studies looked at programs that required youth to be first-time offenders; though 4 of the 13 that had this requirement did make exceptions on a case-by-case basis, only 3 of the studies looked at programs that allowed repeat offenders (Gase et al., 2016, p. 55).

The teen courts used various court models and processes in the study. Of the 20 studies reviewed by Gase et al. (2016), 7 used an adult judge model, 5 incorporated the use of a youth judge, 3 used a combination of an adult judge and a peer jury, 4 used a peer jury model, and 1 used a youth tribunal model. The studies evaluated stated that youth had to admit guilt before participating in the teen court hearing, and two of the studies discussed an assessment or determination of guilt or innocence occurring during the teen court hearing. Eight studies discussed the length of time an offender spent in teen court, ranging from 2 to 24 weeks (Gase et al., 2016, pp. 56–57). Sentences were relatively uniform across the court programs examined and included letters of apology, community service, and future participation on a teen court jury.

Turning our attention to the theoretical orientation of the programs (which we will explore in more detail in the next section), five of the studies discussed being rooted in restorative justice. To help us better understand the procedure of a teen court, a description of a case from the Anchorage Youth Court is given below:

> At 4:00 pm, a youth bailiff for the Anchorage Youth Court steps into a waiting room on the third floor of the Anchorage courthouse and, reading from a docket sheet, calls out Case Number 687432. A 15-year-old girl named Angela stands and begins to move toward the thick courtroom door, along with her mother and father.
>
> Waiting in the courtroom are two teenage defense attorneys (both female) that Angela and her parents met 45 min[utes] before in the basement offices of the Anchorage Youth Court. Two young men in their mid-teens are sitting at a table near the front of the courtroom. They will be serving as the prosecuting attorney for Angela's hearing, and they are currently reading through a case file that describes the incident in which Angela has admitted to being involved. An adult legal advisor sits at the side of the courtroom, near a chair used for witness testimony during daytime hearings in the criminal court. During the youth court hearing, the adult legal advisor will be quiet unless the young people in charge of the courtroom direct a question to him or seek his advice about procedural matters. Angela's parents take their places

on one of the five or six long, wooden, church-style pews at the rear of the courtroom that provide seating for spectators. The youth volunteers study Angela as she enters the courtroom. She has long brown hair and is dressed in jeans and a red shirt. She exchanges nervous glances with her parents as the youth attorneys direct her to come forward to sit near them. Her parents sit directly behind Angela in the spectator area. (Butts et al., 2002, p. 14)

The above quotation from Butts et al. (2002) and the overview of the various program characteristics give us a sense of how these courts work and what they look like in practice. As the description provides, teen courts have some overlap in their procedure with traditional courts and other types of treatment courts, but also distinct characteristics as well, which allow them to serve the distinct needs of teenage populations. We will now turn our attention to the various theoretical orientations which guide teen courts.

Teen Court Theoretical Orientation

Teen courts are a distinct type of treatment court as they frequently involve peers and have a wide variety of models employed. There are several different theoretical models which have been employed as some scholars have argued there has yet to be a fully realized theoretical model for teen courts (DeFosset et al., 2017). As such, we will look at various theories and discuss their influence on teen courts.

Peer Justice

In this section, the theoretical orientations of teen courts will be examined. Since many teen courts programs incorporate peers and a trial-by-peer model, the theoretical perspective to start with and perhaps the one most relevant is peer justice (Center for Court Innovation, 2010). The peer justice model posits that youth peers can pull youth toward delinquent behavior via negative peer pressure; they can also direct youth toward prosocial behaviors via positive peer pressure (Butts et al., 2002). From this perspective, the sentence given by prosocial peers to a youth offender in teen court would be seen as a type of disapproval from their peers. Using the peer justice perspective, youth offenders will view the punishment as more relevant than if the case had been processed and sentencing was given by an adult in the juvenile (or criminal) justice system. As such, the youth offender will be more likely to be driven to engage in the treatment process and make repairs to any harms caused, as well as complete the terms of the sentence (Center for Court Innovation, 2010).

Differential Association

The central idea of differential association is that criminal behavior is learned through direct and repeated interaction with those whose attitudes and behaviors support deviance (Akers, 2000). Through social interactions with these individuals, youth are socialized to have favorable attitudes toward deviant behavior and are taught how to be a criminal. Differential association suggests that if a teenager's antisocial interactions with negative peers are reduced, and exposure to prosocial (anti-deviant/criminal) peers is increased, it would help reduce delinquency. Teen courts have the potential to provide an opportunity for the reduction or elimination of antisocial behaviors by providing prosocial peers instead of criminogenic ones.

Restorative Justice

Teen courts are not strictly a restorative justice-based approach but may incorporate restorative justice and reflect many of the key principles and values of restorative justice approaches (Bouchard & Wong, 2017). Restorative justice focuses on repairing the harm to the community and providing the offender with an opportunity to be actively engaged in the restoration process with the idea that this will prevent future offending. Restorative justice posits that the potential benefits of teen courts are grounded in the focus on community rather than courts and repairing harms instead of getting retribution, as well as owning mistakes and holding oneself accountable (Butts et al., 2002). This restorative approach is in contrast to the retributive model and "get tough" policies which become dominant in the 1970s and 1980s and focus on more punitive measures such as mandatory sentences (Laundra et al., 2013).

Labeling

The application of Howard Becker's labeling theory can be interpreted as teen courts steering youth offenders away from the formal juvenile justice system; as such, the youth offenders are not subjected to the negative labeling that would come with more formal juvenile justice processing (Butts et al., 2002). In addition, since the youth is being judged by a jury of their peers (instead of a more formal representation of the criminal justice system like a judge), they are less likely to internalize a deviant or criminal label in teen court. Through the minimization of stigma and reducing or eliminating the potential to internalize negative labeling (e.g., being a criminal), this theoretical perspective suggests youth offenders may be able to avoid involvement with deviant peer networks, a criminal identity, and additional delinquent or criminal behaviors (Becker, 1963).

Each of the above theories provides a grounding for teen courts. While social bonding theory has received little attention in relation to teen courts, it is possible that the idea of strong bonds and attachments built through the teen court process (with teen peers, victims, parents, and others involved in the process) could also be a viable theoretical grounding for teen courts. Research in the coming years may help clarify which theoretical orientations are applicable in teen courts and best explain their outcomes. We will next turn our attention to evidence supporting the effectiveness of teen courts.

Evidence Supporting the Effectiveness of Teen Courts

Teen courts have proven to be a popular strategy with various potential benefits. Since teen courts have a relatively high rate of program and sentence completion, they are viewed as a useful method in relieving the pressure on the juvenile justice system by decreasing workloads and overcrowding in juvenile facilities and allowing traditional juvenile courts to operate more efficiently (Schneider, 2008). In addition, since volunteers primarily run teen courts, they are seen as beneficial as they have lower operating costs and are more cost effective than traditional juvenile justice processing (Butts & Buck, 2000; Miller, 2008).

In order to consider the potential effectiveness of teen courts, we will look at several outcomes starting with recidivism. To start, utilizing recidivism can be challenging due to different conceptualizations of recidivism and how it is measured. Some earlier studies that have used measures of official recidivism have found post-teen court participation recidivism rates ranging from 3 to 8 percent within 6 to 12 months of participation in teen courts (Butler-Mejia, 1998; McNeece et al., 1996; SRA Associates, 1995). In a 1999 study, Minor and colleagues revealed that 32% percent of teen court youth had reoffended within one year of participation in teen court. In a more recent study examining a teen court in Kankakee County, Illinois, Mason (2019) used a mixed method approach to find that the teen court program successfully reduced recidivism rates.

An area where evidence of the benefits of teen courts is their cost-effectiveness. For example, in 2000, Butts and Buck stated that the voluntary nature of teen courts allows a reasonably large number of cases at a relatively low cost to communities. Dines (2017) provided similar commentary when examining the potential benefits of teen court programs, stating that according to a report from the American Youth Policy Forum in 2005, youth or teen courts saved $480 on average per teen court participant who completes their sentence. Other sources provide more detailed support for the cost savings aspects of these programs. For example, in an article by Stone (2011), the benefits of the cost savings of teen courts are summarized:

> When a teenager goes through the traditional juvenile justice system, he or she is sentenced to probation. It costs about $4,800 to supervise a minor on probation, while it costs about $500 to send a kid to Teen Court. (Stone, 2011, paragraph 15)

In a more recent study, Mason (2019) interview subjects identified several key areas of cost savings generated by the Kankakee County, Illinois, Teen Court, including saving the county the expense of paying employees to process these cases, as well as saving families the cost of fees and fines associated with the juvenile's case (Mason, 2019, p. 26). Another subject in Mason's study stated that the legal fees associated with (formal processing) would be much higher than the cost of pizza and soda (pop) for volunteers in the teen court (p. 37).

The Washington State Institute for Public Policy (2019) published a benefit-cost estimate of teen court vs. traditional juvenile justice court processing. The study revealed the following benefits: to taxpayers ($2,712), participants ($846), others ($5,577), and indirectly ($1,584), the total benefits minus the costs were $12,016 per participant, substantial savings for teen courts relative to the costs of the traditional juvenile justice process. Interestingly, despite their popularity, few sources examined the cost benefits of teen courts, although those existing were supportive overall, such as Dines (2017). Furthermore, we need to consider the short-term cost savings associated with processing youth cases via teen courts compared to more traditional forms of processing and the long-term benefits. Teen courts may pay off in the long run with the investment in the youth participants avoiding stigma and labeling, benefitting in human and financial terms later in life. Ultimately, teen court programs provide cost savings and other potential financial benefits through community service, revitalization of neighborhoods, and lower recidivism rates, saving the criminal justice system, the general public, and the community money in the long run (Dines, 2017).

In addition to recidivism and cost savings, there are other benefits of teen courts. A key area of benefit of youth or teen courts is to members or volunteers in these programs. These programs allow youth to actively participate in the decision-making process for fellow youth involved in delinquency as they gain first-hand experience in the criminal justice system (Dines, 2017). This experience may provide beneficial anticipatory socialization for participants in these programs. To illustrate these potential benefits, Dines (2017) discussed the experience of Ashia Barns, who served on the Brownsville Youth Court for one year. Describing her time serving on the Brownsville Youth Court twice a week on Tuesdays and Thursdays, Barns discussed how the program had a good impact on the community and her personal growth, giving her leadership skills and building her self-esteem as well as helping her build skills in a variety of areas including professionalism, interviewing, and resume writing (Dines, 2017, pp. 197–198).

Teen courts may provide benefits across a variety of areas. Participants in these programs who have their cases heard before the teen court instead of a traditional juvenile court may be less likely to recidivate and benefit from the prosocial role models their teen peers and others involved in the program may provide. Other teens in the program (e.g., peer judges and juries) may benefit from the experience of working in a court-like environment, learning both direct and transferable skills that may benefit their personal and professional growth.

Evidence Challenging the Effectiveness of Teen Courts

While a popular strategy, teen courts have not been without their problems and limitations. In 2000, Butts and Buck discussed various problems with teen courts by conducting surveys of programs to identify operational problems that impact the operations of teen court programs. Respondents were asked to identify if the problem was "serious," "minor," "something in between," or "not a problem at all." This study is of particular interest and importance to our discussion as it provides a touch point as teen courts had been active for quite some time by 2000, and results of the study continued to influence the use of and research on teen courts in the subsequent years. Results of the study found the biggest problem for the teen court programs surveyed was funding, with 40% reporting "some problems" with program funding, 25% reporting some problems with funding, and 15% reporting serious problems with funding. Thirty-eight percent of respondents reported no problems with funding (Butts & Buck, 2000). Another challenge identified in the survey was finding participants in the programs, such as attorneys, judges, and youth volunteers, and having a sufficient flow of referrals to the programs. About 21 percent of the programs reported "some" problems or "serious" problems maintaining teen volunteers. Twenty-nine percent of programs report "some" or "serious" problems with maintaining the flow of referrals for their program (Butts & Buck, 2000). Several other issues were identified as presenting "some" or "serious" problems for the teen court programs, including too much time passing between youth arrest and their referral to the teen court program (19 percent), issues in effectively coordinating the efforts of teen courts with other community agencies (16 percent), problems getting youth volunteers (19 percent), and adult volunteers (20 percent) (Butts & Buck, 2000). Given the voluntary nature of teen courts and the general challenges with getting and maintaining funding for any treatment or prevention strategy, the issues identified by Butts and Buck (2000) were to be expected. Turning our attention to empirical findings, we will see that despite the successes discussed above, there are programs and aspects of teen courts that could be more successful.

Various studies have examined teen court programs, resulting in mixed results on how these programs influence youth behaviors. For example, in their 2002 study, Butts et al. looked at outcomes across fourteen court programs in geographically diverse areas. Two of the programs had much lower recidivism rates after six months for youth who participated in the teen court relative to traditional court, one teen court program had no difference, and the fourth program had a small but not significant trend leaning towards the comparison group.

As with the evidence supporting the effectiveness of teen courts, we will look at some specific outcomes as we consider studies not supporting teen courts. Beginning with recidivism, Schwalbe et al. (2012) used meta-analysis to examine various experimental studies of juvenile diversion programs. The study looked at a subset of studies of teen courts, finding that the six programs examined had a non-significant impact on youth recidivism. A more recent study by Gase et al. (2016) compared teen courts to other types of intervention and found little support for the short- or long-term effectiveness of teen courts in reducing recidivism.

We turn our attention to the effectiveness of teen courts and other types of delinquency, prevention, and intervention programs. Patrick and Marsh (2005) looked at four different types of programs: (1) a teen court, (2) an accountability-based diversion program, (3) traditional juvenile justice processing, and (4) a control group with no treatment, and there were no differences in tobacco-related offenses. In a 2008 study Stickle and colleagues revealed that those who participated in teen courts self-reported higher levels of delinquent behaviors than those formally processed through the juvenile justice system. However, it is worth noting that arrest differences were not significant between the groups. Other studies have reported similar findings with teen court programs, where results were less than encouraging (Povitsky, 2005).

In addition to problems identified with teen courts, empirical studies identify limitations or lack of effectiveness, and there are criticisms of teen courts. Even though they are a widely used strategy with various benefits (as discussed above), teen court programs are not without their critics. The primary criticism is the risk of net widening (Butts et al., 2002, Norris et al., 2011). The net-widening argument is rooted in the concern that teen courts, as a diversion targets low-risk, first-time offenders. A large portion of youth targeted by teen courts are unlikely to reoffend without an intervention like teen courts and would be less likely to receive penalties if they went through traditional juvenile court processing. In other words, since the bulk of youth will only engage in delinquency for a short period of time and at relatively low levels, most will simply age out or stop offending on their own, and do not need to be targeting by programs like teen courts. Those who do agree to be part of a teen court, and tried by a jury of their peers, are more likely to be sanctioned than they would if they went through traditional juvenile juice processing (Butts et al., 2002).

Further, trial by peer is a core part of teen court programs. However, most adult offenders usually do not face a jury in court. Therefore, those in teen courts face more formal, longer, and potentially more intimidating proceedings than if they went through traditional juvenile justice processing, where the prosecutor would likely give them a warning and release. Ironically, teen courts seek to divert youth offenders from the potential stigma and labeling of the juvenile justice system, but participants are likely to have more involvement and contact with the juvenile justice compared with those who are not part of these programs (Bouchard & Wong, 2017).

Future Research

As discussed above, teen courts are popular, and there is some level of support regarding their ability to reduce recidivism, as well as being a cost-effective way to process youth offenders relative to processing through the traditional juvenile justice system (or criminal justice system). As we move forward, we need to consider the need for more apparent evidence regarding outcomes. As noted in a variety of studies, there is such diversity in the evaluation literature on these programs (e.g., some rely on official data, some self-reported measures, and others use information reported from parents) that it is hard to gauge the effectiveness of these programs that are based on the findings in the existing literature. In order to rectify this issue, we need evaluators to work with programs to help create standardized measures (or at least study several programs that measure recidivism the same way) to help get a better understanding of the effectiveness of these programs. Next, we need to consider the role of participation in the programs as an indicator or reflection of other theories, such as social bonding. As we have explored throughout this book so far (and will in the remaining chapters), the bonds and attachments built through treatment court programs are a central factor in how they operate and the related successes of participants. As teen courts primarily operate on a volunteer peer model, the role of the traditional courtroom workgroup may be reduced or muted. As such, we need studies examining the influence of the bonds built between participants and their teen peers volunteering in these programs. Another area of inquiry could be comparing the influence of adult/official members of the courtroom workgroup's role relative to teen peer volunteers on measures of success like recidivism in teen court programs. As of the writing of this chapter, we are out of the lockdown phase related to the COVID-19 pandemic, which hit our society in the spring of 2020. As scholars continue to examine teen court programs, studies will need to examine how the COVID-19 pandemic impacted teen courts and how changes to teen court programs (such as virtual sessions) impacted participants' success. A final area of inquiry could be the influence of teen courts on participants over time. Since teen court is exposing youth to a variety of potential professional directions such as law enforcement, law, and treatment programs, it may have the potential to influence what type of education participants pursue in their respective role as a client of the teen court or a volunteer. Another critical area of future study may be the use of the teen court model for a relatively recently identified population, emerging adults. As with teens, among those in emerging adulthood, approximately ages 18 to 29, there are high rates of behaviors such as binge drinking, substance abuse, and low-level offending that may bring this population to the attention of the criminal justice system (Salvatore, 2018). Like teenagers, many in emerging adulthood still don't have fully developed brains, and as Steinberg (2008) discussed, the same level of self-regulation as older adults. Teen courts could provide a model applicable to emerging adults as well, offering them treatment, guidance, and support from peers through the issues reflective of those in emerging adulthood. Finally, as with many of the other types of treatment courts we are exploring, we need to see the long-term impact of participation in teen courts for participants, and how being part of a teen court program did (or didn't) influence offending trajectories or desistance.

Conclusions

Teen courts represent one of the treatment court model's most exciting and innovative uses. Utilizing peers, these programs have shown some level of evidence in reducing recidivism and being much more cost-effective relative to more traditional juvenile justice processing. Teen courts provide a unique opportunity for youth to work with each other (under the supervision of adults) to reintegrate and restore delinquent youths. While the research to date has been mixed, there is significant promise to what teen courts may offer.

In the coming years, as newer generations of teens head into their peak years of offending, we will likely see teen courts remain a viable option in processing these youth in place of more formal processing through the juvenile justice system. The use of teen courts not only diverts participants from the juvenile justice system, helping them to avoid the stigma of being a youth offender, but it may also spark interest in law enforcement, legal work, or related fields. As society changes and evolves, it will be interesting to see how teen courts change. For example, with the legalization of marijuana in many states and jurisdictions, will we see fewer or more cases for teen courts? As many parents may shift to work-at-home positions (and, in theory, be able to provide more supervision for children and be place managers for their homes), will we see a corresponding decrease in youth offending? In addition, we may need to consider other social changes that occur; will there be future pandemics similar to COVID-19 that cause a societal shutdown? If so, how will (or won't) this impact youth offending? Time will help answer some of these questions, and as they are answered, we will be able to see the role teen courts will play for future youth offenders.

Treatment Court Success Story: Teen Court

Name: Nathan J. Robinson

Location: Sarasota, Florida

Background: Nathan J. Robinson was a volunteer lawyer in the Sarasota, Florida, Teen Court in high school. Like many teen courts across the country, the Sarasota, Florida, Teen Court works with minors arrested for first-time offenses (such as shoplifting, vandalism, or fighting). These minors are provided with the option of going through traditional juvenile court or working with the teen court program to resolve their issues. Those who agree to participate in the Sarasota, Florida, Teen Court need to plead guilty, but their records are expunged once their participation is complete.

Sentencing in the teen court occurs as it would in a "real" court, with a jury of teen peers and an actual judge presiding over the proceedings. Prosecuting teen attorneys provide opening statements, reflecting the state's case, followed by the defendant's teen attorney providing their rebuttal. Defendants take the stand and give their testimony, and questions from both the prosecutor and defense are answered; this is followed by closing arguments. The jury then deliberates and a sentence, typically consisting of community service and serving as a juror on the teen court, is meted out; additionally, some may have to write a letter of apology to victims.

Nathan J. Robinson was a defense attorney in the Sarasota, Florida, Teen Court all throughout high school, working with his teen peer volunteers to go through a docket of cases. The program operated very much like a "real" courtroom requiring professionalism in dress and demeanor from the volunteers. Nathan found the experience a great one for professional development and growth and making friends throughout the experience. Perhaps even more importantly, the Sarasota Teen Court benefitted the participants by helping them avoid the juvenile justice system, getting support from peers, and many participants becoming success stories, such as one participant who went from a serious felony offender as a teenager to a practicing attorney as an adult.

What do teen courts do for participants? Teen courts are empowering for young people, offering some like Nathan J. Robinson the chance to develop the skills that will serve them in their adult careers. For those who participate as defendants, it gives them the opportunity to avoid potentially more punitive punishments of the juvenile justice system, especially lower income youth or minorities who may have been victims of institutionalized discrimination in the criminal justice system.

For more information on Nathan J. Robinson see: https://www.currentaffairs.org/2023/06/in-praise-of-the-teen-court.

References

Administrative Office of the US Courts. (n.d.). Facts and case summary—In re Gault. https://www.uscourts.gov/educationalresources/educational-activities/facts-and-case-summaryre-gault.

Akers, R. L. (2000). *Criminological theories: Introduction, evaluation, and application* (3rd ed.). Roxbury.

Barkan, S. (2001). *Criminology: A sociological understanding* (2nd ed.). Pearson.

Becker, H. (1963). *Outsiders: Studies in the sociology of deviance.* Free Press.

Bouchard, J., & Wong, J. S. (2017). A jury of their peers: A meta-analysis of the effectiveness of teen court on criminal recidivism. *Journal of Youth and Adolescence, 46*(7), 1472–1487. https://doi.org/10.1007/s10964-017-0667-7.

Butler-Mejia, K. (1998). *Seen but not heard: The role of voice in juvenile justice* (Unpublished master's thesis). George Mason University, Fairfax, VA.

Butts, J., & Buck, J. (2000). Teen courts: A focus on research. Juvenile Justice Bulletin. US Department of Justice, Office of Justice Programs. https://www.ojp.gov/pdffiles1/ojjdp/183472.pdf.

Butts, J., Buck Willison, J., & Coggeshall, M. (2002). *The impact of teen court on young offenders: Research report.* Urban Institute Policy Center.

Butts, J. A., & Ortiz, J. (2011). Teen courts: Do they work and why? *NYSBA Journal,* 18–21.

Center for Court Innovation. (2010). *Recommended practices for youth courts: A manual for New York youth court coordinators and practitioners.* The New York Bar Foundation. https://www.courtinnovation.org/sites/default/files/Youth_Court_Manual1.pdf.

DeFosset, A. R., Schooley, T. S., Abrams, L. S., Kuo, T., & Gase, L. N. (2017). Describing theoretical underpinnings in juvenile justice diversion: A case study explicating teen court program theory to guide research and practice. *Children and Youth Services Review, 73,* 419–429. https://doi.org/10.1016/j.childyouth.2017.01.005.

Dines, C. (2017). Minors in the major leagues: Youth courts hit a home run for juvenile justice. *Notre Dame Journal of Law, Ethics & Public Policy, 31*(1), 175–199. https://scholarship.law.nd.edu/ndjlepp/vol31/iss1/5/.

Evans, C. B., Smokowski, P. R., Barbee, J., Bower, M., & Barefoot, S. (2016). Restorative justice programming in teen court: A path to improved interpersonal relationships and psychological functioning for high-risk rural youth. *Journal of Rural Mental Health*, 40(1), 15–30. https://doi.org/10.1037/rmh0000042.

Farrington, D. (1986). Age and crime. In M. Tonry (Ed.), *The handbook on crime and punishment* (pp. 241–268). Oxford University Press.

Gase, L. N., Schooley, T., DeFosset, A., Stoll, M. A., & Kuo, T. (2016). The impact of teen courts on youth outcomes: A systematic review. *Qualitative Review*, 1, 51–67. https://doi.org/10.1007/s40894-015-0012-x.

Laundra, K., Rodgers, K., & Zapp, H. (2013). Transforming teens: Measuring the effects of restorative justice principles in a teen court setting. *Juvenile & Family Court Journal*, 64(4), 21–34. https://doi.org/10.1111/jfcj.;2012.

LoGalbo, A. P. (1998). *Is teen court a fair and effective juvenile crime diversion program?* (Unpublished undergraduate thesis). University of South Florida, New College, Tampa, FL.

Mason, R. J. (2019). Reducing recidivism rates: Teen court solution in Kankakee County. Governors State University. All Capstone Projects. https://opus.govst.edu/capstones/526/.

McNeece, A. P., Falconer, M. K., Bryant, C., & Shader, M. (1996). *Hernando County Teen Court: Evaluation of 1996 continuation grant activity.* Florida State University. Institute for Health and Human Services Research.

Miller, H. V. (2008). Restorative justice and youth courts: A new approach to delinquency prevention. *Sociology of Crime, Law, and Deviance*, 11, 189–205.

Minor, K. L., Wells, J. B., Soderstrom, I. R., Bingham, R., & Williamson, D. (1999). Sentence completion and recidivism among juveniles referred to teen courts. *Crime and Delinquency*, 45, 467–480. https://doi.org/10.1177/0011128799045004004.

National Association of Youth Courts. (n.d.). https://youthcourt.net/.

National Research Council (2013). National Research Council Committee on Assessing Juvenile Justice Reform, Committee on Law and Justice, Division of Behavioral and Social Sciences and Education [National Research Council]. *Reforming juvenile justice: A developmental approach.* Washington DC: The National Academies Press.

Nellis, A. (2011). Addressing the collateral consequences of convictions for young offenders. *The Champion*. National Association of Criminal Defense Lawyers. https://www.sentencingproject.org/wpcontent/uploads/2016/01/Addressing-the-CollateralConsequences-of-Convictions -for-Young-Offenders.pdf.

Norris, M., Will, S., & Kim, C. (2011). Smells like teen spirit: Evaluating a Midwestern teen court. *Crime & Delinquency, 57*(2), 199–221. https://doi.org/10.1177/0011128709354037.

Patrick, S., & Marsh, R. (2005). Juvenile diversion: Results of a 3-year experimental study. *Criminal Justice Policy Review, 16*, 59–73. https://doi.org/10.1177/0887403404266584.

Pickett, R. S. (1969). House of refuge: Origins of juvenile reform in New York State, 1815–1857. Syracuse University Press. https://doi.org/10.2307/j.ctv64h7hd.

Povitsky, W. (2005). *Teen court: Does it reduce recidivism?* (Unpublished master's dissertation). University of Maryland, College Park, MD. https://drum.lib.umd.edu/bitstream/handle/1903/3274/umi-umd-3102.pdf;jsessionid=08FAEB10DBCB4BE6F35DBCA6F82153A9?sequence=1.

Puzzanchera, C. (2022). *Juvenile justice statistics: National Report Series fact sheet, August 2022.* https://ojjdp.ojp.gov/publications/trendsin-youth-arrests.pdf.

Salvatore, C. (2018). *Sex, crime, drugs, and just plain stupid behaviors: The new face of young adulthood in America.* Palgrave Macmillan.

Schmalleger, F., & Marcum, C. D. (2020). Juvenile justice: An active learning approach, SAGE, Los Angeles, CA.

Schneider, J. (2008). *Youth courts: An empirical update and analysis for further organizational and research needs.* NCJ Number 222592. Office of Juvenile Justice and Delinquency Prevention. https://ojjdp.ojp.gov/library/publications/youth-courtsempirical-update-and-analysis-future-organizational-andresearch.

Schwalbe, C., Gearing, R., MacKenzie, M., Brewer, K., & Ibrahim, R. (2012). A meta-analysis of experimental studies of diversion programs for juvenile offenders. *Clinical Psychology Review, 32*, 26–33. https://doi.org/10.1177/2F0044118X87018003005.

Scott, E. S., Duell, N., & Steinberg, L. (2018). Brain development, social context and justice policy. *Washington University Journal of Law &*

Policy, 57. Columbia Public Law Research Paper NO. 14-578. https://scholarship.law.columbia.edu/faculty_scholarship/2087.

Shulman, E. P., Steinberg, L. D., & Piquero A. R. (2013). The age-crime curve in adolescence and early adulthood is not due to age differences in economic status. *Journal of Youth and Adolescence, 42*(6), 848–60. https://doi.org/10.1007/s10964-013-9950-4.

Sprague, W. (1915). *Blackstone commentaries, abridged* (9th ed.). Calaghan.

Stickle, W. P., Connell, N. M., Wilson, D. M., & Gottfredson, D. (2008). An experimental evaluation of teen courts. *Journal of Experimental Criminology, 4,* 137–163.

SRA Associates. (1995). *Teen court evaluation of 1994 activities and goals: Characteristics, backgrounds, and outcomes of program referrals.* SRA Associates.

Steffensmeier, D., & Streifel, C. (1991). The distribution of crime by age and gender across three historical periods 1935, 1960, 1985. *Social Forces, 69,* 869–894. https://doi.org/10.2307/2579479.

Steinberg, L. (2008). A social neuroscience perspective on adolescent risk-taking. *Development Review, 28*(1), 78–106. https://doi.org/10.1016/j.dr.2007.08.002.

Stone, E. (2011). With the right kind of peer pressure, teen courts provide 2nd change for youth offenders. Noozhawk. https://www.noozhawk.com/article/062011_teen_court.

Thompson, K. C., & Morris, R. J. (2016). History of the juvenile justice system. In *Juvenile Delinquency and Disability.* Advancing responsible adolescent development. Springer. https://doi.org/10.1007/978-3-319-29343-1_5.

Washington State Institute for Public Policy. (2019). Teen courts (vs. traditional juvenile court processing). https://www.wsipp.wa.gov/BenefitCost/Program/970.

Zimring, R. E. (2005). *American juvenile justice.* Oxford University Press.

CHAPTER 10

Prostitution Courts: Overview

The focus of this chapter, sex workers, are a unique population relative to those who we have looked at thus far. Some consider sex workers victims of their life circumstances, abusive relationships, or the machinations of pimps. Others consider sex work in general a victimless crime, failing to see or consider the underlying reasons why those working as prostitutes or in other types of sex work are doing such work. Throughout the bulk of the later portions of the twentieth century and into the twenty-first, a punitive approach was applied to prostitution that failed to consider the individual prostitute's experiences with trafficking and sexual exploitation (Muftic & Updegrove, 2019). The fundamental limitation to taking a strictly punitive approach is that it fails to address why individuals become involved in prostitution in the first place, such as childhood sexual abuse (Abramovich, 2005; Wilson & Widom, 2008), substance abuse, or addiction (Clarke et al., 2012; Young et al., 2000). Without addressing the underlying causes of prostitution, those involved in prostitution end up in an endless cycle of arrest and recidivism (Blakey et al., 2017). A variety of issues ranging from emotional and financial to physical harm to individual prostitutes, as well as their communities, are the long-term consequences that result when the causes of prostitution are not addressed (Muftic & Updegrove, 2019). Over time, the criminal justice system has recognized the limitations inherent in applying a punitive approach to addressing prostitution, and has looked to diversion and treatment courts to address the issues underlying involvement in the commercial sex trade (Miner-Romanoff, 2017; Shdaimah & Bailey-Kloch, 2014) and as with the other forms of treatment courts like drug and reentry courts, services typically included in prostitution courts involve education, employment, housing, counseling, and substance abuse treatment (Muftic & Updegrove, 2019).

Prostitution courts have proven a popular approach, with more than twenty prostitution courts and a minimum of eight adult-based prostitution programs in the United States by the middle of the second decade of the twenty-first century (Huddleston & Marlowe, 2011; Legislative Budget Board Staff [LBBS], 2016; Mueller, 2012). The first prostitution court was established in 1993 in Midtown Community Court in New York City (Quinn, 2005). There are a variety of different ways prostitution courts operate. Some employ community-based outpatient programs (Wahab, 2006), others act as pre-sentencing or court-monitored diversion courts (Leon & Shdaimah, 2012; Wahab, 2005), and further some programs drop charges while other programs do not (Muftic & Updegrove, 2019). The lack of standardization in format and structure in prostitution courts makes coming to a consensus about their effectiveness challenging, as well as identifying limitations challenging (we will examine both later in the chapter). Regardless of the approach of the prostitution court, these programs all seek to find a balance between punishment and treatment, with the ultimate goal of addressing the causes of prostitution and helping the prostituted individual desist (Shdaimah, 2010).

The purpose of prostitution courts is to provide prostituted defendants the chance to receive court-supervised, community-based services instead of incarceration (Blakey et al., 2017). Evidence suggests that prostitution courts have benefits such as cost savings for taxpayers provided through the diversion of prostituted defendants from jails and prisons and other forms of community supervision. Below we will examine how prostitution court programs are structured, the expansion of these programs to incorporate human trafficking, the theoretical orientation of prostitution courts, evidence that demonstrates the effectiveness and limitations of these programs, areas of future research, and concluding remarks.

Prostitution Court Structure

As with other treatment court programs examined in this book (e.g., drug courts, reentry courts), there is no standardized model for prostitution courts. In this section, two program models will be presented to help provide a sense of how prostitution courts are structured and operated. The first program we will examine is the PRIDE (Positive Recovery Intensive Diversion Experience), which started in January 2009 as a pilot program and in 2010 became a full-time program in Dallas County, Texas (Mueller, 2012). The PRIDE court program follows the structure of the National Association of Drug Court Professionals' model. Like most drug courts, the treatment team comprises the judge, service providers, district attorney, case manager, and counselors (Mueller, 2012). Participants in the program are referred through the Prostitution Diversion Initiative to PRIDE Court, but a significant portion of the program comes from jail after being arrested for prostitution. Once participants are screened and deemed eligible for the program, they must agree to participate voluntarily; if the program is completed, misdemeanor prostitution charges are dropped (Mueller, 2012). As with most treatment courts, PRIDE Court aims to assist the participant with housing employment, reuniting with family, and to get treatment for substance abuse problems (Mueller, 2012, pp. 29–29). Eligibility is open to males, females, and transgender persons. Potential participants cannot have a violent offending history, face felony charges, or be on probation or parole.

The PRIDE Court program has six different phases and is individualized for program participation; it generally takes about one year to complete the program. Below is a list and description of each phase:

- **Phase I: Inpatient Treatment/Stabilization (0–2 months in the program):** Participants attend inpatient substance abuse treatment during this phase. They attend court every Friday. Any required medications are provided, and urine tests are taken.
- **Phase II: Transitional Housing/Outpatient Treatment (2–4 months in the program):** In the second phase of the PRIDE program, the participant spends 60 days in housing provided by the PRIDE Court team. Intensive and supportive outpatient therapy starts at this phase with the inpatient

treatment provider. As in phase 1, participants report to the court every Friday and case managers weekly. In addition, individual counseling is provided once a week with the court counselor and weekly group sessions; this may include AA and NA meetings (and meetings with sponsors). During phase 2, job searches, education, reuniting with family, obtaining ID and other official documentation, and urine tests occur.

- **Phase III: Independent Living (4–9 months in the program):** At this phase, program participants are provided individual housing through service providers or return to their family home if possible. In addition, they must find employment, get their GED and meet other education goals, and reunite with their children. Alcoholics Anonymous (AA) and Narcotics Anonymous (NA) meetings continue, as well as contact with sponsors. They must report to the court every Friday, to their case manager once a week, and attend individual and group counseling weekly. Participants are subjected to random urine tests during this phase.
- **Phase IV: Graduation Phase (9–12 months in the program):** During this phase, participants report to the court every other Friday, to their case manager every other week, attend individual counseling every other week, and must attend aftercare groups with court counselors once a week. Participants must also maintain sobriety, maintain stable housing and employment, and are subject to random urine tests.
- **Phase V: Graduation:** Participants in this phase will have spent a minimum of one year in the program. At this stage, they have completed all counseling, are employed or in school, and must live independently.
- **Phase VI: Alumni Group:** At this point, former participants are the program alum group members. Attending court sessions voluntarily, former participants are provided the opportunity to mentor active participants; former participants are invited to attend holiday gatherings.

Source: Mueller, 2012, p. 29.

Another program phase structure provided by Mueller (2012) is that of Project DAWN, a treatment court targeting female survivors of commercial sexual exploitation located in Philadelphia, Pennsylvania. A collaborative process between the Philadelphia Municipal Court, the Philadelphia County District Attorney, the Office of Adult Probation, and the Defenders Association refers potential participants. Those who agree to participate in the program sign a contract that diverts them from the traditional criminal justice processing in Philadelphia into DAWN Court. Those who enter Project DAWN enter a plea of nolo contendere (no contest) before the Project DAWN Court (PDC) judge. If accepted, the program participant is put on PDC for probation without a verdict for one year (the typical length of the PDC program) (Mueller, 2012, p. 31). PDC eligibility conditions include having an open case for prostitution or a related offense, having no violence convictions, having at least three prior cases related to prostitution, meeting clinical criteria for substance abuse and mental health treatment, living in Philadelphia County, or being homeless in Philadelphia, being eligible for Medicaid, and agreeing to comply with PDC rules and regulations (Mueller, 2012, pp. 31–32). Upon successful completion of the program, changes are dropped, and if the participant maintains a clear record for one year post PDC, they may be able to have their records expunged (Mueller, 2012, p. 31).

Project DAWN has a four-phase structure. Below is a list and description of each phase:

- **Phase I:** In this phase the women are typically referred to an inpatient substance abuse program, usually a co-occurring disorders treatment program. The goal of phase 1 is to provide treatment that focuses on trauma (typically an inpatient program serving females).
- **Phase II:** Based on each participant's circumstances, the women continue substance abuse treatment and may live in a sober living home, transitional housing unit, or a sober family member's home while getting outpatient treatment.
- **Phase III:** Within 100 days of this phase, sexual trauma therapy starts, which is the program's core focus. The participants are currently doing a combination of individual and group trauma therapy.

- During this phase, women are enrolled in weekly outpatient group therapy sessions with local service providers that specifically address how these women ended up in the sex trade, looking into their backgrounds to heal the intense traumas they have faced during their lives. This phase typically occurs 4 to 6 months after joining the program when they are sober and more stable. Finally, during phase 3, civil legal needs start to be addressed, as well as other goals, such as housing and family reunification.
- **Phase IV:** During this phase, trauma healing is ongoing. In addition, participants work with the program to understand their daily needs after graduation (including housing, mental health, education, employment, and physical health). When a participant completes the program, her cases brought into the court are dismissed with prejudice. If a PDC graduate is not rearrested within one year, charges will be expunged from her record.

Source: Mueller, 2012, p. 32–33.

We will now turn our attention to an offshoot of prostitution courts: sex or human trafficking courts. As stated above, prostitution courts employ a variety of models and structures (like other treatment courts) to varying degrees of success. Both the PRIDE court and Project DAWN provide examples of how prostitution courts may be structured and the context and goals of each phase.

Sex or Human Trafficking Courts

In recent years, there has been a reconceptualization of some prostitution courts or a reformulation of the prostitution court model as a more comprehensive understanding of how coercion or force is used to exploit women and others in commercial sex work (Kulig & Butler, 2019). In addition, concerns regarding sexually transmitted infections, the public outcry to protect females from exploitation from pimps, and the interest in addressing the commercial sex trade led to legislation targeting human trafficking, The Victims of Trafficking and Violence

Prevention Act of 2000 (TVPA), signed into law in late October 2000 by President Clinton (Kulig & Butler, 2019, p. 301).

The TVPA led to a reconceptualization for many, with terms like "prostitute," which lends itself to blaming the victim of exploitation (by conceptualizing the victim as an offender), changing into "trafficking," which views the victim as someone being exploited (Fernandez, 2013). This reconceptualization was critical, as it directed society towards treatment and prevention instead of punishment (Stolz, 2007). The focus on prevention and intervention seeks to rescue rather than punish victims for the commercial sex work they were forced to engage in. The criminal justice system, in turn, can focus efforts on punishing the traffickers instead of the victims (Kulig & Butler, 2019).

As there has been an increase in anti-trafficking policies and strategies across the United States, first responders have been provided more training on how to respond to these crimes (Rollins et al., 2017), and more funding has been provided for victim services (US Department of Justice, 2017). Part of this response has been the use of trafficking courts to address the distinct needs of victims of these crimes. The purpose of these programs is to utilize the treatment-oriented approach to address the ordeals the victims have suffered, including any crimes they may have committed while being exploited (Office for Victims of Crime, n.d.).

In their 2019 study, Kulig and Butler identified 34 trafficking-related courts in 10 states, including Texas, Delaware, Florida, California, Michigan, Tennessee, Ohio, Pennsylvania, Illinois, and the District of Columbia (Kulig & Butler, 2019, pp. 305–306). As with other treatment-oriented courts, there is not a standard model of trafficking courts, but there are many overlapping features from program to program. Trafficking courts are often created due to the interest of the courts, which seek to work with identified or at-risk victims to provide them with rehabilitation and support services. Given the nature of the interactions with the courts and other justice agencies, actors within the criminal justice system may identify victim-defendants (Kulig & Butler, 2019). The enrollment process varies from court to court—some employ trafficking risk assessment tools to identify potential participants (e.g., Eleventh Judicial Circuit of Florida, 2017). Others allow potential participants to apply for the program (The County of Fresno, California, n.d.). Like prostitution courts, most programs will not take on participants with violent or felony convictions or histories (Kulig & Butler, 2019).

Once participants are identified, there are general criteria they must agree to in order to enroll in the program. Some programs require participants to plead guilty to their original charges (e.g., Parker & Pizzio, 2017), and agree to specific program requirements and schedules such as weekly meetings (e.g., Liles et al., 2016). Other programs call on participants to work with police to prosecute their traffickers (e.g., California Courts, 2014). If participants agree to requirements, they are typically offered services like those in other treatment courts, with the goal of "graduating" the program and having their charges expunged (Luminais & Lovell, 2018), and some programs may even forgive fines or forego court costs (e.g., Fishman, 2018). Those who fail to meet program requirements may be placed on probation, returned to traditional court proceedings, or given the sentence they would have faced if they had not been diverted to the trafficking court (Luminais & Lovell, 2018; Read, 2016). Evaluations of sex or human trafficking courts have been limited, and evidence has been mixed to date (Kendis, 2019). However, research may find that these programs have utility in assisting victims of commercial sex trafficking and related crimes. Looking at the more general prostitution court effectiveness may help provide some insights into sex or human trafficking courts. Before we turn our attention to the effectiveness of prostitution courts we need to first understand the theoretical grounding of these programs, which may provide a better understanding of how they work and the factors that we need to consider when examining them.

Prostitution Court
Theoretical Orientation

Philosophically, prostitution courts, as well as sex and human trafficking courts, are grounded in therapeutic jurisprudence. As discussed in previous chapters, therapeutic jurisprudence involves using the courts to provide treatment and support, with judges providing supervision and support (as well as other members of the courtroom workgroup) to assist with addressing the underlying reasons an individual is offending. Further, programs grounded in therapeutic jurisprudence seek to provide direction and support so program participants can address substance abuse issues, financial issues, mental health issues, housing, education, and employment.

Scholarship to date has provided little direct discussion of the theoretical orientation of prostitution courts or their variants. However, there is evidence of the applicability of social bond theory, which argues that attachments to peers, education, and family help prevent delinquency and offending behaviors because of the increased informal and external control these attachments provide (Hirschi, 1969). For example, Schweig and colleagues

(2012) discussed a participant in Midtown Community Court in Manhattan Services to Access Resources and Safety program (STARS) named Lizzie, who stated, "With the help and the support of Midtown Community Court, I made some wonderful steps" (p. 6). In another comment discussing the importance of meetings with the team and how the judge (and the courtroom workgroup) provide a support system that helps prostituted women end connections with traffickers and pimps Lizzie stated, "For me being in front of the Midtown judge was a great eye opener, he gave me another chance" (Schweig et al., 2012, p. 8). What both of these quotations demonstrate is the influence of the social bonds participants build with judges and the courtroom workgroup which may help provide the support and guidance needed to succeed in prostitution courts.

Some have suggested that harm reduction motivates prostitution and human trafficking court (Kendis, 2019). Harm reduction is the theory grounded in social justice that looks at dangerous behaviors such as substance use and sex work, and approaches them from a nonjudgmental perspective. Incorporating a variety of health and social services, harm reduction seeks to provide support across a variety of areas without cessation of the targeted behavior (e.g., substance use) as a requirement (Harm Reduction International, n.d.). From a harm reduction perspective, we can see prostitution or sex trafficking courts supporting participants as they disengage from illegal or harmful behaviors in a similar manner to drug courts and other treatment courts. The idea of providing services and support, while a participant in a prostitution or sex trafficking program is provided tools to reduce the harms associated with commercial sex work, and ideally working towards the individual no longer engaging in sex work, while transitioning to legal employment, housing, and other program-identified goals, could be a valid conceptualization of the harm reduction strategy as it could apply to prostitution and sex treatment courts. As we turn our attention to the effectiveness of treatment courts focusing on commercial sex workers, it is worth noting that there is a need for more expansion and development of theoretical approaches and inquiries. For example, life course theory, with its focus on turning points and transitions, could provide an explanation for why specific life events (e.g., teen pregnancy, parental abuse/neglect) could lead a young person into sex work.

Prostitution Courts: Do They Work?

Evidence Supporting the Effectiveness of Prostitutions Courts

Scholars like Muftic and Updegrove (2019) have pointed out evidence regarding the effectiveness of treatment courts outside of drug courts. While fewer studies have explored the effectiveness of prostitution courts (and sex and human trafficking courts) relative to drug courts, there are some studies that suggest they may assist participants across multiple areas, as well as identify key factors that influence successful programmatic outcomes. For example, Miner-Romanoff (2017) evaluated the Changing Actions to Change Habits (CATCH) program in Franklin County, Columbus, Ohio. Serving human trafficking victims involved in prostitution, this two-year treatment-oriented program yielded several positive outcomes for participants and the criminal justice system. Participants in the program experienced reduced rates of recidivism after being in the CATCH program. As measured by the number of days in jail, the study found that, on average, those who completed the CATCH program spent 0 to 4 days in jail, compared to those who were unsuccessful in completing the program (who spent 20 to 24 days in jail) (Miner-Romanoff, 2017). Other metrics of participant success, such as living conditions, also were improved. Another metric is engaging in education, vocational training, or volunteering. Those who completed the CATCH program during the years 2009 through 2013 had various indicators of successful engagement in education or vocational training, being employed, or volunteering within one year of successful completion of the program, with almost 78% enrolled in education or vocational training, volunteering or employed.

The results of the CATCH program provide a notable example of the potential benefits of treatment courts for commercial sex workers. Regarding benefits for the criminal justice system, Carmen (2010) (cited in Miner-Romanoff, 2017) reported that the CATCH program costs approximately $18,000.00 per year, relative to approximately $200,000.00 for a year in jail. In a more recent study, Muftic and Updegrove (2019) examined the effectiveness of Survivors Acquiring Freedom and Empowerment (SAFE) Court, a prostitution treatment court in Harris County, Texas. The results of the study revealed those who participated in SAFE Court were less likely to be rearrested relative to those who did not participate in the program at a bivariate level (though this was not found at a multivariate level).

As we turn our attention to evidence that challenges the effectiveness of prostitution courts and other treatment courts that work with commercial sex workers it is important to note that research in these areas is ongoing. Future research will likely identify additional evidence regarding the effectiveness of these programs and will be reported in updated editions of this and similar books.

Evidence Challenging the Effectiveness of Prostitution Courts

Unlike other forms of treatment courts, there is less evidence to support the effectiveness of prostitution, human trafficking, and other program models targeting commercial sex workers. Evidence is unclear, and may be rooted in how programmatic success is measured. A key challenge may be that judges in these courts may be reluctant to use sanctions like incarceration for victims of sex trafficking, as these individuals may be under the influence of an abuser or pimp (Kendis, 2019, p. 833). If sanctions are not being applied in the same manner as they would be in other treatment court programs, it makes it hard to gauge the effectiveness of a program and if it is meeting its goals of reducing recidivism.

Another key issue with discussing the outcomes of prostitution and human trafficking courts is that there seems to be very little data on outcomes. Various programs often note that there needs to be better data on victim outcomes, yet it does not seem to be collected (Kulig & Butler,

2019, p. 313). Without ample outcome data reported, making assessments regarding the utility of programs is limited at best.

While evidence of the ineffectiveness of prostitution and human trafficking courts is limited, there are a variety of criticisms applied to these programs. First is the notion of under inclusion. These courts mainly focus on cisgender female victims. This may be the result of policing practices or the perceptions of other actors involved in the court programs who may only view a specific type of person as an "appropriate" victim for the treatment courts, or may be because males and transgendered persons avoid participation due to fear of stigma, transphobia, or other negative influences (Kendis, 2019). Another criticism of prostitution court is the focus on prostitution charges, which may overlook victims forced to commit other crimes trafficking victims are pressured to commit. However, they may not be captured in the scope of prostitution-related charges, thereby overlooking potential victims (Kendis, 2019). Perhaps most important is the need for continued evaluations to examine better the outcomes related to these programs, and to identify not only what works but also what does not.

Future Research

Since prostitution courts began in the early 1990s, they have become a strategy to provide support to prostitution-involved clients. Largely serving women, these programs have some support for their utility. Studies have explored a variety of samples, but most are largely female. Future studies should incorporate more studies exploring the effectiveness of prostitution courts for males.

Also, in need of further research is the role of factors like social bonds built between clients of prostitution courts and members of the treatment court workgroup. For example, the role of judges, which have been found to be critical in studies examining other types of treatment courts such as drug and reentry courts, needs to be more studied to explore their utility for prostitution courts. If these factors are potentially as critical for the success of these programs as they are with other forms of treatment courts, studying them may provide an opportunity to develop recommendations to increase the effectiveness of prostitution courts and related programs. Second, the applicability of various theoretical orientations to prostitution and sex or human trafficking courts needs to be expanded. Other treatment courts, such as drug courts, have applied various theoretical orientations (e.g., developmental life course theory) to their programs. However, little research dealing with the various treatment courts targeting commercial sex workers seems to have the same theoretical focus and inquiry level. A more comprehensive understanding of the theoretical underpinnings of these programs may help guide modifications to provide more effective programming strategies. Next, studies need to examine the role of decriminalizing prostitution and its potential impact on prostitution court outcomes; this may interact with legislation decriminalizing some drugs (e.g., marijuana) and need to be incorporated into studies looking at the decriminalization of prostitution. Another area which needs examination is the utility of prostitution courts for those engaging in sex work via non-traditional venues. There is an endless array of "hook up" apps where there are those willing to exchange money for sex. Are these individuals the same as those engaging in street-level sex work? Or are they simply looking to make extra cash? How does the criminal justice system respond (or not respond) to their app-based solicitations? If they were arrested, would diversion and treatment programs like prostitution courts be necessary or effective? These are just some of the questions that need to be examined when looking at non-traditional sex workers. Finally, as more factors are identified for why individuals go into prostitution, studies will need to incorporate these into new research. Findings in the above-mentioned areas may help improve the overall effectiveness of these programs and help meet the needs of an ever-changing population.

Conclusions

In this chapter, we have looked at a variety of treatment court programs seeking to provide treatment and support services for commercial sex workers. Prostitution, sex, and human trafficking courts all ultimately seek to assist those forced, by pimps, traffickers, or life circumstances, into one of the most risky and dangerous professions. A large portion of the research in this area to date has focused on female participants in these programs, yet slowly but surely, we are seeing more focus on male, transgender individuals, and members of the lesbian, gay, and bisexual communities who may also be engaged in sex work.

As discussed here, treatment courts offer sex workers potential solutions. Support in housing, drug treatment, education, employment, and family therapy are just a few of the areas in which treatment courts can give support and direction. The courtroom treatment group itself may be a resource of support, helping program participants reach goals by mentoring them as they reach programmatic milestones.

Evidence to date about the effectiveness of treatment court to address commercial sex workers is more limited than in the case of other treatment courts (e.g., drug courts), but there is some suggestion regarding their effectiveness and utility to assist those involved with commercial sex work. As time moves on and programs continue to innovate and change, we may see other treatment courts like drug courts and mental health courts absorb the populations which are currently served by prostitution courts. Alternatively, we may see prostitution and related courts continue to refine their mission and target wider populations more explicitly to provide services to a broader group of those involved in commercial sex work. In sum, prostitution and related court programs are an innovative approach to addressing sex workers and their challenges. More research is needed to examine their effectiveness, develop the most effective model, and understand the theoretical roots of these programs.

Treatment Court Success Story: Prostitution/Trafficking Court

Name: "Tammie"

Location: New Castle, Delaware

Background: Like many participants in the Delaware Trafficking Court, Tammie is a survivor of sex trafficking who has struggled with substance abuse. Many participants in the Delaware Trafficking Court were involved in prostitution and face a variety of related charges, including walking on a highway without a light, loitering for drugs, and shoplifting. Most of these charges result in fines, though few can pay them.

The Delaware Trafficking Court worked to support women on probation, many of whom were likely involved in prostitution. The court helps provide housing assistance, legal aid services, and community-based mental health treatment. "Tammie," who had been arrested for shoplifting, initially viewed the court as a way to avoid jail, but eventually spent five years in the program.

Prostitution/Trafficking Court Can Work! "Tammie" graduated from the Delaware Trafficking Court Program, receiving flowers, a team jersey for the Pittsburg Steelers, her favorite team, and graduation certificate from the program.

For more information on Tammie see: https://whyy.org/articles/a-judicial-approach-to-sex-trafficking-prostitution-delawares-sex-trade-part-4/.

References

Abramovich, E. (2005). Childhood sexual abuse as a risk factor for subsequent involvement in sex work: A review of empirical findings. *Journal of Psychology and Human Sexuality, 17*(1–2), 131–146. https://doi.org/10.1300/J056v17n01_08.

Blakey, J. M., Mueller, D. J., & Ritchie, M. (2017). Strengths and challenges of a prostitution court model. *Justice Systems Journal, 38*(4), 364–379. https://doi.org/10.1080/0098261X.2017.1327335.

California Courts. (2014, January 15). *Handbook for STAR ("Succeed Through Achievement and Resilience")*. http://www.courts.ca.gov/documents/LosAngelesSTARCourt-ProgramOutline_ikc.pdf.

Carmen, B. (2010). Saving money, changing lives. *Columbus Dispatch.* http://www.dispatch.com/content/stories/local/2010/05/30/saving-money-changing-lives.html.

Clarke, R. J., Clarke, E. A., Roe-Sepowitz, D., & Fey, R. (2012). Age at entry into prostitution: Relationship to drug use, race, suicide, education level, childhood abuse, and family experiences. *Journal of Human Behavior in the Social Environment, 22*(3), 270–289. https://doi.org/10.1080/10911359.2012.655583.

The County of Fresno, California. (n.d.). Specialty programs. https://www.co.fresno.ca.us/departments/publicdefender/juvenile-delinquency/juvenile-specialty-courts.

Eleventh Judicial Circuit of Florida. (2017). *GRACE court benchbook 2017.* Eleventh Judicial Court. https://www.flcourts.org/content/download/217037/1968168/GRACE_Court_Benchbook.pdf.

Fernandez, K. M. (2013). Victims or criminals? The intricacies of dealing with juvenile victims of sex trafficking and why the distinction matters. *Arizona State Law Journal, 45*, 859–890.

Fishman, M. (2018). Human trafficking court shut down, to be merged with other treatment courts in Delaware. *The News Journal.* https://www.delawareonline.com/story/news/2018/05/05/ human-trafficking-court-merged-other-treatment-courts/570948002/.

Harm Reduction International. (n.d.). What is harm reduction? https://www.hri.global/what-is-harm-reduction.

Hirschi, T. (1969). *Causes of delinquency.* Berkeley, CA: University of California Press.

Huddleston, W., & Marlowe, D. B. (2011). *Painting the current picture: A national report card on drug courts and other problems solving court programs in the United States.* National Drug Court Institute.

Kendis, B. (2019). Human trafficking and prostitution courts: Problem solving or problematic? *Case Western Law Review, 69*(3), 805–841.

Kulig, T. C., & Butler, L. C. (2019). From "whores" to "victims": The rise and status of sex trafficking courts. *Victims & Offenders, 14*(3), 299–321. https://doi.org/10.1080/15564886.2019.1595242.

Legislative Budget Board Staff (LBBS). (2016). *Specialty courts.* https://www.lbb.texas.gov/Documents/Publications/Issue_Briefs/3015_Specialty_Courts_0701.pdf.

Leon, C., & Shdaimah, C. S. (2012). Justifying scrutiny: State power in prostitution diversion programs. *Journal of Poverty, 16*(3), 250–273. https://doi.org/10.1080/10875549.2012.695539.

Liles, B. D., Blacker, D. M., Landini, J. L., & Urquiza, A. J. (2016). A California multidisciplinary juvenile court: Serving sexually exploited and at-risk youth. *Behavioral Sciences & the Law, 34*, 234–245. https://doi.org/10.1002/bsl.2230.

Luminais, M., & Lovell, R. (2018). *Process and outcome evaluation of Cuyahoga County's safe harbor project.* Case Western Reserve University, Cleveland, OH. https://case.edu/socialwork/begun/sites/case.edu.begun/files/2018-10/Safe-Harbor-Project-Report.pdf.

Miner-Romanoff, K. (2017). CATCH court: Changing actions to change habits—A preliminary evaluation study. *Journal of Human Trafficking, 3*(2), 136–162. https://doi.org/10.1080/23322705.2016.1194039.

Mueller, D. (2012). *Treatment courts and court-affiliated diversion projects for prostitution courts in the United States.* Chicago Coalition for the Homeless. https://chicagohomeless.issuelab.org/resource/treat-mentcourts-and-court-affiliated-diversion-projects-forprostitu-tion-in-the-united-states.html.

Muftic, L. R., & Updegrove, A. H. (2019). The effectiveness of a prob-lem-solving court for individuals charged with misdemeanor pros-titution in Harris County, Texas. *Journal of Offender Rehabilitation*, 58(2), 117–132. https://doi.org/10.1080/10509674.2018.1562506.

Parker, M., & Pizzio, C. (2017). *Effectiveness of a prostitution diversion program: RESET* (Unpublished master's thesis). California State University, Sacramento, CA. https://scholarworks.calstate.edu/downloads/0k225b092.

Quinn, M. C. (2005). Revisiting Anna Moscowitz's Kross's critique of New York City's women's court: The continued problem of solving the "problem" of prostitution with specialized criminal courts. *Fordham Urban Law Journal*, 33(2), 101–160.

Read, Z. (2016). A judicial approach to sex trafficking, prostitution -Delaware's sex trade, part 4. *Why*. https://whyy.org/articles/a-judicialapproach-to-sex-trafficking-prostitution-delawares-sex-trade-part -4/.

Rollins, R., Gribble, A., Barrett, S. E., & Powell, C. (2017). Who is in your waiting room? Health care professionals as culturally responsive and trauma-informed responders to human trafficking. *AMA Journal of Ethics*, 19, 63–71. https://doi.org/10.1001/journalofethics.2017.19.1.pfor2-1701.

Schweig, S., Malangone, M., & Goodman, M. (2012). *Prostitution diversion programs*. Center for Court Innovation. https://www.courtinnovation.org/publications/prostitution-diversion-programs.

Shdaimah, C. S. (2010). Taking a stand in a not-so-perfect world: What's a critical supporter of problem-solving courts to do? *University of Maryland Law Journal of* Race, Religion, Gender, and Class, 10(1). https://digitalcommons.law.umaryland.edu/rrgc/vol10/iss1/6/.

Shdaimah, C.S., & Bailey-Kloch, M. (2014). Can you help with that instead of putting me in jail? The Justice Systems Journal, 35 (3), 287–300.

Stolz, B. A. (2007). Interpreting the US human trafficking debate through the lens of symbolic politics. *Law & Policy*, 29, 311–338. https://doi.org/10.1111/j.1467-9930.2007.00257.x.

US Department of Justice. (2017, September 29). *Justice Department invests more than $47 million to combat human trafficking and assist victims* [Press release]. https://www.justice.gov/opa/pr/justice-departmentinvests-more-47-million-combat-human-trafficking-andassist-victims.

Wahab, S. (2005). Navigating mixed-theory programs: Lesson learned from a prostitution diversion project. *Affilia, 20*(2), 203–221. https://doi.org/10.1177/0886109905274571.

Wahab, S. (2006). Evaluating the usefulness of a prostitution diversion project. *Qualitative Social Work, 5*(1), 67–92.

Wilson, H. W., & Widom, C. S. (2008). An examination of risky sexual behavior and HIV in victims of child abuse and neglect: A 30-year follow up. *Health Psychology, 27*(2), 149–158. https://doi.org/10.1037/0278-6133.27.2.149.

Young, A. M., Boyd, C., & Hubbell, A. (2000). Prostitution, drug use, and coping with psychological distress. *Journal of Drug Issues, 30*(4), 789–800.

CHAPTER 11

Policy Applications/Implications for Policy and Change

Introduction

The current American criminal justice system is the result of over 200 years of the country's history and the influence of English Common Law. However, since the 1970s, we have seen the shift from due process to the crime control model, which calls for more focus on punishment and incarceration. The "get tough on crime" approach that accompanies the crime control model, spurred on by the war on drugs, is reflected in incarceration as one of the primary tools to deal with offenders. Popular with politicians who forever seek the favor of the fickle public, this model has resulted in a criminal justice system that so often locks offenders up. As we have seen throughout this book, the idea of "locking offenders up and throwing away the key," is popular but impractical. Most offenders will be released at some point either by their sentencing ending, parole, or other types of early release. When offenders are incarcerated, they are not the only ones who are punished; it's their children, spouses and partners, and communities who often suffer (Shlafer et al., 2013). This is not to say incarceration does not have value and there are not offenders who should be incarcerated, but the reality is that most who are incarcerated are there for non-violent offenses (often drug or related offenses) and would benefit, as would their communities and families, from treatment and diversion from the criminal justice system, rather than being immersed deeper in it. To put it another way, the typical offender has likely committed a non-violent drug offense, is often under the age of 25, and is frequently a racial/

ethnic minority. This person will likely not become a hardened criminal; in fact, they will most likely age out of crime by the time they are 30, as they marry, have children, and get full-time jobs, as these factors influence assimilation into the mainstream, non-criminal culture (Salvatore, 2018). Incarceration of these individuals, contrary to what most talking heads are saying on talk shows or posting on social media, does not make them better; it will likely make them worse, cutting them off from prosocial activities and peers, family members, current or potential employers, and others in the community who might act as mentors like teachers, coaches, or religious leaders.

Instead of locking up people for months or years in jails and prisons, what we need are solutions to help those who are off track, delving into drugs or crime, battling mental illness, trapped in the illegal trade of prostitution, struggling with domestic abuse and family challenges, or for those have been incarcerated, but now released, get the help and support they need instead of punishment. We have this solution in the form of treatment- or problem-oriented courts. Be it a drug court, mental health court, or reentry court, these programs can provide participants with the support and guidance they need to succeed. Treatment courts can help participants address why they committed a crime, such as lack of education, unemployment, mental health issues, family challenges, and substance abuse problems. Treatment courts can also help participants get their education, find a home, get their driver's license, attain medical insurance, open a checking account, establish credit, build a resume, and so many other day-to-day tasks so many take for granted. The support provided by judges, defense attorneys, prosecutors, and others who are part of the treatment court workgroups have been shown to help those in these programs succeed, and in doing so saving the criminal justice system time and money by providing participants in these programs a supportive environment where they are given help and treatment, instead of punitive treatment most have been given from the criminal justice system (Salvatore et al., 2020). In this chapter, we are going to explore how treatment courts may be used to change the criminal justice system and impact public policy in very real and practical ways that can benefit not only participants in these programs, but also the criminal justice system and general society.

General Benefits of Treatment Courts

Treatment-oriented or problem-oriented courts provide support for those with mental health, substance abuse, and other challenges who have been charged with non-violent offenses or convicted of a non-violent crime. These court programs are typically alternatives to traditional criminal justice processing, providing participants the opportunity to be provided treatment and support services in lieu of incarceration; usually participants receive an expungement of their sentence after being arrest free for a year after completion of the program (Salvatore et al., 2011). As examined throughout the previous chapters, treatment courts may reduce recidivism, provide cost savings relative to incarceration for taxpayers, help to increase public safety, and help successfully reintegrate offenders into society (Andrews & Bonta, 2010; Dowden, & Andrews, 2000). In addition to these benefits, treatment court programs may help participants maintain social bonds, avoid or reduce the stigma associated with incarceration, and help meet social justice goals that have become increasingly important in our culture and society. Unlike traditional criminal justice processing, which is rigid in its processing of offenders from adjudication through sentencing, treatment courts, grounded in the philosophy of therapeutic jurisprudence, seek to assist rather than punish, using a non-adversarial approach to working with participants in the program, using judicial actors as agents of therapeutic change (Redlich & Han, 2014). Let us now consider looking at some of the most critical areas of benefit in more detail.

Cost Savings

Perhaps more than any other benefit to treatment courts, the public and political leaders focus on the cost effectiveness of treatment courts. Spending or saving taxpayers' money will always get headlines; as such, the cost savings found by treatment courts is a critical area of benefit. For example, let us look at the cost effectiveness of drug courts, the most popular form of treatment courts relative to incarceration. A 2016 study by the Washington State Institute for Public Policy found it is around $5,000 to provide treatment for an adult via drug court and around

$2,200 for a juvenile. Over ten years these savings build as former offenders cease drug use and offending, at about $12,000 for adults and around $5,000 after ten years for juveniles. The savings can continue to build as time goes on (Washington State Institute for Public Policy, 2016a, 2016b). Evidence supporting the cost effectiveness of treatment courts also is found with other treatment courts such as mental health courts. In their 2015 study, Kubiak and colleagues examined the costs of treatment, arrest, and confinement 12 months after participation in a mental health court (MHC). The results of their study found that the total outcome costs per person for the 12 months after participating in the MHC those who successfully complete the program was $16,964, significantly different than the $32,258 of those who did not complete the program, as well as being significantly different than the comparison groups which cost $39,870 (Kubiak et al., 2015). The results of these studies support the cost effectiveness of treatment courts as an alternative to incarceration. It is critical to convey to the public and policymakers the value of these findings, as treatment courts can save taxpayers money and provide a viable alternative to traditional incarceration in jails and prisons.

Generally, people like to save money, and the cost is a critical measure of success of any treatment or prevention program targeting criminal justice populations. With evidence to support the cost savings associated with many types of treatment courts, policymakers, advocates, and scholars can argue for the expansion of these programs in communities where they are not present, as well as to areas and problems where the treatment court approach has not been applied.

Maintain Social Bonds

Throughout the preceding chapters we have seen, time and again, the effectiveness of treatment court programs in utilizing the social bonds built between participants and these programs, members of the treatment court workgroup, as well as relatives of participants and former graduates of these programs who act as mentors (Salvatore et al., 2011; Salvatore et al., 2020). Social bonds may be the key to the success of treatment courts, building the human connections and support structures critical for participant success in both the short and long term.

However, an additional component of these programs is that they allow participants to stay in communities where they can continue to work, attend school, spend time with friends and family, attend religious services, and engage with neighbors, community leaders, and day-to-day interactions with staff in stores, doctors' offices, and other businesses. These social bonds help integrate and attach someone to a community; as argued by social bond theory (Hirschi, 1969), the more bonded to conventional society an individual is, the less likely they are to engage in delinquency and crime. While it should be noted this is a somewhat simplified conceptualization of social bond theory, it does reflect the basic idea of the theory and makes intuitive sense, with the potential role of social bonds in treatment courts being reflected in examples from the empirical literature provided throughout this book.

It is the informal attachments and bonds in day-to-day life that are critical to weaving participants in treatment courts into the fabric of their communities, and the more connected they are, the less likely they are to engage in future offending behaviors. The fear of losing the prosocial attachments built in their lives with family, coworkers, teachers, friends, and so many others will act to deter behaviors that may risk these bonds, thereby keeping those who have participated in treatment court programs on a prosocial path. In addition, if participants in treatment courts can stay in the community they not only maintain the bonds mentioned above, but they are also there for their children. As studies have shown, children with parents who are incarcerated are more likely to experience a variety of adverse outcomes, including poorer school performance, substance use, and delinquency (Martin, 2017). Not only does it make sense for participants to stay in the community to support, bond to, and supervise their children in the short term, but it makes sense in the long term as well. After all, if their parents can find a way to work with the criminal justice system to resolve their problems to be productive members of society, their children stand a better chance of succeeding in the long run with their parents being present and acting as role models. Social capital is conveyed from generation to generation. If parents participate in treatment courts (instead of being incarcerated in jails and prisons) they may not only benefit themselves in the short term, but also benefit their children and potentially subsequent generations. Imagine a participant in a drug court, who instead of going to jail on a drug charge for a year goes to drug court where they are given guidance on attaining their college degree, assisted in developing a better resume, and guidance in applying for a better paying job. All of these potential aspects of a drug court could help the participants build social capital which they can then transfer to the next generation, helping to address some of the inequities and challenges in our society. If treatment courts can potentially help build social capital and help lift some out of poverty, then they may have more utility than just the short-term reductions in reoffending and relapses and associated cost savings. As such, treatment courts make sense to keep participants in the communities where they can make a difference in the lives of their families and communities, rather than warehouse them in prison where their lack of presence will weaken their families and communities, not strengthen them.

Avoiding Stigma

The idea that social bonds and attachments are a critical component of treatment court success has been a core theme of this book, and they are key elements of the success of treatment court programs. However, an additional factor, not explored in prior sections, has been the role of stigma. Scholars have argued that criminal offenders are a marginalized population that faces some of the highest levels of stigma (LeBel, 2012), who are seen to be responsible for their "criminal" identity, which may result in more negative treatment and outcomes due to this identity (Corrigan et al., 2003). Society has punished those who have a criminal label in a variety of ways. For example, former offenders may find they face restrictions in housing, employment, and other activities and aspects of mainstream society (Pogorzelski et al., 2005). In addition, many in the community tend to believe negative stereotypes of offenders, including that they are dangerous and unintelligent (Hirschfield & Piquero, 2010). To put it another way, those who attain the stigma of being a criminal offender by being arrested, sentenced, and incarcerated are likely to face the stigma or negative perceptions and stereotypes associated with being a criminal. These negative perceptions and stereotypes can lead to more formal challenges such as being eliminated from jobs due to organizational policies restricting the hiring of those with felony convictions or informal issues such as rejection from peers, neighbors, and family members due to having a criminal record or having served time in jail or prison.

Avoiding the stigma associated with being a criminal offender is critical to maintaining social bonds, finding employment, attaining housing, and achieving standing in one's community. Without the stigma of being a criminal offender, individuals engaging in day-to-day activities like getting an apartment, voting, and applying for a job don't face the same barriers. As social bonds with friends, family, and community members may be tenuous and subjected to outside influences such as the stigma surrounding being a criminal, it is critical to avoid individuals attaining this stigma. Treatment courts assist participants with avoiding stigma because instead of going to prison or jail, participants in treatment courts such as drug courts, mental health, or veteran's courts allow them to stay in the community. Treatment court programs not only divert participants away from incarceration, but also the intangible punishments like stigma.

Shift Towards Greater Social Justice

While certainly not a new area of concern, we have seen a marked increase in the interest in social justice outcomes for criminal justice populations from students, scholars, practitioners, and the general public in recent years. As many have become more informed about the costs and issues associated with incarceration, more and more have called for alternatives to incarceration. Further, the long and well-documented history of institutionalized discrimination in the criminal justice system has left many facing punishments from a system that penalizes them based on their demographic characteristics, such as gender, age, and race/ethnicity (Tonry & Melewski, 2008). The prevalence of black males and other marginalized groups in jails, prisons, death row, and so many other areas of the criminal justice system show that despite many changes and reforms, there are other solutions needed to assist criminal justice system populations.

Treatment courts can help the criminal justice system with solutions beyond incarceration and punishment, helping to address long-standing imbalances in society and the criminal justice system. Treatment courts may be one such reform; as examined throughout this book, we have seen examples of treatment courts that have worked with populations who in the past would have been subjected to the revolving door in and out of correctional facilities. Instead, programs like reentry courts have worked with these populations by having judges, prosecutors, and many other criminal justice system actors work with program participants to make prosocial changes, leading participants to employment, housing, and sustainable lifestyles without criminal offending.

Policy Recommendations

As we head towards the conclusion of this book, we need to consider how the programs and practices, as well as the benefits of various treatment courts, can be utilized more expansively to assist more potential participants. While not perfect, treatment courts are an alternative that may offer many the first opportunity to have the criminal justice system work with them instead of against them to reach their life goals. Below is a list of policy recommendations which can be drawn for the examinations of various treatment court models throughout this book.

Adoption of Standardized Models

As demonstrated throughout this book, various program models are utilized in treatment court programs. While most more or less follow the phased structure of drug courts, there can also be significant variation within the type of court program (e.g., drug courts) as well as in the various types of treatment courts (e.g., mental health courts, reentry courts, prostitution courts). It may be challenging or not practical to adopt a universal standardized treatment court model, as there may be significant variations in the needs of participants and the treatment services offered. For example, the needs of a participant in a veteran's court may be focused on providing mental health services, housing, and substance abuse treatment; a reentry court, on the other hand, would be focused on helping participants develop a resume, build credit, find employment and housing, and resolve any lingering issues around their criminal history such as fines. A more effective strategy would be for specific types of programs like drug courts to adopt standardized models based on evidence-based practices (EBP), which are effective at helping program participants reach goals such as reducing recidivism, finding employment, securing housing, and so forth.

By developing and promoting standardized models, treatment courts based on evidence-based practices grounded in empirical research programs can ensure they utilize the most effective practices for their clients and ideally yield better outcomes. Though it is important to note that no matter how much empirical/research-based evidence there is for a program model, there may be a need to adopt specifications that reflect regional cultural differences and meet the specific needs of the client population; that being said, a standardized model could be developed that could account for these differences. Standardized models within specific types of treatment courts (e.g., drug courts) could be promoted via professional associations such as the National Association of Drug Court Professionals, and organizations that reach multiple audiences such as the Academy of Criminal Justice Sciences, which hold events via national and regional conferences and associations, and state and federal agencies such as the National Institute of Justice.

Target Youth Populations:
Special Program Needs of Today's Youth

With each generation of young people, we see distinct needs, challenges, and characteristics. As our society has shifted (and will continue to shift), we have seen young people's maturation process change. A few generations ago (not that long ago in the grand scheme of our society), many married and had children soon after high school. Families could live a middle-class lifestyle with only a high school diploma, sometimes less. They could acquire affordable housing, automobiles, and other components of a successful lifestyle in our society. However, starting in the 1960s, society changed in various ways, including the shift from a manufacturing to a service economy, the delay of finishing education as more and more went to college, and the postponement of marriage and parenthood. These factors typically foster aging out of criminal offending (Salvatore, 2019). As a result, we have seen a new life course called emerging adulthood develop. Neither adolescence nor the young adulthood of the past, emerging adulthood is a distinct stage of the life course, characterized by experimentation with drugs and other forms of identity exploration that can lead young people into the criminal justice system (Salvatore, 2019).

Most behaviors emerging adults will engage in are typically not violent or predatory crimes. However, binge drinking and substance use may lead to arrest and incarceration. The treatment court model could be ideal for the emerging adult population. Utilizing a treatment approach, emerging adults need substance abuse treatment, mental health counseling and support services, and direction in education and career. An "emerging adult" court could help divert emerging adults from jails and prisons and onto prosocial paths. Scholars like Butts and Ortiz (2011) have argued for the potential benefits of teen courts in addressing the behavioral challenges of teenagers. An "emerging adult" court could build on the existing teen and juvenile drug court models, building support and treatment services to address the distinct needs of emerging adults. The use of an "emerging adult" court could be particularly beneficial for colleges and universities to integrate or house on site as these institutions typically have students engaging in behaviors common in emerging adulthood, including binge drinking, substance use, and low-level offending (such as being loud and rowdy in public).

Target Overlooked Populations: *LGBTQIA+ Populations*

As with emerging adults, there are other populations that could be targeted for diversion programs via the treatment court model. Lesbian, Gay, Bisexual, Transgendered, Questioning, Intersex, and Asexual (LGBTQIA+) populations have a high prevalence of risky and dangerous behaviors (see Gonzales & Henning-Smith, 2017) which include unsafe sexual practices, high levels of alcohol use and binge drinking, and high rates of substance use (Salvatore & Daftary-Kapur, 2020). While some of these behaviors (e.g., unsafe sex practices) would generally not come to the attention of the criminal justice system, high rates of drug and alcohol use could bring members of the LGBTQIA+ community to the attention of the criminal justice system. Further, there are high rates of intimate partner violence in the LGBTQIA+ community (see Stiles-Shields & Carroll, 2015) as well, making these populations an ideal target for the diversion offered by a treatment court.

As a historically overlooked and stigmatized population, the LGBTQIA+ community faces a wider variety of health and justice system related issues. Even as of this writing, the LGBTQIA+ community faces legislative restrictions on personal freedoms and the banning of drag performers in some venues and circumstances, members of the public calling for LGBTQIA+ persons to not be allowed to teach or work with young children, and continued negative stereotypes and prejudices, despite victories in areas such as marital rights. The LGBTQIA+ community has long faced discriminatory and hostile treatment from the criminal justice system, including harassment from police (Chauncey, 2019). A treatment court focused on the needs of the LGBTQIA+ community could provide support and treatment for issues related to substance abuse and addiction and address issues such as intimate partner violence by focusing on the unique needs and culture of this community.

Increasing Aftercare

Another area where treatment courts need more standardization is aftercare. Most programs typically require about a year of non-arrest or non-relapse after completion to have records expunged. Many programs offer former participants the opportunity to return to the program to act as mentors to current program members. I have seen firsthand the benefits mentoring can offer for past participants and current ones, and this could be adopted on a larger scale as part of an aftercare component of treatment courts. Not only would it provide current participants in the program the benefit of how the mentors achieved success in areas like employment, but it can also provide an opportunity for aftercare and support from the treatment program to the mentor. Program mentors could be required to be subjected to periodic evaluations or check-ins with treatment court program staff to identify any challenge areas that may have arisen and help refer them to services if needed. After all, recovery and desistance are often a process, not a complete stop, and providing former participants with the opportunity to receive support could help maintain desistance and prevent relapse.

While no standard length of aftercare is recommended for these programs, former participants would likely benefit from support for at least two to five years after program completion. In practice, providing ongoing support post program completion may prove challenging in the long term. Many treatment court programs work on limited budgets, with members of the treatment court teams volunteering their time. However, given the potential benefits, it may be worth pursuing additional grant funding or budget appropriations to ensure the success of participants long-term, not only for their benefit but the crime reduction benefit to the public, as well as the potential cost savings involved with incarceration in jails or prisons. Aftercare programs could be linked to free or low-cost support services that are pre-existing in communities, such as Alcoholics Anonymous or Narcotics Anonymous, to help bridge any service or support gaps for those who have completed treatment courts.

Conclusion

The treatment court model has shown significant promise across its various iterations. Cost savings, reductions in reoffending and relapse, avoiding stigma, maintaining social bonds, and achieving social justice goals are just some of the benefits of these courts. The recommendations above can help direct the use of treatment courts as they move forward and deal with the ever-changing needs of criminal justice populations.

As researchers and evaluators continue to examine existing treatment courts and future programs, additional recommendations and modifications may be made. These may be influenced by a variety of factors outside the box of the criminal justice system, including the aging of the general population, demographic shifts such as people moving to different parts of the country, and economic changes. Treatment courts, while not universally effective or perfect by any means, as no programming model is, do provide many a chance for success and benefit the public and society on many levels.

Applying the treatment court model to populations such as emerging adults and the LGBTQIA+ community may provide an innovative use of tools such as therapeutic jurisprudence to address the challenges facing these distinct populations. The use of treatment courts for a group like emerging adults may call for the merging of different types of treatment court approaches. For example, an emerging adulthood court may in practice mirror much of what a drug court does but could incorporate the peer approach of teen courts or peer mentors seen in veterans' courts. Creative and innovative uses of treatment courts to provide diversions from traditional criminal justice system may provide the tools necessary to reduce offending, help participants address the underlying issues that brought them to the attention of the criminal justice system in the first place, and ultimately prevent or decrease rates of recidivism, a long-standing challenge area in the criminal justice system.

References

Andrews, D. A., & Bonta, J. (2010). Rehabilitation criminal justice policy and practice. *Psychology, Public Policy, & Law, 16*(39), 1–14.

Butts, J. A., & Ortiz, J. (2011). Teen courts: Do they work and why? https://drj.fccourts.org/uploads/Teen%20Court%20Article.pdf.

Chauncey, G. (2019). The forgotten history of gay entrapment. *The Atlantic.*https://www.theatlantic.com/ideas/archive/2019/06/before-stonewall-biggest-threat-was-entrapment/590536/.

Corrigan, P. W., Markowitz, F. E., Watson, A., Rowan, D., & Kubiak, M. A. (2003). An attribution model of public discrimination towards persons with mental illness. *Journal of Health Social Behavior, 44,* 162–179.

Dowden, C., & Andrews, D. A. (2000). Effective correctional treatment and violent reoffending: A meta-analysis. *Canadian Journal of Criminology, 42,* 449–476.

Gonzales, G., & Henning-Smith, C. (2017). Health disparities by sexual orientation: Results and implications from the behavior risk factors surveillance system. *Journal of Community Health, 42,* 1163–1172. https://doi.org/10.1007/s10900-017-0366-z.

Hirschfield, P. J., & Piquero, A. R. (2010). Normalization and legitimation: Modeling stigmatizing attitudes toward ex-offenders. *Criminology, 48,* 27–55.

Hirschi, T. (1969). *Causes of delinquency.* University of California Press.

Kubiak, S., Roddy, J., Comartin, E., & Tillander, E. (2015). Cost analysis of long-term outcomes of an urban mental health court. *Evaluation and Program Planning, 52,* 96–106.

LeBel, T. P. (2012). Invisible stripes? Formerly incarcerated persons' perceptions of stigma. *Deviant Behavior, 33,* 89–107.

Martin, K (2017, March 1). *Hidden consequences: The impact of incarceration on dependent children.* National Institute of Justice. https://nij.ojp.gov/topics/articles/hidden-consequences-impact-incarceration-dependent-children.

Pogorzelski, W., Wolff, N., Pan, K. Y., & Blitz, C. L. (2005). Behavioral health problems, ex-offender reentry policies, and the "Second Chance Act." *American Journal of Public Health, 95,* 1718–1724.

Redlich, A. D., & Han, W. (2014). Examining the links between therapeutic jurisprudence and mental health court completion. *Law and Human Behavior, 38*(2), 109–118.

Salvatore, C. (2018). *Sex, crime, drugs, and just plain stupid behaviors: The new face of young adulthood in America.* Palgrave Macmillan.

Salvatore, C., & Daftary-Kapur, T. (2020). The influence of emerging adulthood on the risky and dangerous behaviors of LGBT populations. *Social Sciences, 9*(12), 1–15.

Salvatore, C., Hiller, M. L., Samuelson, B., Henderson, J., & White, E. (2011). A systematic observational study of a juvenile drug court judge. *Juvenile and Family Court Journal, 62*(4), 19–36. https://doi.org/10.1111/j.1755-6988.2011.01066.x.

Salvatore, C., Michalsen, V., & Taylor, C. (2020). Reentry court judge: The key to the court. *Journal of Offender Rehabilitation, 59*(4), 198–222.

Shlafer, R., Gerrity, E., Ruhland, E., & Wheeler, M. (2013). *Children with incarcerated parents — Considering children's outcomes in the context of family experiences.* University of Minnesota.

Stiles-Shields, C., & Carroll, R. A. (2015). Same-sex domestic violence: Prevalence, unique aspects, and clinical implications. *Journal of Sex & Marital Therapy, 41*(6), 636–648. https://doi.org/10.1080/00926 23X.2014.958792.

Tonry, M., & Melewski, M. (2008). The malign effects of drug and crime control policies on Black Americans. *Crime and Justice, 37*(1), 1–44.

Washington State Institute for Public Policy. (2016a). Drug courts: Adult criminal justice. http://www.wsipp.wa.gov/BenefitCost/Program /14.

Washington State Institute for Public Policy. (2016b). Drug courts: Juvenile justice. http://www.wsipp.wa.gov/BenefitCost/Program/44.

CHAPTER 12

Conclusions

So, we are at the final chapter of this book. What conclusions can we come to? Perhaps most importantly, have we answered the question posed by the title of this book: are treatment courts the solution to the recidivism problem? To answer that question, we need to consider that the purpose of this book was to provide a supplementary text that can give a focused look at the most prevalent types of problem- or treatment-oriented court programs. Across this book we have looked at a variety of these programs, finding that some work better than others and many follow a similar format (with many treatment courts following the format of drug courts), though some have a format that are distinct (such as teen courts). Evidence in the form of cost-effectiveness, reductions in recidivism, success with housing, employment, and reconnecting with family members, have been found in varying degrees with many of these programs, though as noted in their respective chapters, some of these programs (e.g., drug courts) are much more prevalent and have been evaluated to a greater extent than more recent innovations to treatment courts (e.g., reentry courts). Ultimately, we will need evaluation-based research to help understand if treatment courts, especially those with less formal evaluations, are an effective approach in supporting participants and preventing recidivism.

Like any program or strategy, countless variables influence a program's effectiveness, including their time and place in history, location, and the population they are dealing with—what may work for a drug-involved population in the late 1980s and 1990s in Miami, Florida, may not work in Portland, Oregon, in 2020. Ultimately, we may not be able to fully answer the question posed by this book's title, but we can pose some questions that may help address it. To start, what can we conclusively say about treatment courts? Are they a universal fix? Are they magic bullets? Are they more fitting for some criminal justice system clients than others? It is hard for any one book to answer any of these questions conclusively; truth be told it might take an entire career exploring just one type of treatment court to really answer these questions as accurately as possible. After all, our society changes and evolves as culture shifts like a wave; when the first drug court started in 1989, the legalization of marijuana on a large scale might have been unthinkable; 25 years from now, other drugs criminalized today may be legal, or perhaps society may go in the opposite direction with a return to the alcohol prohibition of the early twentieth century (though a look at how that worked last time might be a deterrent in and of itself). Drug markets also change; we have seen marijuana-based drug courts, shifts to cocaine, heroin, and methamphetamines, and the now current fentanyl/prescription opiates crisis tearing through our communities and costing countless lives.

Perhaps the best way to frame this conclusion section would be the way students so often ask me in classes, when (usually at the end of the semester) a student will pose the inevitable question: so what do you really think, not based on the articles or reports, but you as a person? This is always an intriguing question for me to answer. I am likely biased because I just wrote a book about treatment courts. Treatment courts were one of the first programs I evaluated. I have spent several years in various treatment court programs. I have spent a lot of time reading about them, not only in empirical articles, law journal articles, and books, but success stories from the mainstream media. I have also watched countless videos from problem-oriented court programs with moving testimonials of program participants and members of the treatment court team discussing the powerful experiences they have had in these programs and how they have changed their lives for the better. Taking off my "professor" hat and putting on my "Chris (regular person)" hat, I can say from the court programs I have observed (okay, I cannot completely take off my professor hat) these programs are impressive. I will not say they are perfect, and I cannot make a universal statement; as I mentioned above, many factors influence any program's effectiveness, and I cannot ignore them. However, I have witnessed firsthand youth and adults in crisis, whose lives could either continue down a criminal or deviant path, deeper into addiction, dysfunction, and involvement with the criminal justice system, take a radically different turn when a judge, probation officer, or other members of the treatment court workgroup (sometimes the entire treatment court workgroup), or a mentor in a program showed that they were genuinely interested and cared for them. I have sat in conversation (during focus groups) with formerly gang-involved individuals whose lives were once on a path either towards incarceration or early death, who share with me how a treatment court gave the tools they needed to transform their lives and put them on a prosocial path leading to college and a graduate degree instead of a prison cell. I have seen a judge share intimate details about his past with a youth in crisis, sharing how he was just as, if not more, a delinquent at the same age and place in life but made changes and found a better path forward. I have seen court session after court session filled with clients and treatment court team members rejoicing at the victories program participants have reached, such as finding jobs, graduating from high school or college, getting driver's licenses, securing apartments, and purchasing homes. Some of these milestones are small, some large, but almost all were unimaginable for the program participants before they were part of these programs. Does that equate to evidence? Well, the social scientist in me (wearing the professor hat) will tell you these are examples, ones that certainly suggest the benefits of these programs, but more substantial evidence is needed instead of just the anecdotal (such as testimonials on various treatment court websites). Thus far the evidence provided is promising, but not strong enough to make a strong or definitive statement that problem-oriented or treatment courts work. The "professor" would say they show the promise and potential of these courts and what they may offer participants.

While I have seen firsthand, solid evidence for the effectiveness of social bonds between judges, treatment court team members, and participants of treatment courts, these experiences, which have been interesting and rewarding on so many levels, still only represent the lens of one researcher's (and the colleagues who worked with me on these projects) experiences and may only be generalizable to a certain degree. As discussed previously, what works in a juvenile drug court in Philadelphia may not be the same as what works in a juvenile drug court in Las Vegas. Much of my scholarship has incorporated the various incarnations of social bond theory, so I am likely partial to applying the theory to treatment courts. From my firsthand observation of a juvenile drug court and a reentry court program, I saw ample evidence of how social bonds can work—with judges and treatment court team members, as well as engaged family members and mentors providing support for program participants to succeed. I have listened to program participants to state how much it meant that people believed in them and took the time to guide them through the process of everyday activities like opening bank accounts, going to doctor's appointments, learning how to use email, purchasing a mobile phone, and finding a home. These everyday activities, which so many of us have parents, grandparents, or siblings to guide us through in our lives, can seem mystifying to participants in treatment court programs.

Further, I have witnessed evidence of the effectiveness of social bonds in promoting the success of program participants in treatment courts across many studies (some of which are integrated into various chapters in this book), so there seems to be at least some level of effectiveness of social bonds for which we could argue there is support. Of particular interest is the role of judges (a topic examined in this book's introduction, as well as in various chapters). Judges seem to matter, perhaps more than any other member of the treatment court team; as a critical representation of the criminal justice system, judges can represent to program participants the ultimate stern, unforgiving parental figure to chastise and punish them for their wrongdoings. Judges can also represent a supportive, caring figure in the lives of participants; for some who have never had an agent of the criminal justice system treat them with understanding or kindness, this is a revelation. This interest and kindness are critical to success for many participants in treatment courts. As many clients of treatment courts and the criminal justice system have had harsh, abusive, and neglectful childhoods, many may never have experienced genuine interest and support from an adult authority figure, much less a representative of the criminal justice system.

Having a judge, defense attorney, prosecutor, or probation officer express interest and support in their lives can make a huge difference for a client of a treatment court. Having witnessed the judges and staff of treatment courts step out of their traditional roles in the courtroom and into a more supportive role has been enlightening for me as a researcher and person. Seeing the eyes of a juvenile drug court client light up as a room of adult professionals clap for them and award them with a small gift of sunglasses or a gift certificate for accomplishing a goal like graduating high school, as their family looks on, can be an exciting event. A supportive environment may not be enough for all potential clients of problem-oriented or treatment courts. While there are many successes in these programs, there are also failures, and not all treatment court programs are as effective as others.

Some program participants may find treatment courts lacking; after all, does providing a supportive environment undo decade of abuse or neglect? Can a treatment court give someone with no work history a way to enter a challenging labor market which they may lack the communication and technical skills to enter? I argue that they can; programs like reentry courts show that even those without a legal work history can make a change and find a prosocial path to employment, but even those court programs have failures. Only some participants in a program may be amenable to the services a treatment court provides. Some may be too vested in the criminal lifestyle to shift away from it. Others may need services beyond what the court may offer, and others may still be comfortable with the routine stability that institutional life may provide relative to the uncertainty of life in the community.

While treatment-oriented courts have been around for over 30 years, a long time in some respects but not so long in the grand scheme of our society, we may need more time to study these innovative and engaging programs. It may be retrospective research of those early participants in treatment courts that yields clues to what is most effective in these programs. By looking back at their time in the treatment court and reflecting on how the program's goals and treatment team influenced their lives (or perhaps did not), scholars will be able to report to academics, practitioners, and the public what these persons felt had the most influence on their long-term success or failures. By identifying these factors, they can be better integrated into problem-oriented or treatment courts across the country, providing greater levels of success for participants.

As we turn towards the future, we must acknowledge that times and needs change. Treatment court programs must constantly innovate as the needs of the populations may alter as society changes. In 1989, when the Miami-Dade Drug Court first opened its doors, there were mobile phones, but they did not dominate our day-to-day lives as they do today. The same goes for personal computers—sure, laptops were a thing in the late 1980s and early 1990s, as was the Internet. However, for most, these technologies were novelties, especially for those in the largely impoverished clientele of the criminal justice system. Back in the late 1980s and early 1990s, most jobs were posted in newspapers; if you wanted to apply for a job, you did so in person, or you mailed in or faxed a resume and cover letter (probably typed on a typewriter or word processor for most). Within a decade, our world has radically changed; consumer mobile phones exploded, and they became more and more affordable and common for people from every walk of life. With the advent of text messages, and wireless Internet, at the beginning of the twenty-first century, our ways of communicating changed dramatically; much of this technology was pretty easy to use and accessible, but if you had been institutionalized during this time, it might seem strange and foreign, especially to someone incarcerated when pay phones were a common sight. People bought a daily newspaper and could only buy items in person or via mail-order catalogs. The changing technology of the last 40 years is something that treatment court programs like reentry courts have had to adopt to help clients succeed, as many may never have submitted a resume online or even have a mobile phone.

Treatment court programs need to be agile and willing to adapt to the types of changes like technology that occur in our society. In order to do so, they need staff and resources. Many of these programs run on very tight budgets, relying on volunteer judges and attorneys. Some programs run on the very generous out-of-pocket spending of those who volunteer in them, which, while admirable, may limit their ability to serve clients over time. Ultimately this is why books like this as well as other forms of scholarship need to be prompting knowledge about these programs to students, practitioners, fellow scholars, and the general public. As stated above (and throughout many of the chapters), treatment courts are not perfect; there likely is not any perfect program that can reduce the recidivism problem across all populations, but these programs show more than a promise, and that promise needs to be built upon and nurtured. If a program shows success, it must be celebrated and the public informed. Fortunately, many programs have adopted technology and tools like YouTube videos and social media to get the word out about the success of their clients and programs.

At a community level, police departments, religious organizations, schools, and other community groups need to be aware that these programs may offer solutions to populations like drug-involved youth, who may otherwise end up in the juvenile or adult system. The same goes for correctional organizations, which historically left those who completed their sentences or were granted parole to face life in the community, often unprepared. Programs like reentry courts can help prepare these individuals for work, find housing, and deal with any lingering legal issues. However, to do so, the administration of correctional facilities needs to be informed of these programs and their work. To accomplish this, evaluation-based research needs to continue and to be disseminated not only to academic audiences, but to practitioners and the public as well, in order to ensure the potential benefits of treatment courts are widely known.

In closing, perhaps the most needed factor is belief in the value of diversion and treatment programs instead of incarceration. As we have seen time and again, incarceration, while popular with politicians and the public, rarely "fixes" those involved in crime. If anything, incarcerations make them more likely to fail once released. Cutting off prosocial relationships in the communities and exposing those incarcerated to the culture of jails and prisons may influence them to engage in gang activity or other illegal acts in prison. Maybe compassion is vital; not only may it be the secret to the success of treatment courts like reentry and drug courts, but it may also be the factor that spurs those meting out arrests and sentencing to see the potential in those engaging in offending behaviors. While not all treatment courts (or any other prevention or treatment strategy, for that matter) can claim universal effectiveness, they can usually claim at least some success. This success can offer hope, not only to the participants in these programs, but to our society as well, that we can help those on the lowest rungs of society's ladder climb towards a better future.

Index

10 key components of drug
   courts, 60

adolescence, 47, 73, 189, 214, 243
adolescent-limited offenders, 12
aftercare, 48, 103, 110, 219, 244,
   245
age, 3, 7, 12, 16, 32, 43, 55, 80, 95,
   147, 189, 191, 194, 195, 196,
   197, 198, 206, 214, 234, 240
aging out, 12, 243
Animal courts, 27
attachments, 15, 43, 47, 61, 67, 69,
   72, 80, 105, 109, 155, 201, 207,
   224, 238, 239

Bureau of Justice Assistance
   (BJA), 23

childhood abuse, 31, 230
COVID-19, 10, 80, 207, 208
crime rates, 4, 7, 10, 78
criminal justice system, 4, 5, 7, 8,
   9, 12, 13, 16, 21, 22, 23, 27, 30,
   31, 32, 35, 41, 42, 46, 55, 59,
   66, 77, 81, 92, 93, 94, 97, 100,
   101, 102, 103, 106, 107, 108,
   110, 111, 114, 115, 117, 119, 120,
   128, 130, 131, 137, 139, 146,
   148, 149, 151, 154, 157, 162,
   163, 164, 169, 184, 190, 191,
   201, 203, 206, 210, 216, 222,
   225, 226, 228, 234, 235, 238,
   240, 241, 243, 244, 245, 246

dark figure of crime, 6, 7
desistance, 68, 73, 83, 87, 136,
   154, 155, 208, 245
deterrence, 8, 11, 40, 44, 45, 46,
   51, 52, 53, 125, 175, 187
deterrent effect, 11, 45, 175
developmental taxonomy, 12, 18
domestic violence, 29, 37, 42, 119,
   120, 121, 122, 123, 126, 127,
   128, 129, 130, 132, 133, 134,
   135, 136, 137, 138, 139, 140,
   141, 142, 143, 196, 248
domestic violence courts, 42,
   120, 121, 123, 128, 137, 141,
   142
Domestic Violence Courts
   (DVC), 29

domestic violence policy, 120
drug court, 22, 24, 25, 26, 28, 34, 35, 37, 38, 39, 46, 48, 52, 56, 59, 60, 61, 62, 63, 64, 66, 68, 69, 70, 72, 73, 74, 75, 76, 77, 78, 79, 80, 81, 82, 83, 84, 85, 86, 87, 88, 89, 90, 94, 137, 149, 235, 237, 239, 243, 246, 247
Drug Courts Program Office (DCPO), 22
due process, 4, 25, 64, 101, 151, 193, 194, 234

education, 7, 20, 24, 26, 30, 32, 41, 45, 47, 61, 62, 64, 66, 67, 68, 72, 73, 74, 93, 94, 97, 153, 169, 175, 176, 177, 179, 180, 182, 183, 184, 190, 207, 216, 219, 221, 223, 224, 225, 229, 230, 235, 243
emerging adulthood, 207, 243, 246, 247
employment, 14, 15, 16, 23, 26, 30, 32, 41, 43, 45, 47, 51, 61, 62, 66, 67, 68, 72, 73, 74, 82, 93, 94, 97, 102, 112, 147, 149, 159, 160, 169, 173, 175, 176, 177, 178, 179, 180, 182, 183, 185, 190, 216, 218, 219, 221, 223, 224, 229, 239, 240, 241, 242, 244

family, 6, 8, 13, 15, 18, 26, 27, 28, 43, 44, 47, 50, 51, 55, 62, 66, 67, 68, 69, 71, 72, 73, 74, 85, 89, 95, 102, 122, 123, 138, 139, 148, 151, 164, 169, 172, 176, 177, 178, 179, 180, 181, 190, 192, 194, 195, 218, 219, 220, 221,

224, 229, 230, 235, 238, 240, 248
Fathering Court, 29
feminist movement, 137

gender, 3, 126, 190, 214, 240
generalizability, 158, 159, 161, 183
Get Tough, 4, 5, 9, 10, 12, 14, 15

Homeless Courts, 8, 30
housing, 15, 21, 29, 30, 32, 33, 41, 47, 61, 62, 96, 112, 147, 149, 153, 159, 160, 161, 169, 173, 180, 182, 185, 217, 218, 219, 220, 221, 223, 224, 229, 230, 239, 240, 241, 242
human trafficking, 31, 217, 221, 223, 224, 225, 226, 227, 228, 232, 233

identity theory, 153, 157, 165
incapacitation, 11, 13
incarceration, 4, 5, 9, 10, 11, 13, 14, 15, 17, 18, 19, 21, 29, 31, 34, 53, 59, 60, 66, 77, 81, 82, 93, 111, 159, 160, 173, 174, 184, 190, 194, 217, 226, 234, 236, 237, 240, 241, 243, 245, 247
integrative, 49

job training, 29, 33, 60, 130, 173
judges, 18, 21, 24, 25, 34, 39, 43, 44, 46, 51, 60, 67, 72, 81, 95, 102, 110, 121, 122, 124, 129, 130, 131, 133, 136, 137, 138, 140, 171, 172, 174, 176, 177, 178, 197, 204, 223, 224, 226, 227, 235, 241

judicial oversight, 28, 42, 47, 151, 152
Justice and Mental Health Collaboration Program (JMHCP), 23
juvenile drug court, 62, 66
LGBTQIA+, 13, 136, 243, 244, 246
Life course theory, 46, 47, 53, 73
life skills, 21, 30, 60, 75, 112, 173

Martinson Report, 9
mass incarceration, 5, 11, 12, 13, 14, 15, 16, 18, 60, 81, 186
medical model, 9
medical model of incarceration, 9
mental health, 8, 14, 16, 21, 23, 28, 30, 31, 33, 34, 38, 41, 42, 47, 48, 56, 57, 65, 75, 92, 93, 94, 95, 96, 97, 98, 99, 100, 101, 102, 103, 108, 110, 111, 112, 113, 114, 115, 116, 117, 121, 122, 128, 133, 149, 150, 151, 152, 153, 156, 160, 162, 164, 167, 168, 173, 220, 221, 223, 229, 230, 235, 236, 237, 240, 241, 243, 247
mental health courts, 16, 23, 30, 31, 41, 42, 93, 94, 96, 98, 101, 110, 111, 112, 113, 114, 115, 116, 117, 133, 149, 229, 237, 241
mentors, 150, 151, 152, 153, 154, 155, 156, 161, 163, 174, 178, 185, 235, 237, 244, 246
Miami Dade County, 22
military service, 47, 73, 157, 162, 163, 164
military subculture, 148, 162
Monitoring the Future, 65, 87

National Crime Victim Survey (NCVS), 7
National Crime Victimization Survey (NCVS), 5
Netflix, 3

Office of Justice Programs (OJP), 23
Office of Juvenile Justice and Delinquency Prevention (OJJDP), 23, 116

Packer, 4, 18
participant compliance, 97
phases, 26, 62, 67, 95, 218
police, 6, 7, 8, 17, 34, 92, 94, 108, 111, 119, 121, 136, 168, 223, 244
policymakers, 60, 63, 135, 237
procedural justice, 50, 55, 156, 165, 171, 181, 188
prosocial, 13, 15, 16, 43, 47, 51, 66, 69, 73, 74, 80, 82, 95, 102, 109, 150, 161, 164, 176, 179, 185, 190, 200, 204, 235, 238, 241, 243
prostitution courts, 23, 31, 38, 42, 216, 217, 221, 222, 223, 224, 225, 226, 227, 229, 231, 232, 241

race/ethnicity, 3, 240
recidivism, 4, 10, 21, 24, 29, 30, 31, 33, 34, 38, 56, 59, 61, 66, 75, 76, 77, 78, 79, 81, 83, 86, 87, 90, 97, 103, 106, 109, 110, 114, 116, 117, 121, 125, 126, 128, 134, 135, 140, 143, 149, 158, 162, 165, 167, 169, 170, 173, 176, 180, 181, 182, 184, 186, 188,

202, 203, 205, 206, 208, 211,
212, 213, 216, 225, 226, 236,
242, 246
reentry court, 15, 16, 23, 24, 25,
26, 30, 32, 33, 36, 37, 39, 42,
43, 44, 45, 51, 56, 72, 136, 169,
170, 171, 172, 173, 174, 175,
176, 177, 178, 180, 181, 182,
183, 184, 185, 186, 187, 188,
216, 217, 227, 235, 241, 242
reincarnation, 170, 182
reintegration, 111, 169, 180, 184
restorative justice, 5, 33, 40, 48,
53, 55, 102, 103, 109, 113, 114,
153, 156, 157, 167, 191, 198,
200, 212
rewards, 26, 41, 52, 67, 70, 82, 96,
100, 127, 151, 172, 189
risk-need-responsivity (RNR)
model, 45, 175

sanctions, 22, 26, 41, 45, 46, 51,
52, 63, 67, 78, 83, 96, 97, 98,
100, 110, 115, 151, 152, 171,
172, 174, 191, 226
social bond theory, 40, 43, 47, 51,
53, 56, 176, 224, 238
social bonding theory, 44, 46, 51,
52, 156, 175, 201
social bonds, 5, 43, 44, 51, 52, 53,
61, 67, 68, 70, 72, 73, 85, 105,
155, 156, 176, 177, 178, 184,
224, 227, 236, 237, 238, 239,
240, 245
social capital, 176, 178, 179, 184,
188, 239
social control, 43, 44, 52, 67, 68,
74
social justice, 224, 236, 240, 245
social learning theory, 128

social network, 177, 179
social support, 13, 105
social ties, 47, 73, 178
stigma, 109, 154, 170, 190, 201,
203, 206, 208, 227, 236, 239,
240, 245, 247
substance abuse, 14, 21, 22, 26,
28, 30, 31, 33, 52, 53, 61, 66, 67,
69, 74, 78, 82, 83, 99, 113, 122,
146, 148, 149, 150, 151, 153,
156, 157, 161, 162, 163, 164,
173, 180, 207, 216, 217, 218,
220, 223, 229, 235, 236, 242,
243, 244
substance abuse disorders, 62,
146, 148, 153, 173

teen courts, 32, 36, 39, 42, 190,
191, 197, 198, 199, 200, 201,
202, 203, 204, 205, 206, 208,
210, 211, 212, 214, 243, 246
The Federal Bureau of Investigation (FBI), 6
theoretical orientation, 21, 45,
48, 94, 152, 170, 175, 198, 217,
224
therapeutic community, 106
therapeutic jurisprudence, 21, 23,
35, 36, 38, 40, 41, 42, 47, 48,
50, 52, 53, 55, 56, 57, 61, 67, 72,
97, 98, 100, 101, 102, 109, 117,
121, 128, 137, 143, 152, 163,
170, 172, 223, 236, 246, 247
trajectory, 47, 73
turning point, 47, 52, 53, 72, 73,
74

unemployment, 14, 103, 150, 151,
153, 161, 235
Uniform Crime Report (UCR), 5

veterans, 30, 33, 41, 48, 146, 147,
148, 149, 150, 151, 152, 153,
157, 158, 159, 160, 161, 162,
163, 164, 165, 166, 167, 168,
246
Veterans' courts, 33, 42
victimization, 3, 4, 6, 7, 8, 18, 19,
31, 103, 128
Violence Against Women Act,
29, 120
Violent Crime Control Act of
1994, 22

warrior ethos, 148